THE CEO MBA

Your Blueprint to Business Excellence

By

Robert N. Jacobs

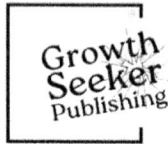

Growth
Seeker
Publishing

"The world rewards leaders who dare to think bigger. Every obstacle you face today is preparing you for the strength and wisdom you'll need tomorrow.

Your journey toward greatness starts with believing you have the power to make an extraordinary difference. Step forward boldly, lead courageously, and create the legacy that only you can build.

Robert N. Jacobs

A Note From The Author

To all aspiring and current CEOs; your path is demanding, but your potential for impact is limitless.

Leadership at the highest level requires more than ambition; it demands resilience, courage, wisdom, and an unwavering commitment to growth. As markets evolve and complexity increases, the most successful leaders are those who embrace continuous learning and boldly navigate uncertainty.

The CEO MBA equips you with the insights, strategies, and real-world frameworks to unlock your full leadership potential. Drawing from proven principles and the success stories of world-class executives, this book is your companion in building a thriving organisation and leaving a meaningful legacy.

Commit to your journey of excellence today. Embrace the challenge, seize the opportunity, and shape the future. The world is waiting for the leader you are destined to become.

Robert N. Jacobs
Author & CEO | Growth Seeker Publishing Ltd.

Introduction

In today's rapidly changing world, where the demands on business leaders are more complex than ever, this book is your guide, whether you are an aspiring CEO or a seasoned leader. Traditionally, mastering leadership, strategic thinking, and business acumen has been a long and costly journey, often only accessible to those pursuing an MBA. However, as leadership evolves, so must the way we learn.

The CEO MBA: Your Blueprint to Business Excellence is crafted to break down the essential elements needed to run and grow a successful business. Each chapter could be a standalone course or even a degree program. However, this book combines knowledge and practical insights in one accessible format. It is for entrepreneurs dreaming of building something new, leaders refining their skills, and business professionals seeking to understand what it truly takes to thrive at the top.

Experienced CEOs might find some familiar concepts here, but the real value lies in fresh perspectives and a reminder of the core principles that drive effective leadership and strategic success. From embracing a resilient mindset to mastering financial metrics or leading high-performance teams, this book offers strategies and reflections from which even the most seasoned leaders can benefit.

You already know that running a business is not about knowing everything; it is about knowing enough about many things to make informed decisions, delegate effectively, manage talent, and inspire confidence in those around you. This book understands that CEOs must be versatile, possessing a broad understanding of various disciplines and the ability to make strategic choices that shape their organisation's future.

Whether you are just beginning your leadership journey or looking to sharpen your skills, I hope this book becomes a valuable resource. Each chapter invites you to think deeply, act strategically, and lead with courage. The path of a CEO is challenging, but with the right tools and mindset, it can be profoundly rewarding. Let this book be your companion as you navigate the complexities of business and strive to make a lasting impact.

Enjoy the journey ahead.

Robert Jacobs
Curious By Design

Table of Contents

Chapter 1
The Ceo's Mindset: Cultivating Leadership And Vision 1
   1.1 - Overview 1
   1.2 Defining The Ceo Mindset 2
   1.3 Visionary Leadership 4
   1.4 Emotional Intelligence 5
   1.5 Decision-Making 7
   1.6 Adaptability 9
   1.7 Inspirational Leadership 11
   1.8 Resilience 15
   1.9 Cultivating Innovation 17
   1.10 Legacy Building 19
   Conclusion 21

Chapter 2
Strategic Planning: The Key To Shaping Your Company's Future 24
   2.1 Overview 24
   2.2 The Essence Of Strategic Planning 25
   2.3 Analysing The Business Environment 26
   2.4 Setting Objectives 28
   2.5 Strategy Formulation 30
   2.6 Execution 32
   2.7 Monitoring And Control 35
   2.8 Adapting To Change 36
   2.9 Involving Your Team 39
   2.10 Case Studies 41
   2.11 Tools And Techniques 43
   Conclusion 47

Chapter 3
Understanding Financial Metrics: The Language Of Business 49
   3.1 Overview 49
   3.2 Financial Statements 101 50
   3.3 Key Performance Indicators (Kpis) 51
   3.4 Budgeting For Success 53
   3.5 Cash Flow Management 55
   3.6 Profit Maximisation Strategies 57

3.7 Cost Management 59
3.8 Investment Appraisal 62
3.9 Financial Risk Management 64
3.10 The Ceo's Role In Financial Leadership..............66
3.11 Learning From The Giants 69
3.12 Case Studies 70
Conclusion 73

Chapter 4
Marketing Mastery: Building Your Brand And Customer
Base 75
4.1 Overview...75
4.2 Understanding Your Market 76
4.3 Building A Strong Brand 78
4.4 Digital Marketing Strategies 80
4.5 Pricing Strategies 83
4.6 Distribution Channels..85
4.7 Customer Relationship Management (Crm)..........87
4.8 Analysing Marketing Data 90
4.9 Global Marketing 93
4.10 Innovative Marketing Tactics 96
4.11 Case Studies In Marketing Excellence 98
Conclusion 101

Chapter 5
Sales Strategies For Growth: Driving Revenue Expansion
....102
5.1 Overview...102
5.2 The Sales Funnel 103
5.3 Effective Sales Techniques.................................105
5.4 Building And Managing A Sales Team 109
5.5 Customer-Centric Selling 112
5.6 Leveraging Technology In Sales.........................115
5.7 Key Account Management 118
5.8 Negotiation Skills 122
5.9 Scaling Sales Operations 125
5.10 Metrics And Kpis For Sales Success 129
5.11 Learning From The Best 134
Conclusion 136

Chapter 6
Operational Excellence: Streamlining For Efficiency........139

6.1 Overview 139

6.2 Understanding Operational Excellence 140
6.3 Lean Management.. 141
6.4 Quality Management Systems 143
6.5 Supply Chain Optimisation... 145
6.6 Technology In Operations 148
6.7 Sustainability In Operations... 151
6.8 Risk Management In Operations 154
6.9 Customer Service Excellence.. 156
6.10 Case Studies In Operational Turnaround..................... 160
6.11 Measuring Operational Success................................... 163
6.12 Conclusion 166
Chapter 7
Innovation And Product Development: Staying Ahead Of The Curve... 169
7.1 Overview 169
7.2 The Innovation Imperative.. 169
7.3 Cultivating A Culture Of Innovation.............................. 171
7.4 The Product Development Process................................. 173
7.5 Customer-Centric Design 174
7.6 Prototyping And Mvps 176
7.7 Scaling Your Product.. 178
7.8 Intellectual Property (Ip) 180
7.9 Leveraging Data In Product Development...................... 182
7.10 Collaborative Innovation.. 184
7.11 Case Studies In Innovation 186
Conclusion.. 188
Chapter 8
Talent Management: Hiring, Developing, And Retaining The Best 190
8.1 - Overview 190
8.2 The Strategic Importance Of Talent Management........... 191
8.3 Attracting Top Talent... 193
8.4 Effective Hiring Processes.. 195
8.5 Onboarding And Integration 197
8.6 Employee Development 200
8.7 Performance Management 202
8.8 Succession Planning.. 205
8.9 Employee Retention Strategies 207

8.10 Diversity And Inclusion **210**

8.11 Learning From Leading Employers **214**

Conclusion **217**

Chapter 9
Corporate Culture And Values: Crafting A Cohesive Identity

.... 220

9.1 Overview 220
9.2 The Power Of Corporate Culture 220
9.3 Defining Your Company's Core Values 222
9.4 Leadership's Role In Culture Building 224
9.5 Communicating Culture 227
9.6 Aligning Culture With Strategy 230
9.7 Cultural Transformation 233
9.8 Engaging Employees 235
9.9 Measuring Cultural Health 239
9.10 Case Studies Of Strong Cultures 242
9.11 Sustaining Culture During Growth And Change 246
Conclusion 251

Chapter 10
Effective Communication: Inside And Outside The Company

.... 254

10.1 Overview 254
10.2 Foundations Of Effective Communication 254
10.3 Internal Communication Strategies 256
10.4 Public Speaking And Presentation Skills 258
10.5 Crisis Communication 260
10.6 Media Relations 263
10.7 Digital Communication 265
10.8 Stakeholder Engagement 268
10.9 Brand Communication 270
10.10 Listening Skills 273
10.11 Case Studies In Communication Excellence 275
Conclusion 277

Chapter 11
Navigating Global Markets: Expansion And Localisation
Strategies

.... 279

11.1 Overview 279
11.2 Market Analysis And Selection 280
11.3 Cultural Sensitivity And Adaptation 282
11.4 Building A Global Team 284

11.5 International Supply Chains 286

11.6 Global Marketing Strategies... 288
11.7 Currency Risks And Financial Management...................... 291
11.8 Legal And Regulatory Compliance 294
11.9 Case Studies Of Successful Global Expansion 297
11.10 Exiting A Market... 300
Conclusion 302

Chapter 12
Corporate Responsibility And Ethics: Building A
Sustainable Future 304
12.1 – Overview.. 304
12.2 - The Importance Of Corporate Social Responsibility (CSR)
.... 295
12.3 - Ethical Leadership.. 307
12.4 - Sustainability Practices 309
12.5 - Social Impact... 312
12.6 - Stakeholder Engagement.. 314
12.7 - Transparency And Reporting 316
12.8 - Ethical Supply Chain Management.............................. 318
12.9 - Crisis Management And Ethical Dilemmas 319
12.10 - Conclusion... 321

Chapter 13
Risk Management: Anticipating And Mitigating Threats. 323
13.1 Overview... 323
13.2 Understanding Risk Management 323
13.3 Identifying Risks 324
13.4 Assessing Risks... 326
13.5 Strategies For Risk Mitigation...................................... 327
13.6 Financial Risks 329
13.7 Operational Risks 331
13.8 Reputational Risks 333
13.9 Crisis Management Planning 336
13.10 Insurance And Risk Transfer 338
13.11 Case Studies In Effective Risk Management 340
Conclusion 341

Chapter 14
Navigating Economic Cycles And Market Changes............ 343
14.1 Overview... 343
14.2 Economic Cycles Overview... 344
14.3 Predicting Market Trends... 346

14.4 Recession-Proofing Your Business.................................. 348

14.5 Capitalising On Economic Growth.................................. 350
14.6 Financial Planning For Volatility.................................. 353
14.7 Innovation During Downturns.................................. 355
14.8 Managing Costs And Efficiency.................................. 357
14.9 Employee Morale And Retention.................................. 359
14.10 Diversification Strategies 361
14.11 Learning From Past Economic Cycles 363
Conclusion 365

Chapter 15
Mergers And Acquisitions – Strategies For Growth And
Consolidation **368**
15.1 - Overview 368
15.2 - Types Of M&A Deals 369
15.3 - Strategic Purposes Of M&A.................................. 371
15.4 - Risks In M&A.................................. 372
15.5 - Strategic Fit 373
15.6 - Conducting Due Diligence 375
15.7 - Integration Planning.................................. 377
15.8 - Cultural Integration 380
15.9 - Measuring Success.................................. 381
15.10 - Common Pitfalls And How To Avoid Them 384
15.11 - Case Studies Of Successful M&As 386
Conclusion 389

Chapter 16
Technology And Digital Transformation: Leveraging The
Digital Age **390**
16.1 Overview.................................. 390
16.2 The Digital Revolution.................................. 391
16.3 Challenges And Opportunities 394
16.4 Strategic Technology Planning 397
16.5 Developing A Technology Roadmap.................................. 400
16.6 Digital Transformation Roadmap.................................. 402
16.7 Adopting New Technologies.................................. 404
16.8 Cybersecurity.................................. 408
16.9 Data-Driven Decision-Making.................................. 412
16.10 Customer Experience In The Digital Age 414
16.11 Digital Leadership.................................. 418
16.12 Innovation Through Digital Channels 421
16.13 Case Studies In Digital Transformation.................................. 424

Conclusion 426

Chapter 17
Leadership In Crisis: Managing Through Turbulence 428
17.1 Overview 428
17.2 Recognising Signs Of A Crisis 428
17.3 Crisis Management Planning 430
17.4 Effective Communication During A Crisis 431
17.5 Decision Making Under Pressure 433
17.6 Maintaining Team Morale And Cohesion 435
17.7 Business Continuity Planning 437
17.8 Learning From Crisis 439
17.9 Rebuilding Trust And Confidence 440
17.10 Resilience And Adaptability 442
17.11 Case Studies In Crisis Leadership 443
Conclusion 445

Chapter 18
Personal Development For Ceos: Continuous Learning And Adaptation 447
18.1 Overview 447
18.2 The Importance Of Self-Awareness 447
18.3 Lifelong Learning 449
18.4 Mentorship And Coaching 451
18.5 Balancing Personal And Professional Life 453
18.6 Adapting To Change 455
18.7 Networking And Building Relationships 458
18.8 Physical And Mental Health 460
18.9 Time Management And Productivity 462
18.10 Personal Branding 464
18.11 Inspirational Reads And Resources 466
Conclusion 467

Chapter 19
Building And Leveraging Networks: The Power Of Relationships 468
19.1 Overview 468
19.2 The Value Of Networking 468
19.3 Building Strategic Partnerships 471
19.4 Effective Networking Strategies 473
19.5 Cultivating Investor Relations 476
19.6 Community Engagement 479
19.7 Alumni Networks 481

19.8 Mastermind Groups And Think Tanks 483

19.9 Navigating Industry Associations 486
19.10 Social Capital 489
19.11 Case Studies In Networking Success 491
Conclusion 494

Chapter 20
The Future Of Leadership: Trends, Challenges, And
Opportunities 496
20.1 Overview 496
20.2 Emerging Leadership Trends 497
20.3 Navigating Globalisation 499
20.4 Sustainability And Ethical Leadership 501
20.5 The Role Of Ai And Technology In Leadership 502
20.6 The Changing Nature Of Work 504
20.7 Inclusive Leadership: Embracing Diversity For Innovation
.... 505
20.8 Personalisation And Customisation: Tailoring Leadership
Approaches 507
20.9 Learning And Development: The Future Of Executive
Education 509
20.10 Entrepreneurship And Intrapreneurship: Cultivating
Innovation 510
20.11 Case Studies In Future-Focused Leadership 511
Conclusion 514

Chapter 1

The CEO's Mindset: Cultivating Leadership and Vision

1.1 - Overview

To embody the mindset of a successful CEO is to adopt a unique fusion of visionary thinking, emotional intelligence, resilience, and strategic insight. This mindset, distinct from other organisational roles, is forward-thinking, consistently optimistic, and deeply rooted in a strong sense of accountability. It is a blend of technical competencies and a profound understanding of the psychological and emotional qualities that underpin successful leadership.

The defining feature of a great CEO is their ability to perceive the broader picture while focusing on the intricate details that drive daily operations. This dual capacity, visionary and pragmatic, enables CEOs to guide their organisations through turbulent periods such as economic recessions, technological disruptions, and global crises while remaining vigilant about future opportunities. To develop such a mindset, aspiring leaders must cultivate heightened self-awareness, maintain a steadfast commitment to lifelong learning, and possess the resilience to overcome challenges with grace. The necessity of continuous self-improvement through learning is a key aspect of a CEO's mindset.

A critical component of a CEO's mindset is their innate ability to **inspire and motivate** others. Leadership is not merely about issuing directives from a corner office but about influencing individuals and empowering them to achieve excellence. This requires a nuanced understanding of human behaviour and, most importantly, empathy. The ability to understand and share the feelings of others is a key aspect of a CEO's mindset, and it is crucial in communicating a compelling vision that unites the organisation in pursuing a shared objective.

This chapter explores the psychological and emotional attributes crucial for effective leadership and long-term vision. Examining the complexities of the CEO mindset, it seeks to equip aspiring leaders with the necessary tools and perspectives to lead with **purpose**, resilience, and innovation.

1.2 Defining the CEO Mindset

The **psychological foundation** of a successful CEO is grounded in several key mental models and mindset shifts that distinguish them from other leaders. One of the most pivotal is the **growth mindset**, a concept introduced by psychologist Carol Dweck. A growth mindset is the belief that abilities and intelligence can be developed through dedication, effort, and learning from failure. CEOs who embrace this mindset are more likely to take risks, embrace challenges, and view setbacks as growth opportunities rather than obstacles. This chapter stresses the need for aspiring leaders to adopt a growth mindset, making them feel the urgency of this mindset for their development.

A prime example is Jack Ma, the founder of Alibaba, who embodies the **growth mindset**. Despite facing numerous rejections and failures early in his career, Ma's dedication to continuous learning and improvement enabled him to create one of the world's largest e-commerce platforms. His resilience and relentless focus on learning from mistakes exemplify the psychological foundation necessary for leadership success, providing aspiring leaders with a model of determination and perseverance.

Another essential component of the CEO mindset is **decisiveness**. CEOs frequently find themselves in situations where they must make high-stakes decisions with limited information and under significant pressure. This demands a mental approach that balances **intuition with analysis** and an ability to trust one's instincts while thoroughly evaluating the available data. Decisiveness does not mean being hasty but reflects the confidence required to make tough decisions, even in ambiguous situations.

Additionally, successful CEOs often demonstrate a **strong sense of purpose** and clarity of vision. They are driven by a deep belief in their organisation's mission and are committed to generating value for shareholders and broader stakeholders. This sense of purpose fuels their capacity to overcome leadership challenges and inspires others to support the organisation's objectives.

The CEO mindset blends growth-oriented thinking, decisiveness, resilience, and a sense of purpose. These elements form the **foundation of effective leadership**, enabling CEOs to navigate the complexities of the business world with confidence and clarity while motivating others to follow their lead.

1.3 Visionary Leadership

Visionary leadership goes far beyond setting ambitious goals; it involves **crafting a compelling and actionable vision** that resonates with every organisation member. A vision is not merely a statement of intent, but a narrative that provides direction, inspires action, and unites the organisation around a common cause.

Creating a compelling vision starts with thoroughly understanding the organisation's core values and mission. A CEO must articulate a vision that reflects these values while also addressing the needs and aspirations of all stakeholders. This requires **strategic foresight** and the ability to anticipate future trends and challenges and plan effectively for them. Equally important is the CEO's ability to communicate the vision in an inspiring and relatable manner.

Elon Musk, for example, demonstrates **visionary leadership** with Tesla, where his vision extends beyond the production of electric vehicles. Musk envisages a future where sustainable energy becomes the global standard, with Tesla leading this transformation. His ability to communicate this vision to his employees and the public has played a critical role in Tesla's success. Musk's vision is clear, actionable, and inspiring, providing a roadmap for the company's future growth while garnering support from diverse stakeholders.

A vision must be broken down into concrete goals and milestones to ensure it is actionable. This involves setting long-term objectives and identifying the key steps required. A compelling vision is both ambitious and achievable, offering a clear path forward while challenging the organisation to reach new levels of success.

Effective communication of the vision is equally crucial. CEOs must ensure their vision resonates with every organisation member, from the executive board to the front-line workers. This involves formal communication channels and **embodying the vision** through daily actions and decisions. When employees see that the CEO is genuinely committed to the vision, they are far more likely to align their efforts with the organisation's goals.

In conclusion, **visionary leadership** is about crafting and communicating a compelling vision that unites and propels the organisation forward. It requires strategic foresight, a deep understanding of the organisation's core values, and the ability to inspire and motivate others. By developing these skills, CEOs can ensure their vision becomes a reality, driving sustained growth and long-term impact.

1.4 Emotional Intelligence

Emotional intelligence (EI) is critical to effective leadership, particularly for CEOs. It encompasses the ability to understand and manage one's emotions and the emotions of others to improve relationships, decision-making, and overall organisational effectiveness.

At the core of emotional intelligence is **self-awareness**, the ability to recognise and understand one's emotions and their impact on thoughts and behaviour. Self-awareness is essential for CEOs, enabling them to remain grounded, make informed decisions, and lead authentically. Leaders with high self-awareness are better equipped to handle the pressures of their role, maintain a balanced perspective, and avoid the pitfalls of ego-driven decisions.

Empathy, another key aspect of emotional intelligence, enables CEOs to connect with their employees on a deeper level. It involves understanding the emotions, needs, and perspectives of others, which is vital for building trust, fostering collaboration, and creating a positive organisational culture. Empathetic leaders make their teams feel valued and understood by demonstrating genuine concern for their well-being.

Indra Nooyi, former CEO of PepsiCo, was renowned for her **high emotional intelligence**. She prioritised personal connections with employees, listened to their concerns, and displayed empathy in all her interactions. This approach helped strengthen the company's culture and contributed to its long-term success by fostering employees' sense of belonging and engagement.

Developing emotional intelligence requires consistent effort and practice. One effective strategy is mindfulness, such as meditation or reflective journaling, which helps leaders become more aware of their emotional states and triggers. Additionally, regular feedback from peers, mentors, or executive coaches offers valuable insights into how a leader's behaviour is perceived, providing opportunities for personal growth.

Active listening is another practical technique for enhancing emotional intelligence. It involves fully focusing on, understanding, and responding to what is being said. By practising active listening, CEOs can better understand their employees' needs and concerns, making them more effective at addressing issues, resolving conflicts, and fostering collaboration.

In conclusion, emotional intelligence is a vital skill for CEOs, enabling them to lead with **empathy, self-awareness**, and authenticity. By developing emotional intelligence, leaders can improve relationships, make better decisions, and create a positive organisational culture that drives long-term success.

1.5 Decision-Making

One of the most critical abilities for a CEO is **decision-making**. At the executive level, decisions often involve high stakes, uncertainty, and incomplete information, making it essential for CEOs to balance intuition with rigorous analysis. Intuition, often described as a gut feeling, plays a significant role in decision-making. It stems from experience, deep knowledge, and a profound understanding of the business environment, allowing leaders to make quick decisions when time is limited.

However, intuition alone is not enough; it must be paired with thorough analysis to ensure that decisions are **informed and aligned** with the organisation's long-term objectives. CEOs who excel in decision-making can combine instinct with critical thinking, ensuring their choices are timely and strategically sound.

Jeff Bezos, the founder of Amazon, is a prime example of a CEO who balances intuition with **data-driven analysis**. Known for his "Day 1" philosophy, Bezos emphasises maintaining a start-up mentality, being agile, customer-centric, and willing to take risks. This approach has guided Amazon's strategic decisions, including developing Amazon Web Services (AWS) and acquiring Whole Foods. While these decisions were supported by extensive data analysis, they also relied heavily on Bezos's intuition and vision for the future.

CEOs can adopt tools and frameworks that promote analytical thinking while tapping into their intuition to enhance their decision-making capabilities. One such tool is the decision matrix, which helps leaders evaluate options based on predefined criteria. Another valuable approach is scenario planning, where CEOs consider multiple future scenarios and develop strategies to address them. This allows leaders to anticipate risks and opportunities, preparing them to navigate uncertainty.

Cognitive biases, such as confirmation bias and anchoring, can affect decision-making. CEOs must remain aware of these biases and actively seek diverse perspectives, challenge their assumptions, and explore alternative viewpoints. By doing so, they can make more balanced and well-rounded decisions.

Moreover, decision-making must strike a balance between **speed and deliberation**. In fast-paced business environments, quick decisions are often crucial. However, it is equally important to ensure that these decisions are well-considered and aligned with the organisation's strategic objectives. Achieving this balance allows CEOs to make informed decisions without sacrificing quality.

In conclusion, effective decision-making requires a delicate equilibrium between **intuition and analysis**. CEOs can make strategic decisions that drive the organisation forward by leveraging both and remaining mindful of cognitive biases. Making sound decisions confidently and quickly is a hallmark of successful leadership and a key determinant of a CEO's effectiveness.

1.6 Adaptability

In today's rapidly changing business environment, one of the most critical attributes for a CEO is **adaptability**. The capacity to navigate uncertainty, pivot strategies, and respond to evolving market conditions distinguishes successful leaders from those who struggle in adversity. Adaptability is essential for CEOs in dynamic environments, such as fast-growing start-ups or industries undergoing significant transformation.

In these settings, CEOs must adjust their strategies swiftly, seize emerging opportunities, and mitigate risks as they arise. This requires an open mindset, a willingness to experiment, and learning from successes and failures.

Satya Nadella, CEO of Microsoft, exemplifies **adaptability** in leadership. When Nadella took the helm in 2014, Microsoft was seen as lagging in the fast-evolving tech industry. Under his leadership, the company shifted to a cloud-first, mobile-first strategy, fostering significant growth and innovation. Nadella's ability to pivot the company's strategy, embrace new technologies, and cultivate a culture of continuous learning highlights the importance of adaptability in the CEO role.

CEOs must first develop a keen sense of external awareness to foster adaptability. This involves staying informed about industry trends, competitor activities, and technological advancements that could impact the business. By maintaining a broad perspective and anticipating change, CEOs can position their organisations to respond swiftly and effectively to new challenges and opportunities.

Internally, CEOs must create a culture that embraces **adaptability**. This includes encouraging experimentation, supporting risk-taking, and fostering an environment where failure is viewed as a learning opportunity rather than a setback. Implementing agile methodologies, which focus on iterative development and cross-functional collaboration, helps organisations remain flexible and responsive to change.

CEOs must also lead by example when it comes to adaptability. This means being willing to shift course when necessary, acknowledging when a strategy is not working, and being open to feedback from all levels of the organisation. By demonstrating a commitment to adaptability, CEOs can inspire their teams to embrace change and seek continuous improvement.

In conclusion, **adaptability** is vital for CEOs, particularly in today's fast-changing business landscape. By staying informed, fostering a culture of adaptability, and leading by example, CEOs can ensure their organisations remain resilient and agile. Adaptability helps CEOs navigate challenges and positions their companies to capitalise on new opportunities, driving sustained growth and success.

1.7 Inspirational Leadership

Inspirational leadership goes beyond simply motivating employees; it is about **cultivating a sense of purpose** and passion that drives individuals to exceed expectations. CEOs who inspire their teams foster a high-performance culture that fuels innovation, promotes collaboration, and leads to exceptional outcomes. Inspirational leadership is essential for building a culture where employees feel valued, empowered, and driven to contribute to the organisation's success.

A key component of inspirational leadership is articulating **a compelling vision** that resonates personally with employees. When leaders communicate a vision aligned with their team members' values and aspirations, they create a powerful sense of shared purpose. This shared purpose motivates employees to work toward common goals and fosters deep loyalty to the organisation.

Richard Branson, founder of Virgin Group, is a notable example of an **inspirational leader**. His charismatic leadership style, bold vision, and genuine enthusiasm for his employees' well-being have been pivotal in creating a company culture that is both innovative and customer-focused. Branson's ability to inspire his teams has contributed significantly to the Virgin brand's longevity and success.

Authenticity is another crucial element of **inspirational leadership**. Employees are more likely to be inspired by leaders who are genuine, transparent, and true to their values. Authentic leaders build trust by being open about their challenges, admitting mistakes, and demonstrating humility in their interactions. This authenticity strengthens the bond between leaders and their teams, making employees feel valued and respected.

In addition to authenticity, recognising and celebrating team members' **achievements** is essential for fostering a culture of inspiration. By acknowledging and rewarding employees' efforts, leaders reinforce positive behaviours and create an environment of appreciation. This recognition boosts morale and encourages a continuous cycle of high performance.

One effective way to inspire teams is through **storytelling**. Stories connect with people emotionally, conveying complex ideas in relatable and memorable ways. By sharing personal stories, experiences, and examples of how the organisation's vision has been realised, CEOs can inspire their teams to believe in the company's mission and see their work as part of a broader, meaningful journey.

In conclusion, **inspirational leadership** fosters purpose, passion, and commitment within an organisation. By articulating a compelling vision, leading authentically, and recognising the contributions of their teams, CEOs can inspire their employees to achieve greatness. This not only drives individual performance but also contributes to the overall success and growth of the organisation.

Strategic thinking is crucial for CEOs, enabling them to plan for the future with agility and foresight. In today's complex and rapidly changing business environment, CEOs must be able to anticipate trends, identify opportunities, and devise strategies that position their organisations for long-term success. Strategic thinking involves more than just setting long-term goals; it requires developing a roadmap for achieving those goals while maintaining flexibility to adapt to changing conditions.

At the heart of strategic thinking is seeing the **big picture** while understanding the detailed elements that drive the organisation forward. This combination of vision and analytical skills allows CEOs to navigate the complexities of their industry and market dynamics. Successful strategic thinking involves planning and positioning the organisation to thrive in uncertainty.

One of the most effective tools for **strategic thinking** is scenario planning. This process involves exploring multiple future scenarios and creating strategies to address them. By considering a range of possible outcomes, CEOs can better prepare for uncertainty and make more informed decisions. For example, during the 2008 financial crisis, companies that engaged in scenario planning were better equipped to navigate the downturn by having contingency plans in place.

Another valuable tool for strategic thinking is the **SWOT analysis**, which assesses the organisation's strengths, weaknesses, opportunities, and threats. This structured framework helps CEOs evaluate the internal and external factors that could influence their organisation's success. By understanding these elements, CEOs can make strategic decisions that leverage strengths, address weaknesses, capitalise on opportunities, and mitigate risks.

Staying ahead of industry trends and technological advancements is also crucial to **strategic thinking**. CEOs must actively seek new information, learn from competitors, and experiment with innovative approaches. This requires a continuous learning mindset and a willingness to challenge conventional thinking. For instance, Indra Nooyi, former CEO of PepsiCo, successfully repositioned the company by focusing on healthier products in response to shifting consumer preferences, ensuring PepsiCo remained competitive.

Strategic thinking also involves collaboration and input from diverse perspectives. CEOs who engage with their executive teams, board members, and key stakeholders foster a culture of **open communication and collaboration**. This ensures that decisions are well-rounded and informed, empowering leaders to craft strategies that propel their organisations toward success.

In conclusion, **strategic thinking** is essential for CEOs, allowing them to plan for the future with agility and foresight. Using tools like scenario planning and SWOT analysis, staying attuned to industry trends, and fostering collaboration, CEOs can develop strategies that position their organisations for long-term success. Strategic thinking is not just about goal-setting; it is about crafting a roadmap to achieve those goals while remaining adaptable to change.

1.8 Resilience

Resilience, the ability to withstand adversity and recover from setbacks, is critical for any CEO. The journey to success is rarely linear, and leadership often involves facing significant obstacles and navigating periods of uncertainty. A resilient CEO can endure challenges and emerge stronger, guiding their organisation through difficulties with perseverance and grace.

Howard Schultz, former CEO of Starbucks, exemplifies the importance of **resilience** in leadership. Schultz grew up in a low-income household and faced numerous challenges throughout his early life. Despite these hardships, he transformed Starbucks into one of the world's most iconic brands. However, Schultz's leadership journey was not without setbacks. In 2008, when Starbucks encountered financial difficulties, Schultz made the tough decision to close hundreds of stores and lay off employees. His resilience, determination, and ability to lead the company through adversity ultimately resulted in a successful recovery, underscoring the importance of perseverance in leadership.

Resilience in leadership is not solely about personal endurance; it also involves fostering a resilient organisation. This means creating a culture where **challenges are viewed as opportunities** for growth and failure is seen as a learning experience rather than a setback. CEOs can build organisational resilience by encouraging open communication, supporting risk-taking, and ensuring employees have the resources and support necessary to overcome obstacles.

A **growth mindset** plays a significant role in fostering resilience. It encourages individuals to see challenges as opportunities for learning and development. By adopting this mindset, CEOs can lead by example, demonstrating that setbacks are not to be feared but embraced as part of the journey toward success.

Adaptability is another key element of resilience. In a rapidly changing business environment, CEOs must be able to pivot and adjust strategies in response to new challenges. Adaptable leaders are better equipped to steer their organisations through periods of uncertainty, ensuring continued success. This requires staying informed about external trends, being open to new ideas, and taking calculated risks.

In addition to organisational resilience, CEOs must prioritise their **mental and physical well-being**. The pressures of leadership can take a toll, and maintaining resilience requires a healthy work-life balance. CEOs can preserve their stamina and lead effectively over the long term by setting boundaries, seeking needed support, and prioritising self-care.

In conclusion, **CEOs' resilience is essential**, enabling them to navigate challenges, overcome setbacks, and guide their organisations through adversity. By cultivating a growth mindset, fostering a resilient culture, and maintaining personal well-being, CEOs can develop the resilience necessary for long-term success. Resilience is not just about surviving hardship; it is about thriving in the face of challenges and emerging stronger.

1.9 Cultivating Innovation

Innovation is the driving force behind business growth and competitive advantage. For CEOs, fostering a culture of innovation within their organisations is essential to remaining competitive in an ever-changing marketplace. Innovation is not limited to developing new products or technologies; it also involves nurturing a mindset of creativity, experimentation, and continuous improvement.

One key element in cultivating innovation is creating an environment where **new ideas can flourish**. This involves encouraging employees to think creatively, take risks, and challenge the status quo. CEOs can promote innovation by providing the necessary resources and support for experimentation, such as dedicated time for research and development, access to cutting-edge technologies, and opportunities for cross-functional collaboration.

Google's "**20% time**" policy is a powerful example of how cultivating innovation can lead to remarkable success. This policy encourages employees to spend 20% of their work time on projects that interest them, even if they are not directly related to their job responsibilities. This approach has led to the development of some of Google's most successful products, such as Gmail and Google News. As a CEO, fostering an environment where employees thrive through innovation can inspire growth and drive organisational success.

In addition to promoting creativity, CEOs must embrace **failure** as an integral part of innovation. Innovation often involves taking risks, and not all initiatives will succeed. However, by viewing failure as a learning opportunity, CEOs can encourage their teams to continue pushing boundaries and exploring new possibilities. This approach fosters innovation and builds resilience as employees learn to persevere despite setbacks.

Collaboration is another essential aspect of innovation. By bringing diverse perspectives and expertise together, organisations can generate more creative solutions and accelerate innovation. CEOs can promote collaboration by breaking down silos, encouraging cross-functional teams, and creating environments where employees can share ideas and work together on innovative projects.

Staying informed about external trends and **emerging technologies** is critical for fostering innovation. CEOs must actively seek new information, engage with thought leaders, attend industry conferences, and stay abreast of technological advancements. By remaining ahead of the curve, CEOs can identify new opportunities for innovation and position their organisations to capitalise on them.

Finally, CEOs must lead by example when it comes to **innovation**. This means being open to new ideas, demonstrating a willingness to take risks, and continually seeking ways to improve and evolve the organisation. By embodying the principles of innovation, CEOs can inspire their teams to embrace creativity and drive the organisation forward.

In summary, **innovation** is essential for CEOs who want to drive their organisations forward in a competitive marketplace. CEOs can create an environment where innovation thrives by fostering a culture of creativity, embracing failure, promoting collaboration, and staying informed about external trends. Innovation is more than generating new ideas; it is about creating a culture of continuous improvement and adaptability that ensures success in an ever-changing world.

1.10 Legacy Building

Building a **legacy** goes beyond achieving financial success; it is about creating a lasting impact that endures long after a CEO's tenure. For many leaders, the ultimate measure of success is the legacy they leave behind and how they have shaped their organisation, influenced their industry and contributed to society. Legacy building involves embedding long-term thinking into daily leadership practices, ensuring the CEO's impact transcends their time in the role.

A CEO's legacy is often defined by the **values and principles** they instil within the organisation. This includes fostering a commitment to social responsibility, ethical business practices, and a focus on sustainability. Leaders who prioritise these values build successful businesses and contribute to the well-being of society and the environment. For example, Paul Polman, former CEO of Unilever, focused on creating a legacy through sustainability. Under his leadership, Unilever committed to ambitious goals, including reducing its environmental footprint and improving the livelihoods of millions. Polman's legacy is not just about Unilever's financial success but its positive impact on the world.

Legacy building involves not just fostering ethical values but also developing **future leaders**. CEOs who invest in mentoring and developing their teams ensure the organisation's long-term success and leave a legacy of strong leadership. By nurturing the next generation of leaders, CEOs ensure that their vision and values continue to guide the organisation after they step down. This can be achieved through leadership development programs, succession planning, and cultivating a culture of continuous learning.

Legacy building extends beyond the organisation, with CEOs making a lasting impact by **contributing to the broader community**. This might involve advocating for industry-wide changes, supporting charitable causes, or investing in initiatives that address social and environmental challenges. Bill Gates, co-founder of Microsoft, exemplifies this legacy building through his philanthropic efforts, particularly in global health and education.

Gates's commitment to using his wealth and influence to make a positive difference in the world highlights the power of legacy building.

Embedding legacy thinking into everyday leadership practices requires CEOs to prioritise **long-term goals over short-term gains**. This means focusing on sustainable growth, investing in people and communities, and making decisions that align with the organisation's core values. By doing so, CEOs create a lasting impact that extends beyond financial success and benefits the greater good.

In conclusion, **legacy building** is about creating an enduring impact beyond a CEO's tenure in the role. By focusing on values, developing future leaders, contributing to the broader community, and prioritising long-term goals, CEOs can ensure that their legacy is one of positive and lasting influence. Legacy building is not just about what a leader achieves during their tenure but also about their impact on future generations.

Conclusion

As explored throughout this chapter, becoming a successful CEO requires more than technical skills or the ability to rise. It demands cultivating **a unique mindset** that blends vision, emotional intelligence, decisiveness, adaptability, and a commitment to innovation and legacy building. The CEO's mindset is more than leading an organisation; it is about shaping its future, inspiring its people, and creating a lasting impact far beyond its tenure.

The journey toward this mindset begins with **self-awareness** and a growth-oriented approach to challenges. CEOs must embrace continuous learning, remain open to feedback, and be willing to pivot when necessary. Their ability to balance intuition with rigorous analysis in decision-making, combined with their resilience to overcome setbacks, positions them to lead their organisations confidently in the face of uncertainty and change.

Visionary leadership and emotional intelligence further distinguish effective CEOs. By crafting and communicating a compelling vision that unites and motivates their teams, CEOs guide their organisations with purpose. By connecting personally with employees and leading with empathy and authenticity, they foster a culture of trust and collaboration, driving long-term success.

Innovation is the **lifeblood of thriving organisations**. CEOs who cultivate a culture of creativity and experimentation and are not afraid to fail ensure that their companies remain agile and competitive in an ever-evolving marketplace. Innovation, strategic thinking, and a commitment to long-term goals enable CEOs to build lasting legacies.

Ultimately, a CEO's success is measured by the **legacy** they leave behind. By embedding sustainability, ethical leadership, and social responsibility into the fabric of their organisations, CEOs create a lasting impact that benefits not only their companies but society at large. Developing future leaders and investing in the broader community ensures that their influence continues to shape their industry and the world for generations to come.

In conclusion, the **CEO's mindset** is a powerful combination of vision, strategy, emotional intelligence, and a focus on legacy. By embracing these attributes, aspiring leaders can achieve their immediate goals and make a lasting and positive impact on their organisations, industries, and society. This mindset is about leading with purpose, resilience, and a vision beyond the boardroom.

Chapter 2

Strategic Planning: The Key to Shaping Your Company's Future

2.1 Overview

Strategic planning is the heartbeat of any successful organisation. It is not simply an optional process but a critical necessity that businesses must engage with to create a clear and effective vision for their future. This plan does more than just establish goals; it defines the **procedures and operations** that will guide an organisation in achieving its vision. In today's business world, where rapid changes constantly introduce new challenges and opportunities, having a solid strategic plan is indispensable for long-term success.

Without a strong strategic plan, companies risk falling behind as they react to problems and opportunities rather than anticipating and shaping them. A robust **strategic plan** helps businesses maintain focus and fosters resilience, allowing them to adapt and thrive amid change. In this chapter, we will explore the essential steps of creating a strategic plan, from conducting **environmental analyses** using tools such as **SWOT** and **PESTEL** to setting **SMART objectives**, formulating strategies, and executing them effectively. By the end, you will have the knowledge and tools to develop a strategic plan that meets your business goals, positions your organisation for growth, and ensures resilience in an unpredictable environment.

Strategic planning is not just about setting goals; it is about understanding the broader landscape in which your organisation operates and aligning all actions towards a unified vision. This unifying function requires continuous assessment, thoughtful strategy development, and a dynamic, adaptive approach to business. We will discuss how to monitor progress, adapt to inevitable changes, and involve your entire team to ensure that your strategic plan becomes a living, breathing document capable of evolving with your business and contributing to its ongoing success.

2.2 The Essence of Strategic Planning

At its core, strategic planning is a proactive endeavour that steers a business's future direction. It sets out an organisation's goals and the most effective use of resources to achieve those goals. This process is pivotal for long-term success, guiding an organisation from its current state to its desired future. A robust strategic plan is a compass that prevents businesses from drifting aimlessly, ensuring they proactively chart a course for success.

The essence of strategic planning is not only about setting objectives but about making sure every decision, action, and resource is aligned with a broader vision. It clarifies the organisation's direction and helps ensure all efforts contribute to its objectives. Consider the case of **Apple's** resurgence during the early 2000s. Under **Steve Jobs'** leadership, Apple's strategic plan was centred around simplicity and innovation. This clear focus allowed Apple to concentrate its resources on a few key products like the iPod, iPhone and iPad, which ultimately revolutionised entire industries.

Strategic planning also plays a pivotal role in guiding **decision-making** within the organisation. When new opportunities or challenges arise, a well-developed strategic plan provides a framework for evaluating whether these options align with the company's long-term objectives. This ensures that businesses stay focused on their overarching goals and do not get distracted by short-term gains that may not contribute meaningfully to their vision.

In summary, strategic planning is more than just goal-setting; it is about ensuring that every aspect of the organisation is aligned with the **long-term vision**. It provides clarity, facilitates better decision-making, and efficiently allocates resources. A well-thought-out strategic plan equips businesses with the tools they need to navigate the complexities of the business environment, ensuring sustained growth and long-term success.

2.3 Analysing the Business Environment

A crucial part of strategic planning involves thoroughly analysing the business environment. This analysis enables businesses to understand internal and external factors affecting their success. Two widely utilised tools in this process are the **SWOT** and **PESTEL** analyses.

The **SWOT analysis** is a framework that helps businesses identify their **Strengths**, **Weaknesses**, **Opportunities**, and **Threats**. By conducting a **SWOT analysis**, companies can take a holistic view of their current position and understand the factors influencing their future performance. For example, a company may identify its strong brand reputation as a key strength while recognising a lack of digital presence as a significant weakness. Opportunities might include an expanding market for the company's products, while threats could arise from emerging competitors. By understanding these internal and external factors, businesses can develop strategies to capitalise on their strengths, address weaknesses, seize opportunities, and mitigate threats.

In addition to **SWOT**, the **PESTEL analysis** provides a framework for understanding the broader external environment. **PESTEL** stands for **Political, Economic, Social, Technological, Environmental**, and **Legal** factors that could affect the business. Using a PESTEL analysis, companies can identify macro-environmental forces that could significantly impact their operations. For example, government regulations, economic trends, or technological advancements can present business challenges and opportunities. A renewable energy company, for instance, might use **PESTEL** to evaluate how environmental regulations and shifts in consumer demand for sustainable products could impact its business strategy.

By regularly conducting **SWOT** and **PESTEL analyses**, businesses can stay informed about the factors shaping their industry and develop **resilient strategies** that can adapt to change. Companies like **Starbucks** have used environmental analysis effectively to adjust their strategies in response to changing market conditions. By recognising the growing

27

consumer demand for ethically sourced products, Starbucks integrated **social responsibility** into its business model, launching initiatives such as ethically sourced coffee and reducing its environmental impact. These initiatives resonated with consumers and helped strengthen the company's brand.

2.4 Setting Objectives

After conducting a thorough analysis of the business environment, the next step in the strategic planning process is to set clear, actionable objectives. These objectives serve as **targets** that the organisation aims to achieve, and they are essential for guiding efforts and measuring progress. The most effective objectives are **SMART**, meaning they are **Specific, Measurable, Achievable, Relevant, and Time-bound**.

Objectives must be specific and provide a clear direction for the organisation. Vague goals, such as "increase sales," are not helpful because they lack clarity. A specific objective, such as "increase sales by 15% in the North American market within the next 12 months," provides much clearer direction and ensures that everyone understands what is expected of them.

Measurable objectives include criteria that allow progress to be tracked. In the example above, the 15% sales increase provides a concrete **metric** that can be monitored over time. This allows the organisation to assess whether it is on track to meet its goals and make adjustments if necessary.

Given the organisation's resources and constraints, **achievable objectives** are realistic and attainable. While it is important to set ambitious goals, they must remain within the realm of possibility. Setting unrealistic objectives can lead to frustration, while **realistic** goals provide a sense of accomplishment and foster momentum.

Relevant objectives are aligned with the organisation's overall strategy and contribute meaningfully to its long-term vision. For instance, a **technology company** focused on innovation might set an objective to "launch three new products that leverage artificial intelligence within the next 18 months." This ensures that the company's efforts are aligned with its broader strategic priorities.

Finally, **time-bound objectives** include a specific deadline, which creates a sense of urgency and helps the organisation prioritise tasks. For example, setting a 12-month deadline for increasing sales by 15% provides a clear timeframe within which progress can be regularly assessed and adjustments made if necessary.

By setting **SMART objectives**, businesses can ensure that their strategic vision is translated into **actionable steps**. This helps to focus efforts and direct resources towards the organisation's strategic goals and establishes clear benchmarks for success. Well-defined objectives guide the organisation's efforts and provide valuable tools for tracking progress and making necessary adjustments.

2.5 Strategy Formulation

Strategy formulation is the next step in the strategic planning process once the business environment has been analysed and SMART objectives have been set. This involves determining the most effective way to achieve the organisation's objectives and allocating resources efficiently to support these efforts. Strategy formulation requires a deep understanding of the organisation's strengths and weaknesses and a keen awareness of the broader market environment.

Several common strategic options exist for businesses, including cost leadership, differentiation, and focus. Each strategy offers a different approach to achieving a **competitive advantage** in the market.

The **cost leadership strategy** focuses on becoming the lowest-cost producer in the industry. By reducing costs and achieving economies of scale, a company can offer its products or services at a lower price than its competitors, attracting price-sensitive customers. This strategy often involves optimising the **supply chain**, improving **operational efficiencies**, and negotiating favourable terms with suppliers. An example of a company that has successfully employed a **cost leadership strategy** is **Walmart**. By leveraging its vast supply chain, operational efficiencies, and buying power, Walmart has consistently offered lower prices than its competitors, attracting many **price-conscious consumers**.

On the other hand, the **differentiation strategy** is centred around offering unique products or services valued by customers and for which they are willing to pay a premium. This approach often involves investing in **innovation**, **branding**, and **customer experience** to create a distinct market position. Companies that pursue a differentiation strategy aim to stand out in their industry through superior quality, exceptional service, or innovative features. A notable example of this strategy is **Apple**. Apple has built its brand around sleek design, premium quality, and a user-friendly experience. By focusing on these attributes, Apple has cultivated a loyal customer base willing to pay a higher price for its products, such as the iPhone and MacBook, which are perceived as premium offerings.

The third common strategic option is the **focus strategy**, which involves targeting a specific **market segment** or niche. In this approach, companies tailor their products or services to meet a particular group of customers' unique needs rather than competing across the entire market. The focus strategy can be further divided into **cost focus** and **differentiation focus**. In terms of **cost focus**, a company aims to be the lowest-cost producer in a specific niche. In contrast, with a **differentiation focus**, the company seeks to offer specialised products or services to a specific customer group. A great example of the focus strategy is **Tesla's** early approach to the luxury electric vehicle (EV) market. Tesla initially targeted high-end consumers interested in electric vehicles, focusing on delivering premium quality and cutting-edge technology. By narrowing its focus, Tesla was able to build a strong brand within this niche before expanding to a broader market with more affordable models.

In strategy formulation, businesses must carefully consider which approach best aligns with their strengths, market conditions, and overall objectives. Whether through **cost leadership**, **differentiation**, or **focus**, the goal is to position the organisation in a way that maximises **competitive advantage** and drives long-term success. Each of these strategies requires a clear understanding of the company's core competencies and the external environment, ensuring that the chosen approach is realistic and achievable given the company's resources and capabilities.

2.6 Execution

While formulating a strong strategy is essential, the real challenge lies in executing that strategy. Execution is where the strategic plan is implemented, translating high-level objectives into concrete steps the organisation must take to achieve its goals. Effective execution requires careful planning, clear communication, and rigorous follow-up to ensure that resources are allocated efficiently and that every organisation member is aligned with the strategic goals.

The first step in execution is developing **detailed action plans** that break down the strategic objectives into specific tasks. These tasks should be clearly defined, with each assigned to the appropriate teams or individuals, along with specific **timelines** for completion. Each task should be directly linked to the organisation's broader strategic objectives, ensuring that every action contributes to the overall goals. A well-structured **action**

plan will outline what needs to be done, who is responsible for each task, and when the task needs to be completed.

Resource allocation is another critical aspect of execution. It is essential to ensure that the necessary financial, human, and technological resources are available to support the strategy's implementation. For instance, if a company's strategy involves launching a new product line, sufficient resources must be allocated for **research and development**, **marketing**, and **production**. Effective resource allocation requires careful **budgeting** and **prioritisation**, ensuring that the most important tasks receive the necessary support while avoiding the misallocation of resources to less critical areas.

Creating **timelines** is an essential part of the execution process. Timelines ensure tasks are completed logically and provide a framework for regularly monitoring progress. Setting **realistic deadlines** for each task, considering the resources available and any potential obstacles, is crucial for keeping the project on track. Clear and realistic timelines also help create a sense of urgency and keep teams focused on meeting **strategic milestones**.

Regular progress reviews are an important part of **monitoring execution**. These reviews should be conducted at predetermined intervals, such as monthly or quarterly, to assess how the organisation is progressing towards its strategic objectives. During these reviews, leaders should evaluate the **strategy's effectiveness**, the **efficiency of resource allocation**, and the **performance of teams**. If any **deviations** from the plan are identified, corrective actions should be taken to ensure that the organisation remains on track to meet its goals. By regularly monitoring progress, companies can make timely adjustments to their strategy, resources, or timelines, ensuring they stay on course.

Finally, successful execution requires the **involvement of the entire organisation**. Clear communication is essential for ensuring that everyone within the company understands the strategic goals and their role in achieving them. Leaders must foster a **culture of accountability**, where each team member takes ownership of their tasks and strives to achieve the best possible outcomes. Consider the example of **Amazon's** strategy to expand its logistics network. The successful execution of this strategy required a massive investment in new **distribution centres**, technology, and personnel. The coordinated efforts of Amazon's teams, driven by clear goals and a sense of accountability, allowed the company to offer faster delivery times and improve the customer experience, ultimately contributing to its long-term success.

Execution is a critical phase of the strategic planning process. Organisations can drive long-term success by translating the strategic plan into actionable steps, allocating resources efficiently, creating timelines, and ensuring team involvement. Effective execution requires careful planning, ongoing communication, and a commitment to following through on strategic initiatives.

2.7 Monitoring and Control

Once a strategy is in motion, it is essential to monitor its progress and continuously make adjustments as necessary. **Monitoring and control** are key components of strategic planning that ensure the organisation remains aligned with its objectives and can respond to any challenges or changes in the business environment.

Key Performance Indicators (KPIs) are an essential tool for monitoring the success of a strategic plan. KPIs are specific **metrics** that provide insights into how well an organisation is performing relative to its strategic goals. For example, a company focused on increasing sales might track revenue growth, the number of new customers acquired, or its market share. Regularly reviewing KPIs allows leadership to assess whether the organisation is on track to meet its objectives or if adjustments need to be made to improve performance. KPIs help **quantify progress**, making evaluating whether the strategic plan works as intended easier.

In addition to KPIs, **control mechanisms** are needed to ensure that the organisation's activities remain aligned with the strategic plan. These mechanisms can take many forms, such as **budget controls**, which help ensure that financial resources are allocated appropriately, or **quality controls**, which ensure that products or services meet the desired standards. By implementing these control mechanisms, organisations can prevent deviations from the strategic plan and maintain focus on their long-term objectives.

Flexibility is another key aspect of monitoring and control. The business environment is constantly changing, and strategies that were effective when the plan was first developed may need to be adjusted to address new challenges or opportunities. Leaders must remain **adaptable** and willing to change their strategy when necessary. For instance, **Netflix** demonstrated its ability to adapt when it shifted from a DVD rental model to a focus on streaming services. By closely monitoring trends in **consumer behaviour** and the **media industry**, Netflix recognised the growing demand for streaming and adjusted its strategy accordingly, investing heavily in streaming technology and original content. This strategic pivot has been a key factor in Netflix's long-term success.

In conclusion, **monitoring and control** are essential elements of the strategic planning process. By regularly reviewing progress, tracking performance through KPIs, implementing control mechanisms, and maintaining **flexibility**, organisations can ensure that their strategies remain on track and respond effectively to business environment changes. Through effective monitoring and control, businesses can achieve their strategic objectives and sustain long-term success.

2.8 Adapting to Change

In a constantly evolving business landscape, even the most well-crafted strategic plans must be flexible enough to accommodate unexpected changes. The ability to **adapt** to change is crucial for ensuring that an organisation can navigate new challenges and seize emerging opportunities. Adapting to change involves recognising when a strategy is ineffective and being willing to pivot or adjust to stay on course.

Recognising the **need for change** is often one of the most significant challenges for business leaders. It requires continuous **vigilance**, including monitoring **internal performance metrics**, competitor activities, and shifts in market dynamics. Early recognition of the need for change can help an organisation respond before challenges escalate into crises. This requires leaders to be attuned to changes in **consumer behaviour**, **technological advancements**, regulatory shifts, and other external factors that could impact the business.

A classic example of an organisation that failed to recognise the need for change in time is **Kodak**. During the rise of digital photography in the early 2000s, Kodak, which had dominated the film photography market for decades, was slow to pivot towards digital technology. Despite recognising the shift towards digital, Kodak remained overly committed to its traditional film business and delayed the development of new digital products. As a result, when Kodak eventually decided to pivot towards digital, it had already lost significant market share to competitors who had embraced digital photography earlier. This failure to adapt promptly highlights the importance of recognising the need for change and acting decisively to address it.

Once the need for change is identified, the next step is to **pivot effectively**. This involves reassessing the organisation's objectives, resources, and capabilities and developing a new plan that addresses current challenges and opportunities. Effective pivoting requires a combination of **open-mindedness** and **decisive leadership**. Leaders must be willing to question long-held assumptions and explore new approaches that may not have been part of the original strategy.

Pivoting effectively also requires **strong communication** and **leadership**. When a significant change in strategy is required, it is important to communicate the reasons for the change clearly to all organisation members. Leaders should explain the new direction and the steps that will be taken to achieve the revised objectives. This ensures that everyone within the organisation is aligned and working towards the same goals. Additionally, leaders must be prepared to address any concerns or resistance during the transition, helping employees understand how the changes will benefit the organisation.

Adapting to change often involves responding to both **internal** and **external factors**. Internally, changes in available resources, capabilities, or leadership can necessitate adjustments to the strategy. Externally, changes in the market environment, such as shifts in **consumer preferences**, **technological advancements**, or regulatory changes, may require a reassessment of the business's strategic approach. For instance, **Netflix's** transition from a DVD rental service to a streaming giant is an excellent example of how a company can adapt to external changes. Recognising the growing demand for online streaming, Netflix pivoted its business model, investing heavily in **streaming**

technology and **original content production**. This strategic shift allowed Netflix to remain competitive and eventually become a leader in the entertainment industry.

Adapting **to change** is essential for any organisation's long-term success. By staying informed, recognising the need for change early, and pivoting effectively, businesses can navigate the challenges of a dynamic market and continue to achieve their strategic objectives. Adaptability requires proactive leadership, strong communication, and a commitment to continuous improvement, ensuring the organisation remains resilient in the face of uncertainty.

2.9 Involving Your Team

Strategic planning should not be confined to senior leadership; it must be a **collaborative process** that involves the entire organisation. Engaging employees at all levels in the strategic planning process fosters innovation and creativity and increases the likelihood of successful execution by generating buy-in and commitment. Involving your team leads to better solutions and creates a shared sense of **ownership** over the company's success.

One key benefit of involving employees in strategic planning is their diverse perspectives. Employees across different levels of the organisation possess unique insights into the company's day-to-day operations, customer needs, and potential challenges. By incorporating these diverse perspectives into the planning process, leaders can develop more comprehensive and well-rounded strategies that address a wider range of issues.

For example, **Southwest Airlines** is well-known for its **employee-centric approach** to strategic planning. When developing its growth strategy, Southwest involved employees from all levels of the organisation in the planning process. This generated valuable ideas and fostered a sense of **community** and **shared commitment** among employees. As a result, the company successfully executed its strategy while maintaining its unique corporate culture. This example highlights how involving employees in strategic planning can lead to better solutions and a stronger commitment to achieving the organisation's goals.

Involving employees in strategic planning also helps to build **buy-in** and **commitment**. When employees feel that their input is valued and that they have a stake in the company's future, they are more likely to be **engaged** and motivated to contribute to achieving the organisation's strategic objectives. This sense of ownership can lead to greater alignment and cooperation during the execution phase. Additionally, involving employees in the planning process enhances **transparency** and fosters collaboration.

Leaders should create opportunities for **participation** and **input** throughout the process, such as brainstorming sessions, workshops, surveys, and open forums where employees can share their ideas and feedback. This inclusive approach strengthens the strategic plan and builds a more **cohesive** and **engaged** workforce.

Clear and effective **communication** is essential when involving your team in strategic planning. Leaders must clearly articulate the organisation's vision, objectives, and the importance of the strategic plan. Additionally, regular updates on the plan's progress should be shared with employees to keep them informed and engaged. Communication ensures that all employees understand the organisation's strategic goals and their role in achieving them.

In summary, involving your team in strategic planning is essential for developing a strong and effective strategy. By leveraging employees' collective knowledge and insights, organisations can create more comprehensive and robust plans better suited to the company's needs. Furthermore, involving employees builds buy-in and commitment, ensuring everyone is aligned and working towards the same goals. Effective communication, transparency, and collaboration are the keys to successfully involving your team in strategic planning.

2.10 Case Studies

Examining case studies of successful **strategic planning initiatives** can provide valuable lessons for organisations looking to craft and execute their strategies. Learning from the experiences of other companies helps leaders understand the key decisions and actions that led to positive outcomes, offering insights that can be applied to their businesses.

One of the most notable examples of a successful strategic turnaround is **IBM's transformation** in the early 1990s. At that time, IBM faced **declining revenues**, an **outdated business**

model, and **increasing competition**. When **Lou Gerstner** became CEO in 1993, he recognised that the company needed a radical change in strategy to survive. Gerstner shifted IBM's focus from hardware to **services** and **software**, positioning the company as a leader in **IT consulting** and **enterprise solutions**. This strategic shift revitalised IBM and allowed it to remain a dominant player in the technology sector. Gerstner's approach to strategic planning offers several key lessons: first, he recognised the need for change and acted decisively to pivot the company's strategy; second, he focused on leveraging IBM's existing strengths in technology and innovation to develop new revenue streams; third, Gerstner emphasised the importance of **execution**, ensuring that the new strategy was implemented effectively across the organisation. Finally, he involved the entire company in the transformation, building buy-in and commitment to the new direction.

Another compelling case study is **Netflix's transition** from a DVD rental service to a global leader in streaming. In the mid-2000s, Netflix recognised the growing demand for online streaming and strategically decided to invest heavily in **streaming technology** and **original content production**. This shift required significant changes to the company's **business model**, **technology infrastructure**, and **content strategy**. By 2010, Netflix had established itself as a leader in the streaming industry, with a global subscriber base and a portfolio of award-winning original content. The key to Netflix's success was its ability to anticipate market trends and adapt its strategy accordingly. The company's leadership demonstrated a willingness to take **risks** and invest in new areas, even when it meant disrupting its existing business model. Additionally, Netflix's focus on **innovation** and **customer experience** helped it differentiate itself from competitors and build a loyal customer base.

These case studies illustrate the importance of **strategic planning**, **adaptability**, and **execution** in achieving business success. By learning from the experiences of companies like IBM and Netflix, leaders can gain valuable insights into navigating challenges, seizing opportunities, and driving long-term growth. The common themes in these success stories include having a **clear vision**, **decisive leadership**, a focus on **execution**, and a willingness to adapt to changing market conditions.

2.11 Tools and Techniques

Organisations must use various tools and techniques to develop and implement a successful strategic plan. These resources enable businesses to analyse their environment, set objectives, formulate strategies, and monitor progress. By leveraging the right tools, companies can ensure that their strategic planning process is thorough, effective, and aligned with their long-term goals.

One of the most widely used tools in strategic planning is the **Balanced Scorecard**, developed by **Robert Kaplan** and **David Norton**. The Balanced Scorecard is a performance management tool that helps organisations translate their strategy into **actionable objectives** and measure progress across four key perspectives: **financial**, **customer**, **internal processes**, and

learning and growth. By using the Balanced Scorecard, companies can ensure that their strategic plan is aligned with their overall vision, tracking progress across multiple dimensions rather than focusing solely on financial outcomes.

For example, a company might use the financial perspective to track **revenue growth**, the customer perspective to measure **customer satisfaction**, the internal processes perspective to evaluate **operational efficiency**, and the learning and growth perspective to assess **employee development**. This comprehensive approach allows organisations to monitor their performance holistically and adjust as needed to stay on track to achieve their strategic objectives. The Balanced Scorecard helps businesses focus on short-term operational outcomes and long-term strategic goals.

Another valuable tool for strategic planning is **Porter's Five Forces**, a framework developed by **Michael Porter**. Porter's Five Forces helps organisations analyse the **competitive forces** within their industry, providing insights into the external factors that could influence their business. The five forces include the **threat of new entrants**, suppliers' bargaining power, customers' bargaining power, substitute products' threat, and the **intensity of competitive rivalry**. Companies can develop strategies that address their industry's key challenges and opportunities by understanding these forces.

For example, in a highly competitive market, a company might use Porter's Five Forces to assess the **threat of new entrants** and **substitute products**. Based on this analysis, the company could develop strategies to strengthen its **competitive position**, such as improving product quality, lowering costs, or enhancing customer loyalty. This tool helps companies anticipate and respond to changes in the market, ensuring that they remain competitive in their industry.

Scenario Planning is another technique that can be invaluable in the strategic planning process. This technique involves developing multiple scenarios based on different assumptions about the future and evaluating how the organisation would respond to each scenario. **Scenario planning** allows businesses to develop more **resilient and adaptable strategies** by considering a range of possible futures. This is particularly useful in industries subject to significant **uncertainty** or **disruption**.

For example, an energy company might develop scenarios based on different assumptions about future government regulations, technological advancements, and consumer demand. By considering a range of potential outcomes, the company can develop a **flexible strategy** to succeed in multiple scenarios rather than being locked into a single approach that may not hold up under changing conditions.

In addition to traditional frameworks, several **software solutions** can support the strategic planning process. Tools like **MindManager** and **Lucidchart** help organisations visualise their strategy, create detailed **action plans**, and collaborate more effectively across teams. Strategic planning software, such as **OnStrategy** and **Cascade**, offers integrated platforms for developing, executing, and monitoring strategic plans, making it easier for leaders to manage the process from start to finish.

These software solutions allow organisations to **track progress** in real-time, making it easier to adjust strategies as needed. By using technology to streamline the strategic planning process, companies can ensure that their plans remain dynamic and responsive to changes in the business environment.

Another popular tool used in strategic planning is **Objectives and Key Results (OKRs)**. **OKRs** are a goal-setting framework used to align an organisation's efforts with its strategic objectives. The framework involves setting specific, measurable goals (called **Objectives**) and identifying the **Key Results** that will indicate progress toward achieving these goals. **OKRs** have been popularised by companies like **Google** and **Intel**, where they have been used to drive focus, alignment, and accountability across the organisation.

For example, a technology company might set an **objective** to "increase market share in the mobile app industry" and define key results such as "launching three new apps by the end of the year" or "increasing downloads by 20%." By regularly reviewing progress toward these key results, the company can ensure that it is on track to achieve its strategic objectives and make adjustments as needed.

In conclusion, numerous tools and techniques are available to support the **strategic planning process**. From frameworks like the Balanced Scorecard and Porter's Five Forces to software solutions and goal-setting methodologies like OKRs, these resources provide valuable guidance for developing, executing, and monitoring strategic plans. By leveraging these tools, leaders can ensure that their strategic planning process is **thorough**, **effective**, and aligned with the organisation's long-term vision.

Conclusion

Strategic planning is the foundation upon which successful businesses are built. It transforms an organisation's **vision** into **actionable steps**, ensuring that every resource, decision, and effort aligns with the company's long-term goals. As we have explored in this chapter, the **strategic planning process** involves a thorough analysis of the business environment, the setting of **SMART objectives**, the formulation and execution of strategies, and the ongoing monitoring and adaptation to change. Through case studies and practical tools, we have seen how companies like **IBM** and **Netflix** have navigated challenges and seized opportunities by implementing effective strategic plans.

In today's **dynamic business landscape**, the importance of strategic planning cannot be overstated. A well-developed strategic plan provides **clarity**, **direction**, and **resilience**, enabling organisations to thrive amidst uncertainty and change. Strategic planning helps organisations anticipate challenges, leverage opportunities, and position themselves for sustained growth.

It is also important to remember that strategic planning is not a one-time event but an **ongoing process** that requires continuous reflection, adaptation, and commitment. Organisations must regularly review and update their strategic plans to remain aligned with changing market conditions, new technologies, and shifting consumer preferences. Adaptability is a key component of long-term success, and leaders must remain flexible and open to change as they guide their organisations forward.

Furthermore, **involving the entire team** in strategic planning is essential to execute the plan effectively. By engaging employees at all levels and leveraging their insights, businesses can develop more comprehensive strategies and foster a shared ownership of the company's future. Clear communication, transparency, and collaboration are critical to successfully implementing a strategic plan.

As you craft your company's strategic plan, remember that **strategic planning** is not a static document but a **living roadmap** that evolves alongside the organisation. By staying informed, being **flexible**, and involving your team, you can position your organisation for **sustained growth** and long-term success in an ever-changing business environment.

Chapter 3

Understanding Financial Metrics: The Language of Business

3.1 Overview

In today's dynamic business environment, a strong financial literacy foundation is beneficial and imperative for any leader aiming to drive organisational success. The ability to understand financial metrics is akin to mastering a new language, the language of business. These metrics provide a comprehensive view of an organisation's health, performance, and potential, enabling CEOs and business leaders to make informed decisions that are pivotal for achieving strategic goals. Whether the objective is to attract investors, effectively manage cash flow, or chart a course for future growth, a deep understanding of financial statements and key performance indicators (KPIs) is essential.

This chapter demystifies the complex world of finance by breaking down the most critical financial statements and metrics that every business leader must be familiar with. It explores the core elements of income statements, balance sheets, and cash flow statements and examines the KPIs that provide the clearest insights into a company's performance. The chapter also discusses practical budgeting strategies, managing cash flow, maximising profits, assessing investments, and mitigating financial risks. By the end of this chapter, readers will have acquired the financial acumen necessary to lead their organisations toward sustained success, armed with confidence and clarity.

3.2 Financial Statements 101

Financial statements are the cornerstone of any business's financial infrastructure. They provide a snapshot of the company's financial health and are essential tools for making informed decisions. Every CEO must be well-versed in the three main types of financial statements: the income statement, the balance sheet, and the cash flow statement. Each document serves a distinct purpose, and when considered together, they offer a comprehensive view of a business's financial status. The **income statement**, often called the profit and loss statement, summarises a company's revenues, costs, and expenses over a specified period. Its primary function is to answer a fundamental question: Is the business profitable? This statement begins with revenue, commonly known as the "top line," and deducts various operating expenses to arrive at the net income, or the "bottom line." Understanding how to interpret the income statement is crucial for CEOs as it helps identify trends in revenue and costs, assess profitability, and make strategic decisions about pricing, cost management, and growth opportunities.

The **balance sheet** offers a snapshot of a company's financial position at a given time. It is divided into three main sections: assets, liabilities, and equity. Assets represent what the company owns, including cash, inventory, and property, while liabilities indicate what the company owes, such as loans or accounts payable. Equity represents the ownership interest after all liabilities are subtracted from assets. The balance sheet is vital for assessing liquidity, solvency, and financial stability, allowing CEOs to determine whether the business has the resources to support its operations and growth plans.

The **cash flow statement** is often considered the most important financial document for understanding a company's financial health. It tracks the movement of cash in and out of the business and is divided into three sections: operating activities, investing activities, and financing activities. Unlike the income statement, which includes non-cash items like depreciation, the cash flow statement focuses on actual cash transactions. This emphasis on liquidity makes the cash flow statement essential for determining a company's ability to meet its short-term obligations and fund future growth.

While understanding these individual financial statements is crucial, the true skill lies in synthesising the data they provide. For instance, a rising net income on the income statement might indicate growth, but weak cash flow could suggest deeper liquidity issues. Similarly, poor cash flow management can undermine a strong balance sheet. A CEO's ability to analyse and integrate information from these financial statements enables them to make strategic decisions that propel their company forward.

3.3 Key Performance Indicators (KPIs)

Key Performance Indicators (KPIs) are crucial for evaluating a company's health and performance. They serve as a business's vital signs, indicating whether it is on the right path or if corrective action is needed. While numerous KPIs can be tracked depending on the business model, several are universally important across industries.

Profit margins are among the most critical KPIs because they directly reflect profitability, which is the lifeblood of any business. The three main types of profit margins, gross profit margin, operating profit margin, and net profit margin, each provide a unique perspective on a company's financial health. Gross profit margin indicates how efficiently the company produces goods or services relative to its sales. Operating profit margin demonstrates the business's effectiveness in managing its operating expenses, while net profit margin shows the overall profitability after accounting for all costs and expenses. Monitoring these margins consistently allows CEOs to identify trends, benchmark against competitors, and adjust pricing or cost structures as necessary.

Return on Investment (ROI) is another critical KPI that measures an investment's efficiency. It is calculated by dividing the net profit from an investment by its cost. ROI is valuable for CEOs when evaluating the potential returns of various projects or investments. For example, when considering the launch of a new product, calculating the expected ROI helps determine whether the investment will be worthwhile. ROI is also useful for comparing different investment opportunities, enabling CEOs to allocate resources to those that promise the highest returns.

Customer Acquisition Cost (CAC) measures the cost of acquiring a new customer, encompassing all marketing and sales expenses divided by the number of customers acquired during a specific period. Understanding CAC is particularly important in industries with high customer turnover or where acquisition costs significantly impact profitability. CEOs must evaluate CAC to assess the efficiency of their marketing strategies and ensure cost-effective customer acquisition. A high CAC might indicate the need for a more targeted marketing approach or improvements in sales efficiency.

Other important KPIs include **Customer Lifetime Value (CLTV)**, which estimates the total revenue a business can expect from a customer over time, and the **Inventory Turnover Ratio**, which measures how efficiently inventory is managed. Tracking these KPIs provides CEOs with a comprehensive view of the company's performance, highlights areas for improvement, and facilitates data-driven decisions that support growth and profitability. Monitoring key metrics such as profit margins, ROI, and CAC ensures companies remain on the right track, empowering CEOs to make informed decisions that drive success.

3.4 Budgeting for Success

Budgeting is one of the most powerful tools in a CEO's arsenal. It involves planning how the company will allocate its financial resources over a specified period to achieve its financial and strategic objectives. A well-constructed budget serves as a roadmap, guiding spending decisions, forecasting revenue, and ensuring the business remains financially stable.

The importance of **budgeting** cannot be overstated. It enables a company to plan for the future, anticipate potential challenges, and allocate resources to areas that will yield the greatest impact. Without a structured budget, businesses are more likely to overspend, encounter cash flow problems, or miss out on growth opportunities due to poor planning.

Creating a successful budget begins with establishing clear financial objectives. These goals may include targets for revenue growth, profitability, or cost reductions. Once financial goals are set, the next step is to forecast income and expenses. This involves realistically estimating expected revenue during the budget period and planning how funds will be allocated across various expense categories. This process requires careful consideration of historical data, market trends, and sales pipelines to ensure accurate revenue forecasting.

On the expense side, it is crucial to account for fixed and variable costs. Fixed costs, such as rent and salaries, remain constant regardless of the company's activity level, while variable costs, such as materials and utilities, fluctuate with production output. By including all potential expenses, CEOs can create a comprehensive budget that avoids unpleasant surprises later on.

Once the budget is in place, it should not be considered static. Regular review and adjustment are necessary to ensure the business remains on track. This involves comparing actual performance against budgeted figures, identifying variances, and making necessary adjustments. For example, if revenue falls short of projections, it may be necessary to reduce discretionary spending or explore new revenue streams to stay within budget.

Budgeting is not solely about controlling costs but also about investing in growth. A well-structured budget allocates resources to initiatives that drive the company forward, such as new product development, marketing campaigns, or market expansion. By aligning the budget with the company's strategic objectives, CEOs can ensure that every financial decision contributes to long-term success.

3.5 Cash Flow Management

Cash flow is the lifeblood of any business. It represents the flow of money in and out of the company, and managing it effectively is crucial for maintaining liquidity and ensuring the company can meet its financial obligations. Poor cash flow management is one of the leading causes of business failure, making it a key focus for any CEO.

Effective **cash flow management** involves monitoring, analysing, and optimising the company's cash inflows and outflows to ensure sufficient cash is available to meet immediate needs. Unlike profit, which may be tied up in accounts receivable or inventory, cash flow reflects the cash available to the business. Even a profitable company can face difficulties if it lacks the cash to pay its bills when they come due.

One of the first steps in managing cash flow is understanding the timing of cash inflows and outflows. This involves creating a cash flow forecast, which estimates the company's cash position at various points in the future based on expected income and expenses. A cash flow forecast allows CEOs to anticipate periods of cash shortfall and proactively address the issue, such as securing short-term financing or delaying non-essential expenditures.

A common challenge businesses face is the mismatch between cash inflows and outflows. For instance, a company may have to pay its suppliers before receiving customer payments, creating a **cash flow gap**. To address this issue, businesses can negotiate better payment terms with suppliers or offer incentives for customers to pay sooner. Maintaining a cash reserve to cover shortfalls when necessary is another effective strategy.

Effective **accounts receivable and payable management** is critical to maintaining healthy cash flow. This involves ensuring that customers pay their invoices on time and that the company is not paying its bills earlier than necessary. Implementing strict credit policies and regularly following up on overdue invoices can improve the timeliness of receivables. On the payables side, taking advantage of early payment discounts or negotiating extended payment terms can help conserve cash.

Inventory management also plays a significant role in cash flow. Holding too much inventory ties up cash that could be used elsewhere, while holding too little can lead to stockouts and lost sales. By optimising inventory levels and using just-in-time inventory systems, businesses can reduce the amount of cash tied up in inventory and improve cash flow.

Effective cash flow management is crucial for ensuring financial stability and success. By understanding the timing of cash inflows and outflows, forecasting cash flow, managing receivables and payables, and optimising inventory levels, CEOs can maintain liquidity and avoid the pitfalls associated with cash flow problems. A well-managed cash flow enables businesses to meet financial obligations, invest in growth, and weather unexpected challenges, contributing to long-term success.

3.6 Profit Maximisation Strategies

Maximising profit is one of the core objectives of any business. While revenue growth is important, increasing profitability drives a company's overall value. **Profit maximisation** involves implementing strategies that increase revenue, reduce costs, or both. As a CEO, understanding and executing these strategies is crucial for the company's financial success.

Cost reduction is one of the most straightforward ways to maximise profit. This involves identifying areas where costs can be reduced without compromising the quality of products or services. For example, businesses can streamline operations by automating repetitive tasks, renegotiating supplier contracts for better pricing, or outsourcing non-core functions to more cost-effective providers. Cost reduction must be approached strategically to ensure that any cuts do not negatively affect the company's ability to deliver value to its customers.

Pricing optimisation is another effective strategy for maximising profit. Pricing is a powerful lever for increasing profitability; even small adjustments can significantly impact the bottom line. CEOs should regularly review pricing strategies to ensure they reflect the value of the product or service, the costs involved, and the competitive landscape. Dynamic pricing, adjusted based on demand, competition, and other factors, can help maximise revenue. Additionally, implementing premium pricing for higher-value offerings or bundling products and services can increase average transaction values and boost profits.

Revenue diversification is another key strategy for maximising profit. This involves expanding the company's revenue streams by introducing new products or services, entering new markets, or targeting new customer segments. Diversification reduces the company's reliance on a single revenue source, making it more resilient to market fluctuations and increasing overall profitability. For example, a company that primarily sells products might introduce complementary services, such as installation or maintenance, to generate additional revenue. Similarly, expanding into international markets can open up new opportunities for growth and profitability.

Improving **operational efficiency** also plays a significant role in profit maximisation. This involves optimising processes, reducing waste, and increasing productivity. For instance, implementing lean manufacturing techniques can help reduce production costs and increase output, while using data analytics to streamline supply chain management can lower lead times and reduce inventory costs. Companies can increase their profit margins by improving operational efficiency and delivering more value to shareholders.

Customer retention is another crucial area to focus on. Acquiring new customers is often more expensive than retaining existing ones, so increasing customer loyalty can directly impact profitability. Implementing loyalty programmes, improving customer service, and regularly engaging with customers to understand their needs can help increase repeat business and reduce customer churn. Satisfied customers are also more likely to refer others, boosting revenue and profitability.

Profit maximisation is a critical aspect of business success. CEOs can significantly increase their company's profitability by implementing cost reduction, pricing optimisation, revenue diversification, improving operational efficiency, and focusing on customer retention. Maximising profit strengthens the company's financial position and provides the resources needed to invest in growth and innovation, driving long-term success.

3.7 Cost Management

Effective cost management is essential for maintaining profitability and ensuring the long-term success of any business. It involves controlling and reducing expenses while maintaining the quality of products or services. As a CEO, managing costs efficiently without sacrificing quality requires strategic planning and careful execution.

The first step in **cost management** is conducting a thorough cost analysis. This involves reviewing the company's expenses to identify areas where costs can be reduced or eliminated. Costs can be categorised into fixed costs, which remain constant regardless of the company's activity level, and variable costs, which fluctuate with the company's output. By analysing these costs, CEOs can identify inefficiencies and opportunities for cost savings without compromising the quality of products or services.

Operational efficiency is a key component of cost management. Streamlining operations, automating processes, and eliminating waste can significantly reduce costs and improve profitability. For example, implementing lean manufacturing techniques can help reduce waste and improve productivity, while automating tasks such as data entry or payroll processing can reduce labour costs and improve accuracy.

Supplier management is another critical area for controlling costs. By negotiating better terms with suppliers, consolidating purchases to achieve economies of scale, or sourcing materials from lower-cost suppliers, companies can reduce their cost of goods sold (COGS). Building strong supplier relationships can lead to favourable payment terms, discounts, and other cost-saving opportunities.

In addition to managing direct costs, controlling **indirect costs**, such as overhead expenses, is equally important. This might include reducing energy consumption, optimising office space, or implementing telecommuting policies to reduce the need for physical office space. For example, many companies that have embraced remote work have significantly reduced overhead costs associated with office space, utilities, and commuting.

Zero-based budgeting is another effective cost management strategy. Unlike traditional budgeting, which uses the previous year's budget as a baseline, zero-based budgeting requires justifying all expenses from scratch for each new budget period. This approach ensures that every cost is scrutinised and aligned with the company's strategic goals, preventing unnecessary spending and improving cost efficiency.

Fostering a **cost-conscious culture** within the organisation is also important. This involves educating employees about the importance of cost management and encouraging them to identify and suggest cost-saving measures. When employees understand how their actions impact the company's bottom line, they are more likely to make cost-conscious decisions that benefit the organisation.

Cost management is a vital aspect of financial leadership that requires a strategic approach and a focus on efficiency. CEOs can reduce expenses without compromising quality by conducting thorough cost analyses, improving operational efficiency, managing supplier relationships, controlling indirect costs, and fostering a cost-conscious culture. Effective cost management enhances profitability and provides the financial stability needed to invest in growth and innovation.

3.8 Investment Appraisal

Investment appraisal evaluates a project or investment's potential returns and risks to determine its viability. It is a critical aspect of financial management, helping CEOs make informed decisions about where to allocate resources for the best possible outcomes. Effective investment appraisal ensures that capital is invested in projects that align with the company's strategic goals and offer favourable returns.

One of the most commonly used methods for investment appraisal is **Net Present Value (NPV)**. NPV calculates the present value of future cash flows generated by an investment minus the initial cost. A positive NPV indicates that the investment is expected to generate more cash than it costs, making it a worthwhile pursuit. Conversely, a negative NPV suggests the investment would result in a net loss. NPV is a powerful tool because it accounts for the time value of money, recognising that cash received in the future is worth less than cash received today.

Another popular method is the **Internal Rate of Return (IRR)**. IRR is the discount rate at which the NPV of an investment is zero. In other words, it represents the rate of return that makes the present value of an investment's cash inflows equal to its initial cost. IRR is useful for comparing the profitability of different investments, as it provides a percentage return that can be directly compared to the company's required rate of return or cost of capital. Generally, an investment is considered attractive if its IRR exceeds the company's required rate of return.

The **payback period** is a simpler method of evaluating investments. It measures the time it takes for an investment to generate enough cash flow to recover its initial cost. While the payback period does not account for the time value of money or cash flows beyond it, it is useful for assessing an investment's liquidity risk. Investments with shorter payback periods are generally less risky, allowing the company to recover its capital more quickly.

The **Profitability Index (PI)** is another method for comparing the present value of future cash flows generated by an investment to its initial cost. It is calculated by dividing the present value of cash flows by the initial investment. A PI greater than 1 indicates that the investment is expected to generate more value than it costs, making it a good investment. PI is particularly useful for ranking investment opportunities when capital is limited, as it provides a relative measure of profitability.

In addition to these quantitative methods, qualitative factors should be considered when evaluating investments. These may include the strategic alignment of the investment with the company's long-term goals, the potential for gaining a competitive advantage, and the associated risks. For example, investing in cutting-edge technology may offer a lower immediate return but could position the company as an innovation leader, providing significant long-term benefits.

An example of a successful investment appraisal is in Alphabet, Google's parent company. Alphabet has consistently invested in projects that align with its long-term vision of advancing technology and innovation. Investments in artificial intelligence, cloud computing, and autonomous vehicles have generated significant financial returns while positioning Alphabet as a leader in multiple high-growth industries.

Investment appraisal is a crucial process that helps CEOs make informed decisions about where to allocate capital. By using methods such as NPV, IRR, the payback period, and the profitability index, as well as considering qualitative factors, CEOs can evaluate the viability and potential returns of investments. Effective investment appraisal ensures that resources are allocated to projects with the best financial and strategic outcomes, driving long-term success.

3.9 Financial Risk Management

Financial risk is an inherent part of running any business, but with the right strategies, these risks can be identified, assessed, and mitigated. Financial risk management is a crucial element of leadership, ensuring a company remains stable and protected from potential threats that could harm its financial position.

The first step in financial risk management is **identifying financial risks** that could affect the business. These risks can be broadly categorised into market, credit, operational, and liquidity risks.

Market risk refers to potential losses arising from changes in market conditions, such as fluctuations in interest rates, currency exchange rates, or commodity prices. For instance, a company heavily reliant on imported raw materials may face currency risk if the local currency depreciates against the currency in which the materials are priced. Companies can use financial instruments such as hedging to manage market risk by taking positions in derivatives like futures or options to offset potential losses.

Credit risk occurs when a counterparty, such as a customer or supplier, fails to meet its financial obligations. This risk is particularly relevant for companies that extend credit to customers. To mitigate credit risk, companies can implement strict credit policies, conduct thorough credit checks on new customers, and diversify their customer base to reduce reliance on any single counterparty. Additionally, companies can use credit insurance or factoring to protect against non-payment risk.

Operational risk arises from internal processes, systems, or people, including fraud, system failures, or human error. To manage operational risk, companies can implement robust internal controls, conduct regular audits, and invest in employee training and technology to reduce the likelihood of errors or system failures. For example, automated inventory management systems can reduce the risk of stockouts or overstocking, while regular security audits can protect against data breaches.

Liquidity risk occurs when a company cannot meet its short-term financial obligations due to a lack of cash or liquid assets. This risk can be mitigated by maintaining a cash reserve, securing lines of credit, and managing cash flow effectively. For instance, a company that regularly monitors its cash flow and maintains a buffer of liquid assets is better positioned to handle unexpected expenses or revenue shortfalls.

After identifying risks, the next step is to assess their potential impact on the business. This involves estimating the likelihood of each risk occurring and the potential financial consequences. By prioritising risks based on severity, companies can focus their risk management efforts on the most significant threats.

To mitigate these risks, companies can develop strategies such as diversifying revenue streams, implementing redundancies in critical systems, or purchasing insurance to cover catastrophic losses. For example, Coca-Cola's hedging strategies to manage currency risk in various countries demonstrate effective financial risk management. Using forward contracts and options, Coca-Cola can lock in exchange rates and protect itself from fluctuations that could negatively impact its profits.

Financial risk management is essential for maintaining a company's stability and success. By identifying, assessing, and mitigating risks related to market conditions, credit, operations, and liquidity, CEOs can protect their businesses from potential threats and ensure they are prepared to navigate the complexities of the financial landscape. Effective financial risk management safeguards a company's financial health and provides the confidence to pursue growth and innovation.

3.10 The CEO's Role in Financial Leadership

The CEO's role in financial leadership extends far beyond setting the company's strategic direction. As the ultimate decision-maker, the CEO ensures that the company's financial vision aligns with its overall goals and that financial resources are managed effectively to support growth and sustainability.

One of the CEO's key responsibilities in financial leadership is setting the company's financial vision. This involves defining the financial goals that the company aims to achieve, such as revenue growth, profitability, and return on investment. The financial vision must align with the company's strategic objectives and provide a clear roadmap for allocating financial resources.

Another critical responsibility is ensuring financial discipline within the organisation. This involves establishing and enforcing policies and procedures that promote sound financial management, such as budgeting, forecasting, and financial reporting. The CEO must ensure that these processes are rigorously followed and that the company's financial performance is monitored and evaluated regularly.

Capital allocation is another key aspect of the CEO's financial leadership role. This involves deciding how to allocate the company's capital to maximise returns and support strategic objectives. Capital allocation decisions may include investments in new projects, acquisitions, share buybacks, or dividend payments. The CEO must carefully assess each option's potential returns and risks and make decisions that balance growth with financial stability.

In times of financial uncertainty or crisis, the CEO's financial leadership becomes even more critical. **Crisis management** requires the CEO to take swift and decisive action to protect the company's financial position. This might involve cost-cutting measures, renegotiating debt, or securing additional financing to ensure the company can navigate difficult periods. Effective communication with stakeholders, including employees, investors, and creditors, is essential for maintaining confidence and support during challenging times.

Furthermore, the CEO must foster a **culture of financial accountability** within the organisation. This involves promoting transparency in financial reporting, encouraging ethical behaviour, and holding employees accountable for their financial decisions. A culture of financial accountability builds trust with stakeholders and ensures that the company's financial resources are managed responsibly.

Warren Buffett, CEO of Berkshire Hathaway, is an excellent example of financial leadership. Buffett is known for his disciplined approach to capital allocation and consistently invests in businesses with strong fundamentals and long-term growth potential. His commitment to financial discipline and ability to navigate financial crises with calm and rational decision-making have made Berkshire Hathaway one of the most successful companies globally.

In summary, the CEO's role in financial leadership is multifaceted and essential to the company's success. The CEO can guide the company toward sustained growth and long-term success by setting a clear financial vision, ensuring financial discipline, making informed capital allocation decisions, managing financial crises, and fostering a culture of accountability.

3.11 Learning from the Giants

Learning from the financial strategies of some of the world's most successful companies provides valuable insights into what works in the complex world of financial management. Companies like Apple, Amazon, and Microsoft have demonstrated the power of effective financial leadership in driving growth, innovation, and shareholder value.

Apple, for instance, has consistently prioritised **cash management** and has built one of the largest cash reserves in corporate history. This financial strategy has allowed Apple to weather economic downturns, invest in new product development, and return value to shareholders through dividends and share buybacks. Apple's disciplined approach to managing cash flow serves as a reminder of the importance of liquidity in maintaining financial stability and supporting long-term growth.

Amazon, on the other hand, has focused on **revenue diversification and long-term investment**. Despite operating on slim profit margins for many years, Amazon's relentless focus on reinvesting in technology, logistics, and customer experience has transformed it into one of the most valuable companies in the world. Amazon's approach underscores the importance of prioritising long-term growth over short-term profits and the value of investing in innovation to build a competitive advantage.

Microsoft's success can be attributed to its **strategic capital allocation**. Under the leadership of CEO Satya Nadella, Microsoft has shifted its focus to cloud computing, making significant investments in its Azure platform. This strategic decision has driven substantial growth in revenue and profitability, positioning Microsoft as a leader in the cloud computing industry. Microsoft's experience highlights the importance of making bold capital allocation decisions to seize emerging opportunities and stay ahead of competitors.

These companies' financial strategies provide valuable lessons for CEOs. Whether Apple focuses on cash management, Amazon takes a long-term investment approach, or Microsoft allocates strategic capital, these examples demonstrate the power of disciplined financial leadership in driving business success.

3.12 Case Studies

Real-world case studies provide concrete examples of how financial strategies have been successfully or unsuccessfully applied in various business contexts. By examining these case studies, CEOs can gain insights into the practical application of financial principles and learn from others' successes and mistakes.

Under the leadership of Elon Musk, Tesla has become a household name in the automotive industry, particularly in the electric vehicle (EV) sector. However, Tesla's journey to profitability was far from smooth. For years, the company struggled with cash flow issues, high production costs, and investor scepticism. Despite these challenges, Tesla's focus on innovation, brand building, and vertical integration allowed the company to eventually turn a profit and become one of the most valuable automakers in the world.

Tesla's financial strategy involved significant investments in research and development to create cutting-edge EV technology and production facilities like the Gigafactory to achieve economies of scale. The company also leveraged its strong brand and loyal customer base to command premium vehicle prices, contributing to higher profit margins. Additionally, Tesla's focus on vertical integration, such as producing its batteries in-house, helped to reduce costs and improve efficiency. The key takeaway from Tesla's case study is the importance of innovation, brand strength, and vertical integration in driving profitability, even in significant financial challenges.

In contrast, Kodak, once a dominant player in the photography industry, provides a cautionary tale of the consequences of failing to adapt to changing market conditions. Despite being a pioneer in digital photography, Kodak was slow to embrace the digital revolution, clinging to its traditional film business for too long. As a result, the company lost market share to more agile competitors and eventually filed for bankruptcy in 2012.

Kodak's failure was partly due to its reluctance to invest in digital technology and its inability to pivot its business model. The company's financial strategy was too focused on preserving its existing revenue streams rather than investing in new growth opportunities. This case highlights the importance of staying ahead of industry trends, being willing to disrupt your business model, and investing boldly in future technologies. The lesson from Kodak's downfall is the need for agility, forward-thinking, and a willingness to embrace change in a rapidly evolving business environment.

Under the leadership of Paul Polman, Unilever successfully implemented a sustainable growth strategy that focused on long-term value creation rather than short-term profits. Polman's approach involved setting ambitious sustainability goals, such as reducing the company's environmental impact and improving the livelihoods of millions of people. This strategy enhanced Unilever's brand reputation and drove financial performance by aligning the company's operations with global trends towards sustainability.

Unilever's financial strategy involved integrating sustainability into every aspect of its business, from sourcing raw materials to product development and marketing. The company also focused on operational efficiency and cost management to fund its sustainability initiatives without compromising profitability. The success of Unilever's strategy demonstrates that sustainability and profitability can go hand in hand when approached strategically. The key takeaway from Unilever's case study is the importance of aligning financial strategy with long-term sustainability goals to create value for shareholders and society.

These case studies illustrate the practical application of financial principles in real-world business scenarios. By learning from the successes and failures of companies like Tesla, Kodak, and

Unilever, CEOs can gain valuable insights into the importance of innovation, agility, sustainability, and strategic investment in driving financial success.

Conclusion

In today's competitive business landscape, financial literacy is not just an advantage but a necessity. Understanding and leveraging financial metrics is crucial for any CEO or business leader striving for success. This chapter has explored foundational financial statements, key performance indicators, budgeting practices, and strategies for managing cash flow, maximising profit, and controlling costs. These elements form the backbone of sound financial management, providing the insights needed to make informed decisions that drive a company forward.

Mastering financial statements, income statements, balance sheets, and cash flow statements gives leaders a comprehensive view of their business's financial health. This understanding, combined with regular monitoring of KPIs, enables leaders to assess performance accurately and adjust their strategies as needed. Effective budgeting and cash flow management ensure businesses remain financially stable, even in challenging times.

Profit maximisation and cost management are ongoing processes that require a strategic approach. By focusing on efficiency, optimising pricing, and exploring new revenue streams, leaders can enhance profitability and build a stronger financial foundation for their businesses. Careful investment appraisal and financial risk management further safeguard companies, ensuring resources are allocated wisely and potential threats are mitigated.

Financial leadership is paramount for a CEO. Setting a clear financial vision, maintaining discipline, and fostering a culture of accountability is essential for guiding a company toward sustained growth and long-term success. Learning from the successes and failures of industry giants like Apple, Amazon, and Microsoft provides valuable lessons that can be applied to business strategies.

In conclusion, the financial knowledge and skills gained from this chapter are powerful tools that will enable leaders to navigate the complexities of business finance confidently. Applying these principles can lead a company toward a prosperous future, ensuring it remains competitive, resilient, and poised for growth in an ever-changing world

Chapter 4

Marketing Mastery: Building Your Brand and Customer Base

4.1 Overview

Marketing is the **driving force** behind any successful business, serving as the bridge between a company and its customers. It facilitates the introduction, positioning, and selling of products and services, making it essential for leaders and entrepreneurs to master its fundamentals. Building a robust brand and cultivating a loyal customer base is pivotal to business success in today's competitive environment. This chapter delves into the essential tools and knowledge to navigate traditional and digital marketing landscapes. Key topics include understanding your market and customers, constructing a strong brand identity, and deploying effective digital marketing strategies. Additionally, it covers critical areas like pricing strategies, distribution channels, and customer relationship management.

The chapter also addresses the importance of marketing data analysis and global marketing challenges, providing insights into innovative tactics that distinguish your brand in a crowded marketplace. By the end, you will be equipped to craft a marketing strategy that drives growth, enhances brand equity, and fosters long-term customer loyalty.

4.2 Understanding Your Market

A successful marketing strategy begins with a comprehensive understanding of your market. Without clear insights into your target audience's needs, behaviours, and preferences, even the most well-crafted campaigns can fall flat. The foundation of effective marketing lies in identifying who your customers are and what they want, then segmenting the market to target the most relevant and profitable groups.

Market research plays a crucial role in this process, involving collecting and analysing data about consumer behaviour, preferences, and trends. This can be achieved through various methods, such as surveys, focus groups, and secondary data analysis, including industry reports. For example, conducting surveys can help gauge demand, understand customer expectations, and identify the features your audience values if you plan to launch a new product.

Market segmentation allows businesses to divide a broad consumer base into smaller, more manageable groups based on specific characteristics. Demographic segmentation, for instance, categorises the market by factors such as age, gender, income, and education. A luxury watch company might focus on high-income individuals who value exclusivity and craftsmanship. Tailoring marketing messages to this demographic enables the company to create a more focused and effective campaign.

Beyond demographics, **psychographic segmentation** considers consumers' values, beliefs, and lifestyles. This is particularly useful for brands that connect emotionally with their customers. For instance, Patagonia segments its market based on a shared commitment to environmental sustainability, fostering a strong and loyal customer following by aligning its brand values with those of its audience.

Behavioural segmentation further refines market understanding by analysing how consumers interact with products and services. This includes usage rates, brand loyalty, and purchasing patterns. Companies like Amazon leverage behavioural segmentation to personalise recommendations and marketing messages based on customers' past purchases and browsing behaviour.

An effective marketing strategy also requires a thorough **competitor analysis** to identify what your competitors offer and how they position themselves. This helps differentiate your brand and uncover opportunities for gaining a competitive edge. For example, if competitors primarily compete on price, you might distinguish your brand by emphasising superior quality or exceptional customer service.

Developing customer personas is invaluable for synthesising these insights. These fictional representations of your ideal customers are based on real data, encompassing demographic information, behaviours, motivations, and challenges. Detailed personas ensure your marketing efforts are tailored to your target audience's needs and preferences.

Understanding your market is essential for crafting a marketing strategy that resonates with your audience and drives business success. By conducting comprehensive research, segmenting the market effectively, and analysing the competition, you can create a well-informed, targeted marketing plan that positions your brand for growth.

4.3 Building a Strong Brand

A strong brand is among a company's most valuable assets. It extends beyond just a logo or tagline to encompass customers' perceptions of the company, which heavily influence their purchasing decisions, loyalty, and engagement. Building a strong brand involves creating a distinct **brand identity**, positioning your brand effectively in the market, and delivering a consistent value proposition that resonates with your target audience.

Brand identity represents your brand's visual and verbal aspects, including logos, colours, typography, and tone of voice. It is how your brand presents itself to the world and how customers recognise it. A memorable and distinct brand identity should be aligned with the company's values and mission. For example, Apple's brand identity revolves around simplicity, innovation, and premium quality, reflected in its minimalist designs and sleek product aesthetics.

Brand positioning is about securing a unique place for your brand in consumers' minds. This requires understanding what sets your brand apart from competitors and why customers should choose your product or service. For instance, Volvo has positioned itself as a leader in automotive safety with product designs, advertising campaigns, and corporate communications that reinforce this positioning.

The **value proposition** is your brand's promise to customers, explaining how your product or service solves a problem or delivers benefits superior to those of competitors. FedEx's value proposition, "When it absolutely, positively has to be there overnight," clearly communicates its commitment to reliability and speed, which are crucial to its customers.

Brand equity refers to the added value a brand brings to a product beyond its functional benefits. Strong brand equity leads to customer loyalty, the ability to command premium prices and resilience against competitive pressures. Companies like Nike and Coca-Cola have established substantial brand equity by consistently delivering on their promises and fostering emotional connections with their customers. For instance, Nike's "Just Do It" campaign is synonymous with empowerment and athletic excellence.

Consistency is key to building a strong brand. Whether customers interact with your brand online, in-store, or through advertising, it is crucial that the brand identity, messaging, and customer experience are aligned. Starbucks exemplifies this by maintaining a uniform brand experience across its global stores, ensuring consistent quality in service, products, and atmosphere.

Storytelling is another powerful tool in brand building. By telling stories that resonate with your audience, you can create an emotional connection that transcends the functional aspects of your products. Patagonia, for example, uses storytelling to communicate its commitment to environmental sustainability, sharing narratives about conservation efforts and the impact of its products on the planet. These stories strengthen Patagonia's brand values and inspire customers with a passion for the environment.

Building a strong brand requires a strategic identity, positioning, and value proposition approach. By crafting a brand that resonates with your target audience, differentiates from the competition, and consistently delivers on its promises, you can cultivate a powerful and enduring brand that drives customer loyalty and business success.

4.4 Digital Marketing Strategies

In today's digital age, a robust online presence is indispensable for any business looking to grow and succeed. Digital marketing encompasses a variety of strategies and tools that help businesses reach a broader audience, engage more effectively with customers, and achieve measurable results. This section explores key digital marketing strategies, such as **search engine optimisation (SEO)**, social media marketing, content marketing, email marketing, and pay-per-click (PPC) advertising, and offers practical insights into their successful implementation.

Search Engine Optimisation (SEO) enhances a website's visibility on search engines like Google, aiming to appear higher in search results for relevant keywords, thereby driving organic traffic to the site. SEO includes on-page strategies, such as optimising content and website structure, and off-page strategies, like building backlinks from reputable websites. For example, an online store selling handmade jewellery might optimise its site for keywords like "handmade silver necklaces" and publish blog posts on jewellery trends to improve its SEO, increasing the likelihood that potential customers will find the store.

Social media marketing is crucial in building brand awareness and engaging with your audience on platforms like Facebook, Instagram, and LinkedIn. Effective social media marketing involves creating meaningful interactions rather than simply posting content. This includes sharing valuable information, responding to customer comments, and running promotions. Influencer marketing, a popular social media strategy, involves partnering with individuals with large followings and credibility in your industry. For example, a fitness brand might collaborate with a well-known influencer to promote its products on Instagram, leveraging its reach to enhance visibility and engagement.

Content marketing focuses on creating and distributing valuable, relevant content to attract and engage a target audience. Content can include blog posts, videos, podcasts, and infographics. For example, a software company providing financial management tools might produce content that addresses common business challenges, such as managing cash flow or understanding taxes, thereby positioning itself as an authority in the field and building trust with potential customers.

Despite the rise of social media, **email marketing** remains a powerful tool for directly communicating with your audience. It enables businesses to share promotions, newsletters, and personalised recommendations, nurturing relationships over time. Segmenting email lists based on purchase history or engagement levels can significantly increase campaign effectiveness. For instance, special promotions can be sent to customers who have not purchased recently, encouraging re-engagement and driving conversions.

Pay-per-click (PPC) advertising is a paid digital marketing strategy where businesses pay for each click on their advertisements. PPC ads can appear on search engines, social media platforms, and websites, driving targeted traffic to your site. While PPC can effectively reach potential customers, it requires careful management to ensure a positive return on investment. Google Ads, for example, allows businesses to bid on keywords related to their products, displaying ads to users searching for those terms.

Digital marketing offers a range of strategies and tools that help businesses build their brand and attract customers online. By implementing effective SEO, social media marketing, content marketing, email marketing, and PPC campaigns, businesses can reach a broader audience, engage customers more effectively, and achieve measurable results that contribute to long-term success.

4.5 Pricing Strategies

Setting the right price for your products or services is one of the most critical decisions a business must make, as it directly impacts revenue, profitability, and market positioning. An effective pricing strategy requires a deep understanding of costs, competition, customer perception of value, and the overall market environment. This section explores various pricing strategies, including **value-based, penetration, premium, cost-plus, and dynamic pricing**, and guides you in selecting the best approach for your business.

Value-based pricing sets prices based on the perceived value of the product or service to the customer rather than focusing solely on production costs. This strategy is effective when your product offers unique benefits or addresses specific customer needs. For example, Apple uses value-based pricing for its products, reflecting the brand's perceived value in innovation, design, and user experience. Customers are willing to pay a premium because they believe they receive greater value than competitors.

Penetration pricing involves setting a low initial price to attract customers and quickly gain market share. It is often used when launching a new product or entering a new market. The goal is to attract customers early, create brand awareness, and establish a market presence. Prices can gradually increase once the product gains traction and customer loyalty is established. For instance, when it first launched its streaming service, Netflix offered low subscription prices, which helped it attract customers from traditional cable providers.

Premium pricing sets a high price to create a perception of exclusivity and superior quality. This strategy is often used by luxury brands or companies offering high-end products. For example, luxury car brands like Mercedes-Benz use premium pricing to position their vehicles as symbols of performance and status, appealing to affluent customers who value the prestige associated with these brands.

Cost-plus pricing is a straightforward method in which prices are set by adding a fixed percentage or markup to the cost of production. While this ensures costs are covered, and a profit margin is achieved, it may not always maximise profitability as it does not consider perceived value or market demand. However, it can be useful in industries where pricing transparency is expected, or competition is primarily driven by cost.

Dynamic pricing is a flexible approach in which prices are adjusted in real-time based on market demand, competition, and other factors. This strategy is commonly used in industries like travel and e-commerce. For example, airlines adjust ticket prices based on booking time, demand, and competitor pricing. Dynamic pricing allows companies to maximise revenue by charging higher prices during periods of high demand and offering discounts when demand is lower.

Selecting the right pricing strategy is essential for achieving your business's financial goals and positioning your brand effectively in the market. Whether opting for value-based, penetration, premium, cost-plus, or dynamic pricing, it is important to consider costs, customer perceptions, competition, and market conditions. By aligning your pricing strategy with your business objectives, you can maximise profitability, attract the right customers, and build a competitive brand.

4.6 Distribution Channels

Distribution channels are the pathways through which your products or services reach your customers. Choosing the right distribution channels is crucial for maximising market reach, ensuring efficiency, and delivering a seamless customer experience. This section explores different distribution channels and offers successful strategies from various industries.

Direct distribution involves selling products directly to customers without intermediaries, giving companies complete control over the customer experience, pricing, and brand messaging. Direct distribution can take multiple forms, including sales through a company's website, brick-and-mortar stores, or a dedicated sales force. For example, Tesla uses a direct-to-consumer model, selling vehicles through its website and company-owned showrooms, enabling it to control the entire customer experience.

Indirect distribution uses intermediaries such as wholesalers, retailers, or distributors to reach customers. This approach helps companies expand their market reach by leveraging the expertise and networks of intermediaries. For instance, Coca-Cola uses a vast network of bottlers, distributors, and retailers to ensure its products are available worldwide.

Hybrid distribution combines direct and indirect distribution elements, benefiting businesses from both strategies. Companies using a hybrid approach may sell products through their website while using retail partners to reach a wider audience. Apple, for example, sells its products through its online store, retail locations, and authorised resellers, enhancing its global presence.

Omni-channel distribution provides a seamless and integrated experience across multiple channels, whether customers interact with a brand online, in-store, or through mobile apps. Retailers like Walmart and Target have successfully implemented omnichannel strategies, allowing customers to shop online, pick up orders in-store, and access customer service through various channels.

Distribution intensity refers to the level of product availability across different channels. There are three main levels: intensive, selective, and exclusive distribution. Intensive distribution aims to make products widely available, while selective distribution limits availability to maintain a higher level of service. Exclusive distribution grants rights to a single retailer or distributor, often used for luxury or speciality products.

Choosing the right distribution channels is vital for reaching customers and ensuring a positive customer experience. Companies can achieve their business goals and maximise market reach by carefully selecting direct, indirect, hybrid, or omnichannel strategies.

4.7 Customer Relationship Management (CRM)

Customer Relationship Management (CRM) is crucial to a successful marketing strategy. It manages and nurtures customer relationships to enhance loyalty, retention, and satisfaction. Effective CRM provides a significant advantage in today's competitive landscape by enabling businesses to build stronger connections with their customers and deliver more personalised experiences.

CRM is important because it fosters long-term relationships that contribute to sustained business growth. Strong relationships with customers can increase customer lifetime value (CLTV), reduce churn, and create brand advocates who are likely to recommend your products or services. Companies like Amazon and Zappos have built their success on exceptional customer service and CRM practices, keeping customers loyal and encouraging repeat business.

A core element of CRM is **customer data management**. By collecting and analysing customer data, businesses gain valuable insights into consumer behaviour, preferences, and purchasing patterns. This information allows companies to personalise marketing messages, offer tailored product recommendations, and provide more relevant offers. For instance, Netflix uses CRM data to personalise user content recommendations based on viewing history, keeping customers engaged and enhancing their overall experience.

CRM tools and software such as Salesforce, HubSpot, and Zoho are essential for effectively managing customer relationships. These platforms enable businesses to centralise customer data, track interactions across various touchpoints, and automate key processes like sales and marketing. CRM tools help businesses deliver consistent, high-quality customer experiences by streamlining operations.

Segmentation is another critical aspect of CRM. By segmenting the customer base into specific groups based on factors like purchase history, age, and engagement levels, businesses can create targeted marketing campaigns that cater to each group's unique needs and preferences. For example, a fashion retailer might segment customers based on their style preferences and send tailored promotions or recommendations to each group, increasing engagement and driving higher conversion rates.

Customer feedback is invaluable for improving CRM efforts. Actively seeking and responding to feedback demonstrates that your company values its customers and is committed to meeting their needs. Feedback can be gathered through surveys, reviews, and social media, providing insights into areas for improvement. Companies like Apple and Starbucks regularly solicit customer feedback to refine their products and services, ensuring they meet and exceed customer expectations.

Implementing **loyalty programmes** is a powerful CRM strategy for increasing retention and encouraging repeat purchases. These programmes reward customers for their continued business with points, discounts, or exclusive offers. For instance, airlines like British Airways use loyalty programmes to reward frequent flyers, encouraging them to continue flying with the airline in exchange for points that can be redeemed for flights or upgrades.

An **omnichannel CRM** approach ensures a seamless and consistent customer experience across all channels, whether online, in-store, or through customer service. Integrating customer data across touchpoints allows companies to provide a more cohesive and personalised experience. For example, a customer who starts a purchase on a mobile app should be able to complete it seamlessly in-store, with the sales associate having access to all relevant information.

CRM is fundamental to building and maintaining strong customer relationships. Businesses can enhance customer loyalty, increase retention, and drive long-term success by managing customer data effectively, utilising CRM tools, segmenting their customer base, gathering feedback, and implementing loyalty programmes. A robust CRM strategy improves customer satisfaction and creates a competitive advantage by differentiating your brand in the marketplace.

4.8 Analysing Marketing Data

In today's data-driven world, analysing marketing data is essential for making informed decisions, optimising campaigns, and demonstrating your marketing efforts' return on investment (ROI). This section explores the importance of marketing analytics, identifies key metrics to track, and highlights how data can drive better marketing outcomes.

Marketing analytics involves collecting, measuring, and interpreting data related to marketing activities. This process provides insights into the effectiveness of strategies, revealing what works, what needs improvement, and where growth opportunities lie. By leveraging marketing analytics, businesses can make data-driven decisions that enhance campaign performance, maximise ROI, and improve overall marketing effectiveness.

Defining **key performance indicators (KPIs)** is crucial for effective marketing analysis. KPIs are specific metrics aligned with your business goals and used to measure the success of marketing efforts. For example, if the goal is to increase brand awareness, relevant KPIs might include website traffic, social media reach, or brand mentions. Alternatively, if the objective is to drive sales, conversion rates, average order value, and customer acquisition cost (CAC) would be more appropriate metrics to track.

Website analytics is a vital component of marketing data analysis. Tools like Google Analytics provide comprehensive insights into how visitors interact with your website, including page views, bounce rate, session duration, and conversion rates. Analysing this data allows businesses to identify high-performing pages, areas where visitors drop off, and opportunities to optimise the site for better user experience and higher conversions.

Campaign performance analysis focuses on evaluating the effectiveness of your marketing campaigns across different channels, such as email, social media, search engines, and display advertising. By examining metrics like click-through rates (CTR), conversion rates, and cost per click (CPC), you can determine which campaigns are driving the most value and identify those that may need adjustments or discontinuation.

Customer data analysis offers deeper insights into audience behaviour, preferences, and purchasing patterns. This involves analysing customer demographics, purchase history, and engagement levels. By segmenting your customer base and analysing these data points, you can create more targeted and personalised marketing campaigns. For instance, identifying a customer segment that tends to make more purchases during seasonal sales can help tailor marketing efforts to capitalise on this behaviour.

Social media analytics provides insights into your brand's performance across platforms like Facebook, Instagram, and Twitter. Key metrics include engagement rates, follower growth, social share of voice, and sentiment analysis. Monitoring these metrics helps assess the effectiveness of your social media strategy, understand how your brand is perceived, and identify opportunities to increase engagement and reach.

Marketing attribution helps determine which marketing activities contributed to a specific outcome, such as a sale or lead conversion. Attribution models range from simple first-touch or last-touch models, which credit the first or last interaction before conversion, to more advanced multi-touch models that assign value to each interaction along the customer journey. Understanding how different marketing touchpoints contribute to overall performance enables businesses to allocate resources more effectively and optimise their marketing mix.

Predictive analytics uses historical data, statistical algorithms, and machine learning to forecast future outcomes. In marketing, predictive analytics can predict customer behaviour, such as which customers are likely to churn or which products will sell well in the future. By leveraging predictive analytics, businesses can make proactive decisions that improve marketing effectiveness and drive better results.

Analysing marketing data is essential for making informed decisions, optimising campaigns, and maximising ROI. Businesses can gain valuable insights that drive better marketing outcomes by defining relevant KPIs, using tools like Google Analytics, tracking campaign performance, and employing advanced techniques like predictive analytics. Data-driven marketing enables businesses to allocate resources more effectively, personalise campaigns, and precisely achieve their business goals.

4.9 Global Marketing

As businesses expand globally, understanding the challenges and opportunities of global marketing becomes essential. Global marketing involves promoting and selling products or services in multiple countries, each with unique cultural, economic, and regulatory environments. This section addresses key considerations for global marketing, including market entry strategies, cultural adaptation, and overcoming the challenges of international expansion.

Market entry strategies are a crucial consideration when expanding into international markets. Several approaches exist, each with its advantages and risks:

- **Exporting** is the simplest method, involving producing goods in the home country and selling them abroad. This approach involves lower financial risk but offers limited control over the brand's presence in the foreign market.

- **Licensing and franchising** involve granting a foreign partner the rights to produce and sell products under the company's brand name. This allows for faster market entry and reduced financial risk but may compromise control over the brand. For example, McDonald's has successfully expanded globally through franchising, establishing a presence in over 100 countries.

- **Joint ventures and partnerships** involve collaborating with local businesses to enter a foreign market. This strategy enables companies to share risks and rewards while benefiting from the local partner's knowledge and resources. Starbucks, for example, formed a joint venture to enter the Chinese market, helping the company navigate local complexities and adapt to consumer preferences.

- **Direct investment or wholly-owned subsidiaries** involve establishing a company's operations in a foreign market. This approach offers the highest level of control and potential returns but comes with higher risks and costs. Companies like Toyota and BMW have built manufacturing plants in various countries to produce vehicles locally, enabling them to respond more quickly to market demands.

Cultural adaptation is essential in global marketing, as each market has norms, values, and consumer behaviours that influence how products are perceived and accepted. Companies must adapt their marketing strategies to align with local cultures while maintaining brand identity. For example, Coca-Cola faced challenges translating its brand name into Chinese characters but eventually selected "Kekou Kele," meaning "tasty and joyful," resonating with Chinese consumers.

Product adaptation is often necessary to meet local tastes, regulatory requirements, or market conditions. McDonald's customises its menu in different countries to reflect local preferences. In India, where beef consumption is limited, McDonald's offers vegetarian and chicken-based options like the McAloo Tikki burger.

Pricing strategies in global markets must consider local purchasing power, competition, and currency exchange rates. Some companies adopt uniform pricing across all markets, while others adjust prices based on local conditions. Luxury brands like Louis Vuitton maintain premium pricing worldwide to preserve exclusivity, while electronics brands like Samsung may adjust pricing to reflect regional economic conditions.

Overcoming regulatory and logistical challenges is a major consideration in global marketing. Countries have varying regulations regarding product safety, advertising, and trade. Navigating these regulations requires careful planning and often the assistance of local legal and regulatory experts. Logistics and supply chain management can also be complex in global markets, necessitating reliable distribution networks and effective management of cross-border shipping and customs processes.

Digital marketing offers powerful tools for global expansion, allowing companies to reach customers worldwide without needing a physical presence in each market. However, digital marketing strategies must be adapted to local preferences and regulations. While platforms like Facebook and Google dominate many Western markets, platforms like WeChat and Baidu are more popular in China.

Global marketing presents both challenges and opportunities for businesses looking to expand internationally. Businesses can successfully tap into new markets and grow their global presence by carefully selecting market entry strategies, adapting to cultural differences, and navigating regulatory and logistical complexities. A well-executed global marketing strategy enables businesses to reach new customers, increase revenue, and build a strong brand on a global scale.

4.10 Innovative Marketing Tactics

Standing out from the competition in today's crowded marketplace requires creativity and innovation. Employing innovative marketing tactics such as guerrilla marketing, viral campaigns, experiential marketing, and influencer marketing can help create buzz, drive engagement, and capture the attention of your target audience. This section explores these tactics and provides examples of brands that have successfully used them to their advantage.

Guerrilla marketing is a creative, low-cost strategy that uses unconventional methods to promote a product or service. It aims to surprise and engage the audience memorably, often creating intrigue or excitement. This approach is particularly effective for small businesses or startups with limited marketing budgets, as it can generate significant exposure without expensive advertising campaigns. A notable example of guerrilla marketing is T-Mobile's "Flash Mob" campaign. In 2009, T-Mobile organised a flash mob at London's Liverpool Street Station, where hundreds of dancers performed a choreographed routine, surprising commuters. The event was filmed and quickly went viral, generating millions of views and reinforcing T-Mobile's brand as fun and innovative.

Viral marketing involves creating content that is so engaging or entertaining that it spreads organically across social media and other platforms. Successful viral marketing taps into emotions such as humour, inspiration, or curiosity, creating content that resonates with a broad audience. One of the most impactful viral campaigns was the "Ice Bucket Challenge" in 2014, which raised awareness and funds for ALS (Amyotrophic Lateral Sclerosis). Participants were nominated to dump ice water over their heads or donate to the ALS Association, with the challenge spreading rapidly on social media and raising over $115 million for ALS research.

Experiential marketing involves creating immersive and interactive experiences that allow customers to engage with a brand memorably. This type of marketing goes beyond traditional advertising, offering customers the chance to interact with a product or service in real-world settings. For instance, Airbnb's "Night At" campaign transformed unique locations into temporary accommodations, such as the Great Wall of China or the Paris Catacombs. Winners of these experiences could spend the night at these iconic venues, generating significant media coverage and reinforcing Airbnb's brand as a provider of unique and memorable travel experiences.

Influencer marketing leverages social media influencers' credibility and large followings to create authentic, relatable content that resonates with potential customers. Companies can significantly enhance visibility and engagement by partnering with influencers who align with their brand values and target audience. The Swedish watch brand Daniel Wellington successfully used influencer marketing by sending free watches to influencers and encouraging them to post product photos. This strategy quickly built brand awareness and drove sales, contributing to the brand's rapid growth in the watch industry.

Interactive content is another innovative tactic for engaging customers by creating a personalised experience. Quizzes, polls, surveys, and interactive videos encourage participation and sharing, leading to higher engagement. For instance, BuzzFeed's interactive quizzes have been highly successful, generating significant traffic, social media shares, and increased brand awareness.

Pop-up shops and events provide an effective way to create buzz and engage customers in a unique setting. These temporary retail spaces or events create a sense of urgency and exclusivity, attracting customers curious about the limited-time offering. Beauty brand Glossier has used pop-up shops in various cities to create excitement and offer customers an in-person experience, bridging the gap between online shopping and physical retail.

Innovative marketing tactics such as guerrilla marketing, viral campaigns, experiential marketing, influencer marketing, and interactive content can help brands stand out in a crowded marketplace. By thinking creatively and taking risks, businesses can create memorable experiences that engage their audience, generate buzz, and build brand loyalty. These unconventional approaches are particularly effective for small businesses or startups looking to make a significant impact with limited resources.

4.11 Case Studies in Marketing Excellence

Learning from the successes of well-known brands offers valuable insights into effective marketing strategies. This section presents case studies of companies that have excelled through innovative and impactful marketing tactics, providing lessons that can be applied to your business.

Nike's "Just Do It" Campaign, launched in 1988, remains one of history's most iconic and successful marketing campaigns. The slogan "Just Do It" became synonymous with motivation, empowerment, and the pursuit of excellence, resonating with a broad audience ranging from professional athletes to everyday fitness enthusiasts. The campaign's success lies in its ability to tap into a universal desire for self-improvement and achievement, combined with compelling storytelling that showcases athletes overcoming challenges. By consistently using this messaging across various platforms, Nike solidified its position as a global athletic footwear and apparel leader, building a strong emotional connection with consumers.

Old Spice's "The Man Your Man Could Smell Like" Campaign reinvented the brand to appeal to a younger audience. Featuring actor Isaiah Mustafa, the humorous and memorable commercials used wit and charm to engage consumers while blending humour with product promotion. The campaign became a viral sensation on social media, garnering millions of views on YouTube and sparking conversations across platforms. Old Spice capitalised on the campaign's popularity by creating personalised video responses from the campaign's star, engaging directly with fans. This revitalised Old Spice's brand, significantly increasing sales and relevance among younger consumers and demonstrating the power of humour, creativity, and social media engagement.

Red Bull's Content Marketing and Brand Experience strategy has established the company as an energy drink and a lifestyle brand associated with adventure, adrenaline, and extreme sports. One of Red Bull's most notable campaigns was the "Red Bull Stratos" project, where skydiver Felix Baumgartner jumped from the edge of space, breaking the sound barrier during his freefall. This event captivated millions worldwide and aligned perfectly with Red Bull's brand message. The company's content marketing strategy includes producing high-quality media that showcases extreme sports and adventurous lifestyles, positioning Red Bull as a leader in both the energy drink market and the world of extreme sports.

Dove's "Real Beauty" Campaign challenged traditional beauty standards by promoting a more inclusive definition of beauty. The campaign featured real women of various shapes, sizes, and ages rather than professional models, conveying that beauty is diverse and every woman should feel confident in her skin. The campaign resonated with women worldwide, spreading media coverage and sparking conversations about beauty, body image, and self-esteem. Dove's authentic and empowering approach helped the brand build a deep emotional connection with consumers, driving significant sales growth and positioning the brand as a champion of diversity and self-acceptance.

These case studies highlight the power of innovative and impactful marketing strategies. Whether Nike's powerful storytelling, Old Spice's humour and social media engagement, Red Bull's content marketing, or Dove's purpose-driven messaging, these brands have successfully differentiated themselves and created lasting connections with their audiences. By studying these examples, businesses can gain valuable insights into creating marketing strategies that resonate with customers and drive success.

Conclusion

This chapter explores the essential marketing elements critical for building a strong brand and cultivating a loyal customer base. From understanding your market and crafting a compelling brand identity to navigating the complexities of digital marketing and implementing innovative pricing strategies, each section provides the tools necessary to develop a comprehensive and effective marketing plan.

Marketing is more than just promoting products; it involves creating value for your customers, building meaningful connections, and consistently delivering on your brand's promise. The case studies and innovative tactics discussed throughout this chapter illustrate that successful marketing requires creativity, data-driven decision-making, and a deep understanding of your target audience.

Adaptability and continuous learning are key as the marketing landscape evolves with new technologies, consumer behaviours, and global trends. By staying informed, embracing innovation, and remaining true to your brand's core values, businesses can navigate these changes and maintain a competitive edge in the marketplace.

Ultimately, mastering marketing is about building a lasting brand that resonates with customers, stands out in the market, and drives long-term business success.

Chapter 5

Sales Strategies for Growth: Driving Revenue Expansion

5.1 Overview

Sales are the primary driver of business growth. Without a robust and effective **sales strategy**, even the most innovative products and services may fail to reach their full potential. For any leader or entrepreneur, mastering sales fundamentals is crucial for driving **revenue expansion**, building strong **customer relationships**, and securing long-term success.

This chapter delves into the essential knowledge and tools needed to craft and implement sales strategies that lead to growth. We will explore everything from understanding the **sales funnel** and refining **sales techniques** to building a high-performing **sales team** and leveraging technology. Additionally, we will highlight the importance of a **customer-centric approach**, which goes beyond a strategy and represents a mindset that places the customer at the heart of the business.

Focusing on customer needs and cultivating strong relationships can create a sales strategy that boosts loyalty and drives repeat business. We will cover key **metrics** and **KPIs** to track sales performance and share insights from top sales organisations that have consistently achieved revenue growth. By the end of this chapter, you will have a comprehensive understanding of how to design and execute a sales strategy that meets and exceeds your business objectives.

5.2 The Sales Funnel

The **sales funnel** is a fundamental concept in sales strategy. It represents the journey potential customers take from their first interaction with your brand to the point of purchase. Understanding and optimising each funnel stage is essential, as this can significantly enhance **conversion rates** and drive revenue growth.

The sales funnel typically includes the following stages: **awareness, interest, consideration, intent, evaluation**, and **purchase**. At the top of the funnel, the focus is on generating **awareness** and attracting leads. As prospects move through the funnel, the emphasis shifts to nurturing their interest, addressing their needs, and guiding them toward a purchasing decision. At the bottom of the funnel, the goal is to close the deal and convert prospects into customers.

During the **awareness** stage, potential customers become aware of your brand, product, or service. The objective is to reach as many people as possible and inform them about your offer. Effective strategies include **content marketing, social media campaigns**, and **SEO** to capture attention and drive traffic to your website or store.

Once prospects know your brand, they may show **interest** in your product or service. At this stage, they might research more about what you offer, compare it with competitors, and engage with your content. Providing valuable information that educates and engages prospects is essential to maximise impact here. **Blog posts, case studies, webinars**, and **product demos** can all help demonstrate the benefits of your offering.

Prospects actively evaluate whether your product or service fits their needs during consideration. They may seek more in-depth information, such as product specifications, pricing, or customer reviews. To move prospects through this stage, it is critical to offer detailed, easily accessible information and personalise your content as much as possible. Tools like **email marketing, targeted ads**, and **retargeting strategies** can be particularly effective.

At the **intent** stage, prospects have shown interest and are seriously considering your product or service. They might add items to a shopping cart, request a quote, or sign up for a free trial. To encourage them to take the next step, it is important to address potential objections and offer incentives such as discounts, limited-time offers, or free shipping.

In the **evaluation** stage, prospects make a final decision before purchasing. They weigh the pros and cons, consider alternatives, and may seek reassurance from **customer testimonials** or peer recommendations. Personal contact from a **sales representative** can be highly effective here, as it provides the opportunity to answer any remaining questions and offer tailored solutions.

Finally, the **purchase** stage is where the prospect becomes a customer. Ensuring a smooth purchasing process and providing excellent post-purchase support are crucial for turning one-time buyers into loyal customers.

Optimising the sales funnel involves continuously analysing each stage to identify bottlenecks where prospects drop off. For example, if many leads drop off at the consideration stage, it might indicate that your content is not compelling enough or that there are barriers to accessing it. Monitoring and refining your approach is essential for improving conversion rates and moving more prospects through the funnel.

Companies like **HubSpot** have mastered the sales funnel by providing valuable resources at each stage. From free marketing tools and educational content at the top to in-depth product demos and personalised consultations at the bottom, HubSpot ensures that prospects receive the right information at the right time, guiding them smoothly through the funnel.

5.3 Effective Sales Techniques

Sales techniques are the tactical tools that sales professionals use to engage with prospects, overcome objections, and close deals. The effectiveness of these techniques can vary depending on the context, the product or service being sold, and the target market. However, mastering and knowing when to apply these techniques is crucial for any successful sales strategy.

Cold calling is one of the oldest and most direct sales techniques. It involves contacting potential customers who have not previously expressed interest in your product or service. While cold calling can be challenging and often met with resistance, it can still be effective when done correctly. Success in cold calling relies on thorough **research, a clear pitch**, and the ability to handle objections gracefully. Personalisation is key; by understanding the prospect's specific needs and pain points, you can tailor your message to resonate more effectively.

Consultative selling is a more customer-centric approach focusing on building relationships and understanding the customer's needs before offering a solution. Instead of pushing a product, the salesperson acts as an advisor, asking questions to uncover the customer's challenges and goals. This technique is particularly effective in B2B sales, where customers seek customised solutions and the purchasing process is more complex.

A successful consultative selling strategy involves **active listening, empathy**, and a deep understanding of the customer's industry and business. For instance, a software sales representative might start by asking the prospect about their current processes and pain points, then tailor their product presentation to demonstrate how the software can specifically address those challenges. They build credibility and trust by positioning themselves as trusted advisors, leading to stronger, longer-term customer relationships.

Solution selling is closely related to consultative selling but with a stronger focus on how the product or service solves a specific problem for the customer. In solution selling, the salesperson identifies a pain point and positions their offering as the ideal solution. This approach requires a deep understanding of the product and the customer's needs.

For example, if a company struggles with data management, a solution-selling approach would demonstrate how a particular software solution can streamline data processes, reduce errors, and save time. The key to solution-selling success is clearly articulating the value proposition and showing how the solution delivers measurable benefits.

SPIN selling is a technique developed by Neil Rackham based on research into what makes sales calls successful. SPIN stands for **Situation, Problem, Implication,** and **Need-Payoff**, the four types of questions that guide the sales conversation. By asking these questions, the salesperson helps the prospect articulate their needs and realise the urgency of addressing them.

For instance, a SPIN selling conversation with a manufacturing company might begin with questions about their current production processes (Situation), followed by inquiries about inefficiencies or challenges they face (Problem). The salesperson would then discuss the potential impact of these inefficiencies on the company's bottom line (Implication) before introducing a solution that improves productivity and reduces costs (Need-Payoff).

Handling objections is a critical skill in sales. Objections are inevitable, but they should not be seen as roadblocks; rather, they are opportunities to address concerns and reinforce the value of your offering. Common objections might include price, timing, or whether the product meets the customer's needs. The key to overcoming objections is to listen carefully, empathise with the customer's concerns, and provide clear, well-reasoned responses that address those concerns directly.

For example, if a prospect objects to the price of a product, the salesperson might respond by highlighting the long-term cost savings or return on investment that the product offers. "I understand that the initial investment might seem high, but let us look at the cost savings you will achieve over time and how this solution can save you money in the long run."

Closing techniques are the final step in the sales process, where the goal is to secure a commitment from the customer. Various closing techniques exist, such as the **assumptive close** (where the salesperson assumes the sale is a done deal), the **urgency close** (creating a sense of urgency by highlighting limited availability or time-sensitive offers), and the **summary close** (recapping the benefits and confirming that the solution meets all of the customer's needs).

For instance, an assumptive close might sound like, "Great, I will go ahead and set up the delivery for next week." This approach subtly nudges the prospect toward an agreement without putting them on the spot. The key to a successful close is ensuring the prospect feels confident and comfortable with their decision and that all their concerns have been addressed.

5.4 Building and Managing a Sales Team

A high-performing sales team is the backbone of any successful sales strategy. Building and managing such a team requires a clear vision, strong leadership, and a commitment to ongoing development and motivation. This section will explore the key elements of recruiting, training, and managing a sales team to achieve consistent results.

Recruiting the right talent is the first step in building a successful sales team. The ideal sales candidate should possess the necessary skills and experience and demonstrate personal attributes that align with your company's goals and culture. When recruiting, it is important to seek individuals skilled in sales techniques and those who are **resilient, adaptable**, and possess a strong work ethic, which is essential for thriving in the dynamic and often challenging sales world.

Training and development are essential to ensuring your sales team has the knowledge and skills to succeed. A comprehensive training program should cover product knowledge and sales techniques and provide insights into **industry trends, customer psychology**, and sales tools and technology. Ongoing development is equally important, as it allows salespeople to refine their skills continuously, stay updated on best practices, and adapt to market changes.

For example, Salesforce, a leading provider of CRM tools, invests heavily in training and development for its sales team. Salesforce offers various resources, including online courses, workshops, and one-on-one coaching, to ensure its sales professionals are at the top of their game. By providing continuous learning opportunities, Salesforce ensures its sales team remains competitive and effective in a rapidly evolving industry.

Motivating a sales team is key to driving performance. Sales can be demanding and sometimes stressful, so it's important to create an environment that motivates and rewards high performance. Motivation can come through **financial incentives, such as commissions and bonuses**, as well as non-financial rewards, such as recognition, career development opportunities, and fostering a positive work culture.

Incentive structures should align with both individual and team goals. For instance, bonuses based on team performance can foster collaboration and a shared purpose, while individual commissions drive personal accountability. **HubSpot**, for example, uses a combination of financial incentives and a supportive work environment to motivate its sales team. Regular recognition of top performers, career progression paths, and a strong sense of mission all contribute to a motivated and high-performing sales force.

Sales management involves more than simply overseeing day-to-day activities; it requires setting a vision, aligning the team with that vision, and ensuring that each team member is supported in achieving their goals. Effective sales managers are skilled in sales and excel in **coaching, mentoring**, and providing constructive feedback.

A best practice in sales management is setting clear, achievable goals and **KPIs** for the team. These goals should align with the company's broader objectives and be communicated clearly to the sales team. Regularly reviewing progress against these goals helps keep the team focused and allows for timely adjustments. For example, a sales manager might set quarterly **revenue targets** and KPIs such as the number of new leads generated, conversion rates, and average deal size. Tracking these metrics enables the manager to identify areas for improvement and provide targeted support to team members who may be struggling.

Coaching and mentoring are essential components of effective sales management. Sales managers should provide regular feedback, helping team members improve their performance by offering praise for successes and constructive advice on areas needing development. This could involve role-playing sales scenarios, reviewing sales calls, or offering guidance on handling objections. **Google** encourages sales managers to take a coaching approach, helping their teams develop their skills and grow their careers. This focus on development improves individual performance and contributes to a positive and supportive team culture.

Communication is another critical aspect of sales management. Open lines of communication should be maintained, ensuring everyone on the team is informed, aligned, and engaged. Regular team meetings to discuss progress, challenges, opportunities, and one-on-one check-ins for personalised support are crucial for maintaining an effective sales organisation.

You can build and manage a sales team that consistently delivers results by recruiting talent, providing continuous training, creating a motivating environment, and offering strong leadership. Effective sales management ensures that targets are met and fosters a culture of excellence and collaboration within the sales team.

5.5 Customer-Centric Selling

Adopting a customer-centric approach is crucial for successful selling in today's competitive market, where customers have more options and information than ever. Customer-centric selling involves deeply understanding the **buyer's needs, challenges, and goals** and tailoring the sales approach to meet those needs. This strategy builds trust and fosters long-term relationships, leading to higher **conversion rates and customer loyalty**.

The foundation of customer-centric selling lies in understanding **buyer behaviour**. This involves identifying your customers and comprehending their **decision-making processes, pain points**, and the motivations that drive their purchasing decisions. For example, in B2B sales, the decision-making process is often complex and involves multiple stakeholders. Recognising these dynamics enables sales teams to craft more targeted approaches, addressing the specific needs of each decision-maker and building a more compelling case for your solution.

Tailoring your sales approach is fundamental to customer-centric selling. It is not just about presenting a product or service but about aligning your messaging and offerings with what is most important to the customer. For instance, if you are selling a product that offers long-term cost savings but your customer is more concerned with initial costs, it is essential to focus on how the product can provide immediate value. Personalising your pitch to highlight the benefits that resonate most with the customer's current situation demonstrates empathy and understanding, which are key to building a strong relationship.

Active listening is a critical skill in customer-centric selling. It goes beyond simply hearing what the customer says; it involves understanding their underlying concerns and responding in a way that shows you have truly grasped their needs. This can involve asking open-ended questions, encouraging the customer to share more about their situation, and then using that information to guide the conversation. For example, suppose a customer mentions that they are worried about scalability. In that case, you might ask, "Can you share more about how your business plans to grow and what challenges you anticipate?" This builds rapport and provides valuable insights to help you position your product or service as the best solution.

Building trust is another cornerstone of customer-centric selling. Trust is established through honesty, transparency, and delivering on promises. For example, suppose a customer asks about a feature your product does not have. In that case, it is better to be upfront about its limitations while highlighting your product's strengths and benefits. This honesty builds credibility and helps set realistic expectations, preventing disappointment and frustration later.

Personalisation is an effective tool in customer-centric selling. Customers expect a personalised experience tailored to their specific needs. This could include customised product demos, tailored content, or personalised recommendations based on their past behaviour or stated preferences. For instance, an e-commerce company might use data to provide personalised product suggestions, enhancing the customer experience and increasing the likelihood of a sale. Such personalisation shows that the company values the customer as an individual, not just a transaction.

Another essential aspect is the **customer experience**. This includes every customer interaction with your brand, from the first contact to post-purchase support. Ensuring a seamless, positive experience at every customer journey stage is crucial for building long-term relationships. Companies like **Amazon** excel in customer-centric selling by focusing on convenience, personalisation, and exceptional customer service. Their customer-centric approach is evident in everything from the ease of navigating their website to the speed and reliability of their delivery services.

Customer feedback is invaluable for improving customer-centric selling. Actively seeking and responding to feedback shows customers that their opinions are valued and that your company is committed to meeting their needs. Feedback can be gathered through surveys, reviews, or direct customer conversations. Many companies use this information to refine their products and services, ensuring they continue to meet their customers' evolving needs.

The ultimate goal of customer-centric selling is to cultivate **customer loyalty**. Loyal customers are more likely to repeat purchases, refer others, and advocate for your brand. By consistently providing value and focusing on the customer experience, businesses can turn one-time buyers into long-term, loyal customers who contribute to the company's success for years.

5.6 Leveraging Technology in Sales

In the modern business landscape, leveraging technology has become essential for enhancing sales performance, streamlining processes, and driving revenue growth. Various tools, such as **Customer Relationship Management (CRM) systems, sales automation software**, and **artificial intelligence** (AI), can help sales teams operate more efficiently and improve their overall success. This section explores key technologies that can be used to achieve sales goals and offers insights into selecting and implementing the right tools for your business.

CRM systems are at the core of effective sales management. A CRM system helps businesses manage and analyse customer interactions throughout the sales lifecycle, from lead generation to deal closure. By centralising customer data, CRM systems provide a comprehensive view of each customer's history, preferences, and interactions with the company. This information is invaluable for personalising sales approaches, tracking progress, and ensuring no missed opportunities. For instance, **Salesforce**, a leading CRM platform, enables sales representatives to track customer interactions, manage pipelines, and collaborate with team members in real-time, fostering a more organised and effective sales process.

Sales automation tools are essential for reducing the time spent on repetitive tasks, allowing sales professionals to focus on higher-value activities. Automation can handle tasks such as data entry, email follow-ups, and lead scoring, ensuring that these crucial steps in the sales process are completed accurately and on time. For example, **HubSpot Sales** enables teams to automate various aspects of the sales process, such as sending email sequences and following up with prospects. These automation tools ensure that leads are nurtured consistently and that follow-ups occur without delay, allowing sales representatives to focus on relationship-building and closing deals.

Sales analytics and reporting tools provide valuable insights into sales team performance, helping to identify trends, measure success, and make data-driven decisions. These tools can track various metrics, from individual salesperson performance to overall pipeline health. For example, tools like **Microsoft Power BI** integrate with CRM systems to provide real-time dashboards and detailed reports, enabling sales managers to monitor key performance indicators (KPIs) such as conversion rates, average deal size, and sales cycle length. This level of insight helps teams identify areas for improvement and take action accordingly.

Artificial intelligence (AI) and **machine learning** increasingly integrate into the sales process, offering predictive analytics, lead scoring, and personalised recommendations. AI-powered tools can analyse vast amounts of data to identify patterns and predict which leads are most likely to convert, enabling sales teams to prioritise their efforts more effectively. For instance, **Salesforce's Einstein AI** uses machine learning to analyse customer data and suggest the best next steps for engaging with leads. AI helps sales teams focus on the most promising opportunities, increasing the likelihood of closing deals and improving the overall sales process.

Sales enablement platforms provide sales teams with the resources, content, and tools they need to engage with customers effectively. These platforms often include features such as content management, training modules, and collaboration tools, all of which empower sales teams to perform at their best. For example, **Seismic**, a sales enablement platform, provides sales representatives access to up-to-date content, training materials, and real-time analytics to help them close deals more effectively.

Social selling tools are also becoming increasingly important in today's sales landscape. Platforms like LinkedIn, Twitter, and Facebook allow sales professionals to identify potential customers, engage with them, and build relationships over time. Tools like **LinkedIn Sales Navigator** provide sales teams with valuable insights and recommendations, helping them connect with the right prospects at the right time.

Mobile sales tools ensure that sales professionals can maintain productivity even when they are on the move. Mobile CRM apps allow sales representatives to access customer data, update records, and communicate with team members from anywhere. For example, the **Salesforce mobile app** enables sales representatives to manage their pipelines, track leads, and close deals while away from the office, ensuring they can remain productive and responsive to customer needs.

Choosing the right technology for your sales team requires careful consideration of your business's specific needs, budget, and scalability. It is important to select tools that integrate seamlessly with your existing systems and processes and that are flexible enough to grow with your business. Additionally, it is crucial to ensure that your sales team receives proper training on using these tools effectively, as the value of any technology is realised only when it is used to its full potential.

Leveraging technology in sales is essential for staying competitive in today's fast-paced business environment. CRM systems, sales automation tools, AI-driven insights, and social selling platforms are all critical components of a modern, effective sales strategy. By selecting and implementing the right tools, businesses can empower their sales teams to work more efficiently, close deals faster, and achieve consistent success.

5.7 Key Account Management

Key Account Management (KAM) is a strategic approach to managing and nurturing relationships with a company's most valuable customers. These key accounts often contribute a significant portion of a company's revenue, making it essential to take a personalised approach to ensure long-term satisfaction and loyalty. This section explores the principles of effective KAM, focusing on strategies for identifying key accounts, building strong relationships, and maximising the value of these critical customer partnerships.

Identifying **key accounts** is the first step in developing a successful Key Account Management strategy. Key accounts are typically customers who represent a substantial share of revenue or offer significant growth potential. They may also provide strategic value, such as industry influence or market insights. When identifying key accounts, evaluating revenue contribution, profitability, and strategic alignment with your business goals is essential. For example, a B2B software company might identify a large enterprise customer generating a significant portion of its revenue as a key account. In addition to their financial value, this customer might serve as a valuable reference or case study, enhancing the company's credibility in the market.

Building **strong relationships** with key accounts is at the heart of effective Key Account Management. Unlike traditional sales relationships, KAM focuses on creating long-term, mutually beneficial partnerships. This requires a deep understanding of the customer's business, challenges, and goals and a commitment to delivering value beyond the initial sale. A key strategy for building strong relationships is personalisation. This involves tailoring your products, services, and communication to meet the specific needs of the key account. For instance, a key account manager might collaborate with customers to develop customised solutions that address their unique challenges, providing dedicated support to ensure success.

Collaboration is a key element of KAM. Successful key account managers work closely with their customers to co-create solutions that deliver mutual value. This collaboration may involve joint product development, shared marketing initiatives, or collaborative problem-solving. For instance, a key account manager at a manufacturing company might collaborate with a customer to design a new product that meets industry-specific requirements, leading to a win-win outcome for both parties. Cross-selling and upselling are also essential strategies for maximising the value of key account relationships. By identifying additional needs within the key account, sales teams can introduce complementary products or services that enhance the overall value of the partnership.

Maintaining **regular communication** with key accounts is essential for building trust and ensuring the relationship's long-term success. This goes beyond simply responding to inquiries or requests; it involves proactively engaging with the customer, offering insights, and identifying new opportunities for collaboration. Regular check-ins allow key account managers to stay informed about the customer's evolving needs and ensure that the solutions provided continue to meet those needs. In addition to regular communication, actively seeking **feedback** from key accounts is crucial. Understanding how satisfied key customers are with your products and services allows you to make adjustments that improve the partnership.

Measuring the success of your **Key Account Management strategy** involves tracking specific metrics and Key Performance Indicators (KPIs) that reflect the health and value of the relationship. These metrics may include revenue growth from key accounts, customer satisfaction scores, retention rates, and the overall contribution of key accounts to your business. For example, if a key account's satisfaction scores are declining, it may indicate a need for more frequent communication or additional support. By staying attuned to these indicators, key account managers can proactively address issues and ensure that key accounts remain loyal.

The ultimate goal of Key Account Management is to create long-term value. This means continuously identifying new ways to add value through innovative products, personalised services, or enhanced support. By focusing on long-term value creation, key account managers can build partnerships lasting years and deliver substantial benefits for both parties.

In conclusion, **Key Account Management** is a strategic approach focusing on nurturing and growing relationships with a company's most valuable customers. Businesses can create long-lasting partnerships that drive significant revenue growth by identifying key accounts, building strong relationships, collaborating to deliver mutual value, and maintaining regular communication. Effective KAM requires a commitment to personalisation, continuous improvement, and a deep understanding of the customer's needs and goals.

5.8 Negotiation Skills

Negotiation is a pivotal skill for any sales professional, as it directly influences the ability to close deals and build long-term customer relationships. Effective negotiation requires balancing meeting the customer's expectations and achieving favourable business outcomes. This section delves into essential negotiation tactics and strategies to help sales professionals craft win-win solutions that satisfy both parties.

Preparation and research form the foundation of any successful negotiation. Before entering into discussions, gathering as much information as possible about the customer's needs, constraints, and priorities is crucial. Understanding the customer's budget, decision-making process, and potential objections allows you to anticipate concerns and develop strategies to address them. For example, suppose you know a customer is sensitive to price. In that case, you can prepare by highlighting the unique value propositions of your product that justify the cost, such as long-term savings or superior quality. By entering the negotiation well-prepared, you position yourself as a knowledgeable partner ready to offer solutions that meet the customer's specific needs.

Active listening and building rapport are critical components of effective negotiation. Active listening involves fully concentrating on what the customer is saying, understanding their message, and responding thoughtfully. It is about hearing their words and interpreting their emotions and motivations. This approach helps identify the key issues that must be addressed and craft responses that align with the customer's concerns. For instance, if a customer expresses worry about the delivery timeline, you can delve deeper by asking, "Can you share more about how delays might impact your operations?" This demonstrates empathy and shows you are committed to finding a solution that works for both parties.

Creating value and finding common ground is essential for reaching mutually beneficial agreements. Instead of viewing negotiation as a zero-sum game, where one party wins and the other loses, aim to create additional value for both sides. This might involve offering bundled services, extended support, or flexible payment terms that meet the customer's needs while benefiting your business. For example, if a customer is hesitant about upfront costs, you might offer a discount for a larger volume purchase or a longer contract term. This approach addresses the customer's concern and increases the deal's overall value.

Managing objections is a crucial skill in negotiation. Objections are a natural part of the process and should be viewed as opportunities to provide additional information and reassurance. Common objections might relate to price, timing, or the product's suitability for the customer's needs. The key to overcoming objections is to listen carefully, empathise with the customer's concerns, and respond with clear, well-reasoned answers. For example, suppose a customer objects to the price.

In that case, you might respond by emphasising your product's long-term cost savings or unique benefits, such as increased efficiency or reduced maintenance costs. This shifts the focus from the initial expense to the value delivered over time.

Flexibility and knowing your limits are also vital in negotiation. It is important to be willing to make concessions and adapt your approach, but you should also clearly understand your non-negotiables, points beyond which you cannot compromise. Setting these boundaries before entering the negotiation ensures you do not agree to terms that could harm your business. For instance, if a customer is pushing for a price that would result in a loss, you might offer additional services instead of reducing the price further. This approach allows you to maintain profitability while meeting customer needs.

Closing the deal effectively is the final step in a successful negotiation. Once an agreement has been reached, it is important to summarise the key points, confirm the details, and ensure that both parties are clear on the next steps. This helps avoid misunderstandings and sets the stage for a smooth agreement implementation. For example, after agreeing on terms, you might say, "Just to confirm, we will proceed with the agreed pricing and delivery schedule, and I will send the contract details by the end of the day. Does that work for you?" This clear communication reinforces the agreement and ensures alignment between both parties.

Effective negotiation requires **preparation, active listening, value creation, and flexibility**. By approaching negotiations with a collaborative mindset and focusing on long-term relationships, sales professionals can secure deals that benefit both the customer and the business. Successful negotiation helps close deals and lays the foundation for ongoing collaboration and growth.

5.9 Scaling Sales Operations

As businesses grow, scaling sales operations becomes essential to meet increasing demand while maintaining efficiency and effectiveness. Scaling a sales organisation involves expanding its capacity to generate revenue while ensuring that processes, people, and technology evolve to support sustainable growth. This section explores the critical steps for scaling sales operations, including standardising processes, investing in technology, hiring and training talent, and maintaining customer satisfaction during growth.

Standardising sales processes is a key element of scaling effectively. As sales teams grow, having clear and repeatable processes ensures consistency across the board, making it easier to manage an expanding team and maintain high performance. Standardisation improves operational efficiency, simplifies onboarding for new hires, and ensures everyone follows best practices throughout the sales cycle. For example, developing a **sales playbook** that outlines key steps in the sales process, from lead generation to closing deals, helps standardise procedures across the team. The playbook should include guidelines on handling objections, customer communication templates, and strategies for each sales funnel stage. This consistency ensures that every team member can deliver a high-quality experience to customers, regardless of their experience level.

Investing in technology for scalability is crucial as sales operations expand. As the volume of leads, customers, and transactions increases, leveraging sales technology ensures that teams can manage these demands without compromising quality. Customer Relationship Management (CRM) systems, sales automation tools, and analytics platforms help sales teams streamline processes, track performance, and make data-driven decisions. For instance, a CRM system like **Salesforce** allows sales teams to manage customer interactions efficiently, maintain accurate records, and ensure that leads are nurtured effectively. Automation tools, such as email follow-up sequences and lead scoring, reduce the time spent on manual tasks and allow salespeople to focus on building relationships and closing deals. Analytics platforms provide insights into the performance of different sales activities, enabling teams to optimise their strategies continuously.

Hiring and training for growth is another critical aspect of scaling sales operations. Expanding the sales team becomes necessary as the business grows to meet increased demand. However, hiring the right people is crucial to maintaining the effectiveness and culture of the sales organisation. Effective hiring involves focusing on both technical skills and cultural fit. While sales techniques can be taught, finding candidates who share the company's values and are passionate about the product or service is essential for long-term success. For instance, **Zappos** emphasises cultural alignment during the hiring process, ensuring that new hires are capable salespeople enthusiastic about delivering exceptional customer service.

Once the right talent is in place, **training and development** are essential to ensure that salespeople have the knowledge and skills to succeed. A comprehensive training program should cover product knowledge, sales techniques, industry trends and customer psychology insights. Ongoing development is equally important, as it allows salespeople to continuously refine their skills, stay updated on best practices, and adapt to market changes. For example, **Salesforce** invests heavily in training and development for its sales team. It offers a range of resources, including online courses, workshops, and one-on-one coaching, to ensure its sales professionals are at the top of their game.

Maintaining customer satisfaction during growth is crucial for long-term success. With increased sales volume, there is a risk that customer interactions may become less personal or efficient. Ensuring that your customer service and support teams scale in line with sales growth is critical to providing a seamless experience. Investing in customer support technology and expanding the support team can help manage customer inquiries and issues more efficiently. For example, companies like **Zappos** have maintained their reputation for excellent customer service even as they have grown by ensuring that their support infrastructure scales along with their sales efforts. Maintaining a **customer-centric approach** during scaling also involves understanding and meeting customer needs. Personalisation, proactive engagement, and timely responses should remain a priority even as the number of customers increases.

Expanding into new markets is often a key part of scaling sales operations. Entering new geographic regions or targeting new customer segments requires careful planning, a deep understanding of local customer needs, and a tailored sales strategy. Expanding into new markets can present regulatory, cultural, and logistical challenges, which must be addressed to succeed. For instance, **Uber's global expansion** required adapting its sales and marketing strategies to align with each region's cultural norms and regulations. The company tailored its messaging, worked closely with local partners, and navigated regulatory challenges to ensure successful market entry. Scaling into new markets can also involve introducing new products or services that meet the specific needs of those markets. Understanding the unique demands of different regions or customer segments allows businesses to refine their value proposition and create more targeted sales approaches.

Monitoring and adjusting sales strategy is essential as a business scales. What works at one growth stage may not be effective at the next. Continuous review of sales processes, tools, and performance metrics allows teams to identify areas for improvement and make necessary adjustments. For example, **HubSpot** regularly reviews its sales data to identify trends, optimise processes, and refine its approach. This iterative process allows the company to remain agile and responsive to market changes, ensuring its sales strategy continues to drive growth as it scales.

Scaling sales operations is a complex but critical process for growing businesses. Companies can scale effectively by standardising processes, investing in technology, hiring and training the right talent, maintaining customer satisfaction, expanding into new markets, and continuously monitoring and adjusting the sales strategy without compromising the quality of their sales efforts. Effective scaling ensures that sales teams remain efficient and motivated and deliver consistent results.

5.10 Metrics and KPIs for Sales Success

Tracking the right **metrics and Key Performance Indicators (KPIs)** is essential for measuring sales success and driving continuous improvement. These metrics provide valuable insights into your sales team's performance, help identify areas for enhancement, and guide data-driven decision-making. This section will explore key sales metrics and KPIs and offer guidance on setting targets and measuring performance effectively.

Revenue growth is one of the most critical metrics for any sales team. It measures the increase in sales revenue over a specific period and serves as a direct indicator of business success. Monitoring revenue growth allows sales teams to assess the effectiveness of their strategies and identify trends that can inform future planning. For instance, if revenue growth is slowing, it may indicate the need to explore new markets, adjust pricing strategies, or invest more resources in sales efforts. By closely tracking revenue growth, businesses can ensure that their sales strategies align with their overall business objectives.

Another important metric is **sales pipeline coverage**, which provides visibility into the health of the sales pipeline. Pipeline coverage is typically measured as the ratio of the total value of opportunities in the pipeline to the sales target for a given period. A healthy pipeline coverage ratio ensures that enough opportunities are in the pipeline to meet or exceed sales targets. For example, a 3:1 pipeline coverage ratio means that for every £1 of the sales target, there are £3 worth of opportunities in the pipeline. This buffer accounts for deals that may not close, helping to ensure that sales targets are achievable.

Conversion rate is a key KPI that measures the percentage of leads converted into customers. It is an important indicator of the effectiveness of the sales process, from lead generation to closing deals. By tracking conversion rates at each sales funnel stage, teams can identify where prospects are dropping off and optimise those stages to improve performance. For example, losing many leads after product demonstrations may indicate a need for more compelling product demos or more effective follow-up. Monitoring conversion rates allows sales teams to refine their approach and increase the likelihood of closing deals.

Average deal size tracks the average value of closed deals over a specific period. This metric helps businesses understand the revenue potential of each sale and identify trends in customer spending. Monitoring the average deal size can help sales teams adjust their strategies, such as focusing on upselling or cross-selling opportunities to increase deal value. For example, if the average deal size increases, it may indicate that the sales team successfully sells higher-tier products or services or that customers are more willing to invest in larger purchases. Conversely, a decreasing average deal size could suggest a need to adjust pricing strategies or improve the perceived value of the offering.

Sales cycle length measures the average time to close a deal, from the initial contact with a lead to the final purchase. A shorter sales cycle is generally desirable, indicating that the sales team is closing deals more quickly and efficiently. However, longer sales cycles may also occur in more complex sales processes or high-value deals, where more time is required for decision-making. Tracking sales cycle length allows businesses to identify bottlenecks in the sales process and implement strategies to accelerate deal closure. For example, if the sales cycle is longer than expected, it might signal that prospects require more information or reassurance before committing to a purchase.

Customer acquisition cost (CAC) is a critical metric that measures the total cost of acquiring a new customer, including marketing, sales, and onboarding expenses. Understanding CAC is important for determining the profitability of sales efforts. A lower CAC indicates that customers are being acquired cost-effectively, while a higher CAC may signal inefficiencies in the sales and marketing processes. For example, suppose a company's CAC is increasing. In that case, it may be necessary to explore more cost-effective lead generation channels, optimise the sales process, or improve the efficiency of customer onboarding. By comparing CAC to customer lifetime value (CLTV), businesses can assess their sales efforts' overall return on investment (ROI) and ensure that acquisition costs align with long-term profitability.

Customer lifetime value (CLTV) estimates the total revenue a customer is expected to generate throughout their relationship with the company. CLTV is important for understanding the long-term value of each customer and guiding decisions about how much to invest in acquiring and retaining customers. A high CLTV indicates that customers provide significant ongoing value, while a low CLTV may suggest that efforts should focus on increasing customer loyalty and repeat business. By comparing CLTV to CAC, sales teams can assess the profitability of their customer acquisition strategies and ensure that they are generating high-value, profitable customers.

Win rate measures the percentage of deals won out of the total number of opportunities in the sales pipeline. It is a key indicator of a sales team's effectiveness and the competitiveness of the company's offerings. A higher win rate suggests that the sales team is successfully closing deals and overcoming objections. In comparison, a lower win rate may indicate that additional training, improved product positioning, or more targeted sales efforts are needed. For example, suppose a company's win rate is declining. In that case, it might be necessary to re-evaluate the sales approach, provide additional coaching to the sales team, or reassess the competitive landscape.

Sales rep performance tracking is essential for understanding the productivity and effectiveness of individual team members. Key metrics to monitor include the number of leads generated, meetings booked, deals closed, and revenue generated by each salesperson. These metrics provide insights into each team member's contributions and highlight areas where additional coaching or support may be needed. For instance, if a sales rep consistently exceeds their targets, they may serve as a model for best practices, while underperforming reps may benefit from additional training or mentorship.

Customer satisfaction and retention are crucial for long-term sales success. Metrics such as **Net Promoter Score (NPS)**, customer satisfaction (CSAT) scores, and churn rate provide valuable insights into how well the sales team meets customer expectations and builds lasting relationships. For example, a high churn rate, where customers do not renew or continue using the product, may indicate customer onboarding, product fit, or ongoing support issues. By tracking customer satisfaction and retention metrics, businesses can identify potential areas for improvement and take steps to enhance the overall customer experience.

Setting targets and monitoring progress are essential for driving performance and accountability. Targets should be based on historical data, industry benchmarks, and company goals. For example, a company might target increasing its win rate by 5% over the next quarter or reducing its sales cycle length by one week. Regularly monitoring progress against these targets ensures that the team remains focused on achieving its objectives. Periodic reviews allow for adjustments in strategy or tactics as needed, ensuring that the business stays on track to meet its sales goals.

5.11 Learning from the Best

Success leaves valuable lessons, and studying the strategies of top-performing sales organisations offers insights that can be applied to other businesses. This section highlights several companies renowned for their sales excellence, providing case studies of how they consistently drive revenue growth through effective sales strategies.

Salesforce: Customer-centric selling is one of the hallmarks of Salesforce's approach. The company's sales teams are known for their deep understanding of customer needs and for providing tailored solutions that deliver real value. This customer-first approach has enabled Salesforce to build long-lasting client relationships, leading to high customer satisfaction and retention. Salesforce focuses on **consultative selling**, where sales reps act as trusted advisors, helping customers address their unique challenges. This approach is supported by a robust training and development program, ensuring its sales teams have the knowledge and tools to succeed.

HubSpot: Inbound Sales and Data-Driven Success have been crucial to its growth. HubSpot focuses on attracting leads through valuable content and nurturing them through the sales funnel with relevant, personalised interactions. The company aligns its sales process with the buyer's journey, ensuring prospects receive the information they need at the right time. HubSpot's **data-driven approach** also plays a significant role in its success. The company uses analytics to track every aspect of the sales process, from lead generation to deal closure. By closely monitoring these metrics, HubSpot optimises its strategies and makes data-driven decisions that enhance performance.

Zendesk: Key Account Management and Customer Success are central to Zendesk's strategy. The company focuses on identifying high-value accounts and providing them with tailored support, which builds loyalty and increases customer retention. The emphasis on customer success drives Zendesk's sales strategy. By prioritising the success of their key accounts and offering personalised solutions, Zendesk strengthens relationships and creates long-term partnerships, turning customers into advocates for the brand.

LinkedIn: Social Selling and Sales Enablement have been crucial to the company's success. LinkedIn's sales team leverages its platform's data and networking capabilities to excel in social selling. Tools like LinkedIn Sales Navigator help sales professionals identify and engage with prospects in a personalised, relationship-driven manner. LinkedIn's comprehensive **sales enablement program** equips its sales team with the right content, tools, and training, ensuring they are well-prepared to engage with prospects and close deals.

Amazon: Personalisation and Data-Driven Sales have been key to the company's sustained growth. Amazon's deep understanding of customer preferences allows it to deliver tailored recommendations, driving higher conversion rates and customer loyalty. The company's ability to analyse vast amounts of data enables it to optimise the customer experience and adjust its sales strategies based on real-time insights. For example, Amazon's **recommendation engine** uses machine learning algorithms to provide personalised product suggestions, enhancing the customer experience and encouraging repeat purchases.

Gartner: Thought Leadership and Consultative Selling have been instrumental in its sales success. Gartner's sales team positions itself as an expert resource, providing clients with valuable insights and recommendations based on their needs. This approach builds strong, long-term client relationships and reinforces Gartner's reputation as a research and advisory services leader.

By examining these case studies, businesses can gain valuable insights into creating effective sales strategies that drive revenue growth. Whether through **customer-centric selling, inbound sales, key account management**, or leveraging **data and technology**, these companies have demonstrated the importance of aligning sales efforts with customer needs and continuously refining their strategies to stay ahead.

Conclusion

This chapter has explored the fundamental components of successful sales strategies, providing a comprehensive overview of the techniques and approaches that drive revenue growth and long-term business success. Each element is critical in shaping a robust sales strategy, from mastering the sales funnel and employing effective sales techniques to building high-performing sales teams and leveraging technology.

The **customer-centric approach**, emphasised throughout the chapter, remains at the heart of effective selling. By placing the customer's needs, goals, and challenges at the forefront of every sales interaction, businesses can build lasting relationships that close deals, foster loyalty, and encourage repeat business. As businesses grow and scale their sales operations, **technology**, such as CRM systems, sales automation tools, and data-driven insights, becomes indispensable. These tools allow sales teams to work more efficiently, handle increased complexity, and maintain high personalisation and customer engagement levels.

We also discussed **monitoring key metrics and KPIs** to measure sales success and drive continuous improvement. Metrics such as revenue growth, win rates, and customer satisfaction provide valuable insights into the effectiveness of sales strategies, ensuring that businesses remain agile and responsive to changing market conditions.

Finally, we explored the successes of leading sales organisations like Salesforce, HubSpot, and Amazon, drawing valuable lessons from their strategies. Their approaches demonstrate the importance of customer-centricity, data-driven decision-making, and continuous innovation in achieving sustained revenue growth. Ultimately, mastering sales strategies is an ongoing process that requires adaptability, a deep understanding of customer needs, and a commitment to continuous improvement. By staying focused on the customer, leveraging the right tools and techniques, and learning from industry leaders, businesses can build sales organisations that consistently meet and exceed their growth objectives.

Chapter 6

Operational Excellence: Streamlining for Efficiency

6.1 Overview

Operational excellence is a cornerstone of sustainable business success. It involves the ongoing pursuit of efficiency, quality, and agility across all operational facets, enabling businesses to deliver consistent value to their customers while safeguarding profitability. In a highly competitive and rapidly changing business environment, organisations that demonstrate operational superiority are better positioned to adapt to change, manage risks, and scale their operations effectively. Without a solid foundation in operational excellence, even the most innovative products and services may struggle to achieve their full potential.

This chapter explores the key insights and tools necessary for streamlining operations to achieve operational excellence. It delves into methodologies such as **Lean Management**, highlighting technology's critical role in managing and optimising operational processes. Additionally, the chapter discusses the importance of implementing quality management systems and integrating sustainability into operations. By focusing on these areas, businesses can develop a robust operational framework that enhances efficiency, minimises costs, and ultimately builds a resilient and high-performing organisation capable of thriving in an ever-evolving marketplace.

6.2 Understanding Operational Excellence

Operational excellence goes beyond being a buzzword; it represents a systematic, structured, and disciplined approach to managing and improving business operations to achieve superior performance. At its core, it involves a relentless commitment to **continuous improvement**, a fundamental concept that allows organisations to adapt to changing business environments. This approach focuses on efficiency and consistently delivering high-quality products and services. Operational excellence aims to create customer value by refining processes, minimising waste, and maximising resource utilisation. It is not a one-time achievement but a continuous journey toward betterment.In today's business landscape, operational excellence is a strategic enabler that helps companies meet their objectives. By reducing operational costs, enhancing productivity, and elevating customer satisfaction, businesses can gain a competitive edge, improve profitability, and secure long-term sustainability. A prime example is **Toyota**, whose renowned success in the automotive sector is largely attributed to its rigorous focus on operational excellence through the **Toyota Production System (TPS)**. This system prioritises efficiency, quality, and continuous improvement, ultimately helping Toyota maintain its leadership position in the industry.

The key principles underpinning operational excellence include focusing on **customer value, process optimisation, waste**

reduction, and **employee empowerment**. These principles guide organisations in aligning every aspect of their operations to deliver maximum customer value. For instance, companies like **Amazon** have built their operational strategies around providing fast, reliable, and convenient service, driving their global success.

6.3 Lean Management

Lean Management is a systematic approach to enhancing efficiency and quality by eliminating waste and focusing on activities that create value for the customer. Originating from the **Toyota Production System (TPS)**, Lean Management has evolved into a widely adopted methodology across various industries, including manufacturing, healthcare, and services. The primary objective of Lean Management is to streamline operations, reduce costs, and deliver products or services that meet customer needs with minimal waste.

The guiding principles of Lean Management are centred around **continuous improvement (Kaizen)** and **respect for people**. These foundational principles ensure that operations are optimised to deliver maximum customer value. One of the core tools within Lean Management is **Value Stream Mapping**, which involves visualising the flow of materials and information throughout the production process. By mapping the value stream, businesses can identify inefficiencies, bottlenecks, and waste areas, enabling them to streamline processes and focus on activities that add value.

Lean Management also emphasises the importance of **waste reduction (Muda),** which identifies seven forms of waste that can occur in any process: overproduction, waiting, transportation, excess inventory, motion, overprocessing, and defects. The primary goal of Lean is to eliminate or minimise these wastes to boost efficiency. For example, adopting a **Just-In-Time (JIT)** production approach ensures that products are manufactured only when needed, reducing excess inventory and associated costs.

The principle of **Kaizen** lies at the core of Lean Management, emphasising small, incremental improvements to processes. Rather than waiting for breakthroughs, Lean advocates for a focus on daily, ongoing changes that enhance quality and efficiency. This approach empowers employees at all levels to propose and implement improvements to their daily work. This practice has been a key contributor to the global success of companies like Toyota.

Lean Management also promotes **standardised work** to ensure consistency and quality. Standardised work involves defining the most efficient way to perform a task and ensuring that all employees adhere to this standard. This reduces variability, improves efficiency, and facilitates troubleshooting when issues arise. For example, standardised work procedures in fast-food restaurants may outline specific steps for food preparation, ensuring speed and consistency across all locations.

A critical tenet of Lean Management is the **respect and value placed on employees**. Recognising that employee engagement and empowerment are essential to the success of Lean initiatives, Lean principles encourage organisations to foster a collaborative work environment where employees' contributions are valued. Companies such as Toyota and Danaher excel in creating cultures where employees are actively engaged in problem-solving and continuous improvement efforts.

The success of Lean Management has been widely demonstrated across various sectors. For instance, **Boeing** adopted Lean principles to enhance production efficiency and reduce costs. By streamlining its production processes, Boeing reduced aircraft production times while maintaining high-quality standards. Similarly, the **Virginia Mason Medical Center** in Seattle applied Lean principles to healthcare, resulting in better patient care, reduced waiting times, and significant cost savings.

6.4 Quality Management Systems

Quality Management Systems (QMS) provide a formal framework for helping organisations consistently deliver products and services that meet or exceed customer expectations. A robust QMS is essential for maintaining high operational standards, ensuring regulatory compliance, and fostering a culture of continuous improvement. When implemented effectively, a QMS can enhance product quality, reduce costs, improve efficiency, and boost customer satisfaction.

In industries where quality is paramount, such as healthcare, pharmaceuticals, and automotive manufacturing, a well-implemented QMS ensures that products and services consistently meet the highest standards. A QMS provides a structured approach for managing quality across all stages of operations, from design and production to delivery and after-sales service. Companies like **BMW** and **Mercedes-Benz** implement rigorous QMS frameworks to ensure their vehicles adhere to stringent safety, reliability, and performance standards.

The steps involved in implementing a Quality Management System include securing **leadership commitment**, conducting **process mapping and documentation**, and ensuring **employee training and engagement**. A successful QMS requires the full commitment of top leadership, as seen at **General Electric (GE)**, which attributes its long-standing reputation for excellence to the unwavering focus of its leadership on quality. The process mapping and documentation phase involves identifying and documenting key operational processes, which is critical for achieving consistency in quality control. In the pharmaceutical industry, for example, documenting each step in drug production ensures compliance with stringent regulatory requirements.

A well-functioning QMS depends on employees' active engagement and involvement in maintaining and improving quality standards. Companies such as Toyota invest heavily in training employees on quality procedures, creating a work culture prioritising quality at every organisational level. A QMS is not a static implementation; it requires regular **monitoring, auditing,** and **updating** to maintain high-quality standards. For example, Boeing incorporates **Six Sigma** methodologies into its QMS to identify and address defects in production, continuously improving quality and minimising variability.

A critical function of a QMS is ensuring compliance with industry standards and regulations. Regular audits and updates are necessary to maintain compliance with evolving standards. For instance, **Intel** maintains rigorous quality control systems that are continuously reviewed and updated to ensure its products consistently meet stringent benchmarks.

By implementing a robust QMS, businesses can enhance operational standards, ensure compliance with regulatory requirements, and deliver products and services that meet or exceed customer expectations. When integrated with ISO standards, such systems provide a framework that enables businesses to achieve operational excellence.

6.5 Supply Chain Optimisation

Supply chain optimisation is essential for operational excellence, as it directly impacts a company's ability to operate efficiently, reduce costs, and meet customer demands. A well-optimized supply chain enables businesses to deliver products and services promptly and at minimal cost while reducing waste and improving overall performance. In today's highly competitive and globalised markets, companies that master supply chain management enjoy significant competitive advantages.

Optimising the supply chain enhances operational efficiency, improves customer satisfaction, and reduces operational costs. When businesses streamline their supply chains, they can reduce lead times, lower inventory costs, and ensure timely product availability, directly contributing to a better customer experience. Companies like **Amazon** and **Walmart** have built substantial competitive advantages through their highly efficient supply chains, allowing them to deliver products faster and at lower prices than their competitors.

Several strategies contribute to the optimisation of supply chains, including accurate **demand forecasting**, effective **inventory management**, strong **supplier relationships**, and the integration of **advanced technologies**. Accurate demand forecasting is essential for aligning production, inventory, and distribution processes with customer demand. Companies that leverage advanced analytics and machine learning tools can predict demand more accurately, reducing the risk of stockouts or excess inventory. **Procter & Gamble**, for instance, employs sophisticated forecasting models to ensure their products are available when and where customers need them.

Proper inventory management balances customer demand with cost efficiency. Techniques like **Just-In-Time (JIT)** inventory management, safety stock optimisation, and inventory segmentation allow businesses to reduce carrying costs while ensuring product availability. **Dell's** build-to-order model is an excellent example of JIT inventory management, enabling the company to keep stock levels low while meeting customer demand for custom-built products. Effective **supplier relationship management** is another key component of supply chain optimisation. Building strong partnerships with suppliers ensures timely delivery, improves communication, and enhances overall quality. For example, **Toyota's** long-standing relationships with its suppliers have been instrumental in maintaining its operational efficiency and quality, allowing the company to respond quickly to changes in demand and supply conditions.

Technology integration is revolutionising supply chain management. Advanced tools like the **Internet of Things (IoT)**, **blockchain**, and **artificial intelligence (AI)** provide real-time visibility, automation, and data-driven decision-making capabilities. For instance, IoT-enabled sensors allow businesses to track goods in real-time, providing insights into potential delays or inefficiencies. Blockchain enhances supply chain transparency and security by creating immutable records of transactions, which can help reduce fraud and increase trust among stakeholders.

Several companies have demonstrated the transformative power of supply chain optimisation. **Unilever**, for example, achieved a 15% reduction in inventory levels by implementing advanced demand forecasting tools, resulting in significant cost savings and improved customer service. Similarly, **Cisco** optimised its supply chain by leveraging digital platforms that provide real-time visibility into every aspect of its operations. This enabled the company to manage risks more effectively, track shipments in real-time, and maintain high levels of efficiency across its global supply chain.

In conclusion, supply chain optimisation is vital to achieving operational excellence. By employing accurate demand forecasting, effective inventory management, strong supplier collaboration, and advanced technologies, businesses can create a more resilient and responsive supply chain that drives long-term success.

6.6 Technology in Operations

Technology has become a central driver of operational excellence, transforming how businesses manage efficiency, quality, and agility. From **automation** and **artificial intelligence (AI)** to **data analytics** and the **Internet of Things (IoT)**, modern technology offers businesses the tools to streamline operations, improve decision-making, and enhance productivity.

Automation significantly enhances operational efficiency by performing routine tasks more quickly, consistently, and accurately than human labour. Automation can be applied across various operational areas, including manufacturing, logistics, customer service, and data management. By automating repetitive tasks, businesses can reduce labour costs, minimise errors, and allow employees to focus on higher-value activities.

For example, automation can handle assembly, packaging, and quality control tasks in manufacturing. Companies like **Tesla** have adopted advanced automation systems to scale production and maintain high-quality standards. In logistics, automation ensures faster and more accurate order processing. **Amazon's** fulfilment centres, for instance, use robotics and automated systems to manage inventory and ship products efficiently, significantly reducing delivery times and operational costs.

The impact of **AI and machine learning** is profound in transforming business operations. These technologies enable businesses to analyse vast amounts of data, identify patterns, and optimise decision-making processes. AI is particularly valuable in supply chain management, where it can predict demand, optimise inventory, and adjust production schedules in real-time based on market conditions. AI-powered tools also improve customer service by automating routine inquiries and personalising responses, enhancing customer experience. For example, **H&M** uses AI to streamline customer service through chatbots, providing personalised fashion recommendations and efficiently handling customer queries. This has improved response times while reducing the burden on human customer service agents.

Leveraging **data analytics** for process improvement is another powerful way to achieve operational excellence. Data analytics provides real-time insights into performance and efficiency, allowing businesses to make data-driven decisions. In retail, for example, data analytics can optimise inventory levels, ensuring product availability while avoiding overstocking. In manufacturing, predictive maintenance utilises data analytics to monitor equipment performance and predict when maintenance is required, preventing costly downtime and extending the lifespan of machinery.

The **Internet of Things (IoT)** transforms operations by offering real-time monitoring and control over various business processes. IoT-enabled sensors collect data on equipment performance, energy consumption, and inventory levels, enabling businesses to make data-driven decisions that enhance efficiency. IoT devices monitor crop and soil conditions in agriculture, allowing farmers to optimise water usage and improve yields. IoT-enabled smart factories monitor production processes in manufacturing to reduce energy consumption and increase output.

The benefits of technology in operations are demonstrated through case studies of companies that have successfully integrated these tools into their processes. **UPS**, for example, uses its ORION system, which employs AI and GPS data to optimise delivery routes. This system has helped the company reduce fuel consumption, lower delivery times, and decrease operational costs. Similarly, **Adidas** has embraced 3D printing technology and automation in its Speedfactory, enabling rapid production of customised athletic shoes. This innovative approach has allowed Adidas to respond quickly to market demands while improving product delivery speed.

In conclusion, technology is a powerful enabler of operational excellence. By leveraging automation, AI, data analytics, and IoT, businesses can optimise processes, enhance productivity, and achieve greater efficiency. Companies that effectively integrate these technologies into their operations are better equipped to respond to market demands, mitigate risks, and maintain a competitive advantage in an increasingly complex business environment.

6.7 Sustainability in Operations

Sustainability is increasingly becoming a critical component of modern business operations. Companies recognise the need to integrate environmental and social responsibility into their operations to ensure long-term growth, profitability, and a positive brand image. Incorporating sustainable practices into operations helps reduce environmental impact, enhances customer loyalty, and improves operational efficiency. This section will explore the significance of sustainability in operations and highlight examples of companies successfully implementing sustainable practices.

The growing emphasis on sustainability is driven by increasing awareness of environmental and social issues, including climate change, resource depletion, and inequality. Companies that adopt sustainable practices contribute to mitigating these challenges while ensuring their operations remain resilient and future-proof. Businesses can align their operations with broader social goals and regulatory requirements by reducing their environmental footprint, conserving resources, and supporting fair labour practices.

Incorporating **green practices** into operations involves making sustainable choices at every stage of the supply chain, from sourcing raw materials to production, distribution, and disposal. Examples of green practices include reducing energy consumption, minimising waste, using renewable or recyclable materials, and adopting circular economy principles. Companies like **IKEA** and **Patagonia** have successfully made sustainability a core part of their operational strategies, using renewable resources and designing products built to last, reducing the need for frequent replacement.

Reducing energy consumption is one of the most effective ways to lower operational costs and minimise environmental impact. Businesses can achieve energy efficiency by optimising production processes, adopting renewable energy sources, and using energy-efficient technologies. For example, **Google** powers its data centres with 100% renewable energy, drastically reducing its carbon footprint while ensuring operational efficiency.

Minimising waste is another crucial strategy for achieving sustainability in operations. Waste reduction can be achieved through recycling, reusing materials, and adopting zero-waste initiatives. **Unilever** has committed to ensuring that all waste generated in its manufacturing processes is reused, recycled, or converted into energy, helping the company significantly reduce its environmental footprint.

Responsible sourcing involves choosing suppliers that adhere to ethical and environmental standards. This includes using renewable, biodegradable, or recyclable materials and ensuring fair labour practices throughout the supply chain. **Starbucks**, for example, sources its coffee beans through a sustainable sourcing program that ensures environmental protection and supports the livelihoods of coffee farmers.

The concept of the **circular economy** is an innovative approach to sustainable operations. A circular economy is a model of production and consumption designed to minimise waste and make the most of available resources. It involves extending the lifecycle of products by reusing, repairing, refurbishing, and recycling existing materials. This approach contrasts with the traditional linear model, which follows a "take, make, dispose" pattern. For instance, **Philips** designs products that are easy to disassemble, repair, and recycle. Philips also offers "product-as-a-service" models, where customers lease products such as lighting systems instead of purchasing them outright. This approach allows Philips to retain control over the materials and ensures that products are reused or recycled at the end of their lifecycle.

Several companies have successfully integrated sustainability into their operations. **IKEA** has implemented several sustainability initiatives, such as using renewable and recycled materials in its products. The company is committed to becoming climate-positive by 2030, meaning it will reduce more greenhouse gas emissions than it emits across its value chain. IKEA's focus on sustainable sourcing, renewable energy, and recycling programs has strengthened its brand and attracted a loyal customer base that values environmental responsibility.

Patagonia is another company known for its environmental activism and commitment to sustainability. The company uses organic cotton, recycled materials, and fair labour practices in its production processes. Patagonia encourages its customers to repair and reuse their clothing rather than buy new items, promoting a circular economy approach.

In summary, sustainability in operations is no longer a niche concern but a core business imperative. Companies that adopt sustainable practices benefit from increased **operational efficiency**, **cost savings**, and enhanced **brand reputation**. As demonstrated by companies like IKEA, Patagonia, and Google, sustainability is not just an operational advantage but a societal responsibility. Businesses that integrate sustainability into their operations are well-positioned to meet the demands of environmentally conscious consumers and navigate the challenges of a rapidly changing world.

6.8 Risk Management in Operations

Risk management is a vital element of operational excellence. It ensures businesses can identify, assess, and mitigate potential risks that threaten their operations or overall performance. Effective risk management allows companies to remain resilient in the face of challenges, whether internal (such as equipment failures) or external (such as supply chain disruptions or natural disasters).

Identifying operational risks is the first step in developing a robust risk management strategy. Operational risks can take various forms, including supply chain disruptions, equipment breakdowns, regulatory changes, and unforeseen events such as natural disasters or cyberattacks. Companies must conduct comprehensive risk assessments that evaluate their operations' internal and external threats. For example, a manufacturing company may identify equipment failures as a major operational risk, while a retailer might focus on the risk of supply chain disruptions.

Once risks have been identified, businesses must implement **mitigation strategies** to reduce their impact. Common strategies include **supplier diversification**, **business continuity planning (BCP)**, and investing in technology to monitor and predict potential risks. For example, companies reliant on a single supplier for key materials may diversify their supplier base to ensure continuity in case of disruptions. Similarly, a well-developed BCP outlines procedures for responding to risks such as natural disasters, cyberattacks, or equipment failures, enabling companies to maintain critical operations during disruptions.

Technology plays a crucial role in modern risk management, offering tools for **real-time monitoring**, **predictive analysis**, and rapid response. Predictive analytics, for example, can help businesses anticipate equipment failures or supply chain disruptions, enabling them to take preventive action before these risks materialise. **IoT devices** and sensors provide real-time data on operational performance, allowing businesses to identify potential risks as they arise. Cybersecurity is another critical aspect of risk management, as businesses rely more heavily on digital systems and data. Implementing robust cybersecurity measures, such as encryption, firewalls, and regular system audits, is essential for protecting sensitive information and ensuring the integrity of digital operations.

Several companies provide valuable insights into effective risk management. For instance, Toyota faced significant supply chain disruptions after Japan's 2011 earthquake and tsunami. In response, the company implemented a comprehensive risk management strategy that included diversifying its suppliers and increasing inventory levels of critical components. This proactive approach allowed Toyota to maintain operational continuity during future disruptions, such as the COVID-19 pandemic. Similarly, **UPS** uses advanced algorithms and real-time data to monitor risks such as weather disruptions and geopolitical events. This allows the company to maintain reliable delivery services and uphold operational excellence, even in challenging conditions.

In conclusion, risk management is critical for achieving operational excellence and ensuring business continuity. By identifying potential risks, implementing mitigation strategies, and leveraging technology, companies can minimise the impact of disruptions and protect their operations. Companies like Toyota and UPS demonstrate the importance of proactive risk management in navigating challenges and maintaining long-term success.

6.9 Customer Service Excellence

Customer service excellence is a crucial aspect of operational excellence. Delivering consistently high-quality customer service can set a business apart from competitors in a crowded marketplace. Operations efficiency and reliability directly influence a company's ability to meet or exceed customer expectations.

Efficient and reliable operations are the backbone of great customer service. With streamlined processes, businesses can respond faster to customer inquiries, fulfil orders promptly, and resolve issues quickly. Efficient operations reduce errors, enhance product quality, and lead to quicker delivery times, improving the customer experience. Companies that excel in operational efficiency are better equipped to handle customer needs and adapt to fluctuations in demand. For example, **Zappos**, an online retailer known for its exceptional customer service, has built its reputation on operational efficiency. By optimising its supply chain and order processing systems, Zappos can provide fast shipping, easy returns, and a seamless customer experience that keeps customers coming back.

Personalisation is becoming an expectation for today's customers, and operational efficiency enables businesses to offer customised services that enhance customer satisfaction. Companies can use data analytics and technology to understand customer preferences and behaviours to provide personalised experiences that build stronger relationships. For example, **Netflix** uses data analytics and machine learning to provide personalised recommendations to its users. By tracking viewing habits and preferences, Netflix ensures its customers receive tailored content suggestions, improving the overall user experience. This level of personalisation is possible due to the company's highly efficient data collection and processing systems, which operate seamlessly behind the scenes.

Responsiveness is a key factor in customer service excellence. Customers expect timely responses to inquiries, quick issue resolution, and on-time delivery of products and services. Companies that excel in operational efficiency can meet these expectations by maintaining streamlined processes and agile operations. **Amazon's** operational strategy is centred around speed and reliability, allowing the company to fulfil customer orders within hours or days. With its optimised logistics network, including fulfilment centres powered by robotics and automation, Amazon can offer rapid delivery, even during peak shopping seasons. This operational excellence translates directly into high levels of customer satisfaction and loyalty.

Operational excellence also involves empowering employees to deliver great customer service. Employees given the tools, training, and autonomy to resolve customer issues are better equipped to provide positive experiences. For example, the **Ritz-Carlton** hotel chain is renowned for its exceptional customer service, partly due to its employee empowerment policies. Ritz-Carlton employees are authorised to spend up to $2,000 per guest to resolve any issue or improve the guest experience. This level of autonomy, supported by a culture of operational excellence, ensures that employees can address customer needs quickly and effectively, contributing to the brand's reputation for outstanding service.

Consistency is critical to maintaining high levels of customer satisfaction. Customers expect a uniform experience every time they interact with a brand, whether they purchase products, receive support, or use services. Standardised operational processes help ensure consistency in product quality, service delivery, and customer interactions. **McDonald's** is a company that has perfected consistency through operational excellence. By standardising its processes, from food preparation to customer service, McDonald's ensures that customers receive the same level of quality and service regardless of the location they visit. This operational consistency has helped McDonald's build a global brand synonymous with reliability.

To achieve customer service excellence, businesses must regularly measure and assess their performance. Key metrics such as **customer satisfaction scores**, **Net Promoter Scores (NPS)**, and **customer retention rates** provide valuable insights into how well a company meets customer expectations. These metrics help businesses identify areas for improvement and refine their operations to serve their customers better. For example, **Apple** uses customer feedback gathered through surveys and NPS data to continuously improve its retail and online customer service. By tracking these metrics, Apple can identify customer satisfaction trends and adjust its service operations, ensuring that it maintains its reputation for delivering top-tier customer experiences.

In conclusion, customer service excellence is a key outcome of operational excellence. By optimising operations, empowering employees, and focusing on personalisation, responsiveness, consistency, and reliability, businesses can provide outstanding customer experiences that drive long-term loyalty and growth. Companies like Zappos, Netflix, Amazon, Ritz-Carlton, and McDonald's exemplify how efficient operations and exceptional customer service work together to create a competitive advantage in today's marketplace.

6.10 Case Studies in Operational Turnaround

Operational turnarounds are critical for companies facing significant challenges, such as financial instability, declining performance, or inefficiencies in production and service delivery. Successful operational turnarounds require identifying the root causes of problems, implementing strategic changes, and focusing on long-term improvements. This section will explore case studies of companies that achieved remarkable operational turnarounds and the strategies that led to their recovery and success.

In the early 2000s, **Ford Motor Company** faced financial losses, declining market share, and inefficient production processes. The company's operational inefficiencies were compounded by a fragmented global structure, with different regions producing different models, leading to increased complexity and costs. Under the leadership of CEO Alan Mulally, Ford initiated a comprehensive turnaround strategy called the **One Ford initiative**, which aimed to streamline operations and unify the company's global product development.

Key elements of the One Ford initiative included product simplification, cost reduction, and a cultural shift towards transparency and teamwork. Ford reduced its global vehicle models, focusing on fewer platforms that could be sold across multiple markets. This simplification enabled Ford to cut production costs, improve quality, and increase efficiency. Cost-cutting measures included closing underperforming plants, renegotiating labour contracts, and improving supply chain management. Mulally also fostered a new culture of accountability and collaboration within Ford, encouraging transparency and teamwork across all levels of the organisation.

Ford's turnaround was a success. The company returned to profitability without requiring a government bailout during the 2008 financial crisis. Ford regained its competitive position in the global automotive market by focusing on operational excellence and streamlining its processes.

In 2008, **Starbucks** faced declining sales, overexpansion, and operational inefficiencies that threatened its brand and financial health. Founder Howard Schultz returned as CEO to lead a turnaround, focusing on revitalising the company's core values and improving the customer experience. Schultz closed hundreds of underperforming stores and reinvested in the customer experience by retraining baristas to emphasise coffee-making craftsmanship, reinforcing the brand's focus on quality. The company also renovated its stores to create a more inviting customer atmosphere. It embraced digital innovation by launching a mobile app that allowed customers to order and pay ahead of time, reducing wait times and improving convenience.

These changes helped Starbucks regain its status as a leading global coffee brand, with improved financial performance and a renewed focus on the customer experience. Starbucks' turnaround demonstrates the power of returning to core values and focusing on quality and customer experience in driving business recovery.

In the early 2000s, **LEGO** struggled with overexpansion, declining sales, and rising operational costs. The company had diversified its product offerings too widely, leading to increased complexity in its operations and a loss of focus on its core products. By 2003, LEGO was on the verge of bankruptcy. However, under the leadership of Jørgen Vig Knudstorp, who became CEO in 2004, LEGO embarked on a significant operational turnaround that saved the company and transformed it into one of the most successful toy brands in the world.

Knudstorp simplified LEGO's product lines, focusing on core brick sets and key themes like LEGO City and LEGO Technic. This reduction in product complexity allowed LEGO to streamline its operations, lower production costs, and concentrate on delivering high-quality products that resonated with its customers. LEGO also implemented lean manufacturing principles to reduce waste and optimise production processes. This focus on operational excellence enabled LEGO to improve its profitability while maintaining its commitment to product quality. Furthermore, LEGO invested in innovation by introducing new product lines, such as LEGO Star Wars and LEGO Harry Potter, and expanding into digital platforms with successful video games and apps.

LEGO turned its fortunes around by focusing on operational efficiency, product simplification, and innovation. Today, the company is a market leader in the global toy industry and continues to grow through its commitment to operational excellence and innovation.

These case studies illustrate several important lessons for businesses facing operational challenges. Simplifying product offerings and focusing on a company's core strengths can help reduce complexity, lower costs, and improve operational efficiency. Enhancing operational efficiency through streamlining production processes, reducing waste, and optimising supply chains is essential to improving overall performance. Additionally, revitalising the customer experience by focusing on quality, personalisation, and convenience can help rebuild a company's reputation and drive growth. Finally, embracing innovation and leveraging new technologies can give businesses the tools to achieve long-term success.

Successful operational turnarounds require strong leadership, a clear strategy, and a commitment to continuous improvement. By addressing the root causes of their challenges and focusing on operational excellence, companies like Ford, Starbucks, and LEGO were able to regain their competitive edge and achieve sustainable growth.

6.11 Measuring Operational Success

Measuring operational success is crucial for ensuring that efforts to improve efficiency, quality, and performance deliver the desired outcomes. **Key Performance Indicators (KPIs)** provide valuable insights into how well operations function and help businesses identify areas for further improvement. This section explores the KPIs and metrics for measuring operational success and how companies can use data to drive continuous improvement.

KPIs are essential tools that help businesses monitor and evaluate their operational performance. Without measurable goals, companies may struggle to identify inefficiencies or opportunities for optimisation. By tracking KPIs, businesses can ensure they meet customer expectations, control costs, and achieve operational goals. For instance, metrics such as **Overall Equipment Effectiveness (OEE)** and **First Pass Yield (FPY)** are widely used in manufacturing to measure production efficiency and quality. A high OEE score indicates that equipment is being used efficiently, while a high FPY indicates that products are produced correctly without rework, highlighting the effectiveness of the production process.

Establishing benchmarks for KPIs is essential for driving continuous improvement. These benchmarks can be based on historical performance, industry standards, or company goals. For example, if a company's current OEE score is 75%, it might target 85% by implementing lean manufacturing practices and reducing downtime. Similarly, if the on-time delivery rate is 90%, the company might aim for 98% by optimising logistics and production scheduling.

Technology plays a critical role in measuring and improving operational performance. Advanced analytics tools, the **Internet of Things (IoT)**, and **artificial intelligence (AI)** provide real-time data and insights that enable businesses to monitor KPIs more precisely. IoT sensors in manufacturing equipment can track performance and alert managers to potential issues before they lead to costly downtime. Predictive analytics can help businesses anticipate future operational challenges, such as equipment breakdowns or supply chain disruptions, allowing them to take proactive measures.

Several companies have successfully used KPIs to measure and improve their operational performance. **Toyota**, for instance, is known for using Lean Manufacturing principles and rigorously tracking KPIs such as OEE, cycle time, and FPY. This continuous improvement and measurement focus has contributed to its reputation for operational excellence and high product quality. Similarly, **Intel** uses a range of KPIs, including cost per unit, lead time, and on-time delivery, to measure performance across its global manufacturing operations. Intel has optimised its processes, reduced costs, and improved product quality by tracking these metrics. **UPS** also tracks KPIs such as lead time, on-time delivery, and cost per unit to monitor the efficiency of its logistics operations. The company's use of real-time data analytics helps it maintain high operational performance and customer satisfaction levels, even in the face of complex logistical challenges.

Measuring operational success is essential for ensuring businesses operate efficiently and effectively. By tracking KPIs such as OEE, cycle time, lead time, and cost per unit, companies can identify areas for improvement and optimise their processes to deliver better results. Setting benchmarks, monitoring progress, and leveraging technology are key to achieving long-term operational excellence.

6.12 Conclusion

Operational excellence is a holistic approach that integrates **efficiency**, **quality**, **customer satisfaction**, and **sustainability** across all facets of a business. This chapter has explored key elements such as Lean Management, Quality Management Systems, supply chain optimisation, and the transformative role of technology. By continuously improving and leveraging the right tools and methodologies, businesses can streamline operations, reduce costs, and deliver exceptional customer value.

A key takeaway is that operational excellence is not a one-time goal but a continuous journey. Businesses must regularly evaluate their processes, embrace innovation, and adapt to changing market conditions to maintain a competitive edge. The case studies of Ford, Starbucks, LEGO, and others illustrate how even the most challenging operational environments can be turned around through strategic efficiency, leadership, and innovation improvements.

One of the recurring themes throughout the chapter is the importance of aligning operations with **customer needs**. A customer-centric approach ensures that all operational decisions, from process improvements to technological investments, are made to enhance customer value. Companies like Amazon, Zappos, and Ritz-Carlton demonstrate how operational excellence and customer satisfaction are closely intertwined, focusing on delivering consistent, high-quality experiences at every touchpoint.

In today's business environment, operational excellence also involves a strong commitment to **sustainability**. As companies increasingly recognise the need to reduce their environmental impact, integrating sustainable practices into operations is key to achieving long-term success. Companies like IKEA, Patagonia, and Tesla have shown how sustainability can improve operational efficiency, strengthen brand reputation, and attract environmentally conscious consumers.

The role of **technology** in driving operational excellence cannot be overstated. Technology offers businesses the tools to optimise processes, reduce costs, and improve decision-making, from automation and artificial intelligence to IoT and advanced analytics. Companies that effectively leverage technology, such as UPS and Intel, are better positioned to respond to market demands, mitigate risks, and maintain a competitive advantage.

Achieving operational excellence requires a **culture of continuous improvement**, where every level of the organisation is committed to identifying and implementing improvements. Leadership plays a crucial role in fostering this culture by setting the vision, empowering employees, and ensuring that resources are allocated to support operational initiatives. The examples of Toyota's Kaizen philosophy and

Starbucks' leadership-driven turnaround highlight the importance of strong leadership in driving operational excellence.

To ensure that operational excellence efforts deliver the desired results, businesses must regularly measure performance using relevant KPIs. Metrics such as overall equipment effectiveness (OEE), cycle time, and on-time delivery provide valuable insights into how well operations function and where improvements can be made. Setting benchmarks and tracking progress against these KPIs is essential for maintaining a focus on continuous improvement and operational success.

In sum, operational excellence is a multifaceted approach that requires a deep commitment to efficiency, quality, and customer value. By adopting the principles and strategies outlined in this chapter, businesses can optimise their operations, achieve sustainable growth, and build a foundation for long-term success. As the global marketplace becomes increasingly competitive and complex, continuously improving and adapting will be the key to maintaining operational excellence and thriving in the future.

Chapter 7

Innovation and Product Development: Staying Ahead of the Curve

7.1 Overview

Innovation and **product development** are essential pillars for any company aiming for long-term success. Staying ahead is crucial in a marketplace characterised by rapid technological advancements and evolving consumer preferences. Companies continuously innovating and introducing new products are better positioned to maintain a **competitive edge**, meet consumer needs, and achieve **sustainable growth**. This chapter delves into how organisations can foster a culture of innovation and develop products that respond to current market demands and anticipate future trends. We will explore the key stages of the product development process, from **ideation** to **launch**, highlighting best practices and real-world examples to help leaders navigate this complex journey. Mastering innovation and product development strategies is vital for any business leader, guiding a **start-up** or steering an established company.

7.2 The Innovation Imperative

In today's dynamic business landscape, **innovation** is no longer optional but a **strategic imperative**. Companies that fail to innovate risk losing market relevance and falling behind competitors. **Technological advancements** and changing market conditions require businesses to be agile and forward-thinking. Successful companies understand that innovation is not just about launching new products but transforming how they operate, engage with customers, and envision the future.

Incremental innovation involves making small, continuous improvements to existing products, services, or processes. This approach keeps companies competitive by enhancing features, improving quality, or reducing costs. **Apple**, for example, consistently employs incremental innovation with its iPhone series, introducing regular updates such as improved camera quality and new user features while maintaining the core design. On the other hand, **disruptive innovation** refers to breakthroughs that create new markets or reshape existing ones by offering simpler, more accessible alternatives. **Netflix** illustrates this perfectly, evolving from a DVD rental service to a streaming giant, transforming how consumers access content.

In addition to these types, businesses must consider **sustaining** and **radical innovation** in their strategies. **Sustaining innovation** focuses on enhancing existing products and services to serve better current customers rather than creating new markets. This is common in industries like automotive manufacturing, where companies like **Ford** and **Toyota** continuously improve vehicle safety features and performance. Conversely, **radical innovation** involves developing revolutionary technologies or business models that can significantly change industries. **Tesla's** introduction of electric vehicles (EVs) is a notable example, challenging the traditional automotive sector and promoting a global shift towards sustainable transportation.

Moreover, innovation is a strategic tool that enables businesses to anticipate market shifts, address emerging customer needs, and seize new opportunities. Companies that embed innovation into their core strategy tend to be more adaptable and better positioned for long-term success. A prime example is **3M**, renowned for its commitment to innovation. By allowing employees to dedicate 15% of their time to projects of their choosing, **3M** fosters a culture of creativity that has resulted in iconic products like Post-it Notes. Innovation also encompasses reimagining business models and customer engagement strategies. Organisations must remain agile and open to new ideas to stay ahead in today's rapidly changing business environment.

7.3 Cultivating a Culture of Innovation

Creating a culture that encourages **innovation** is one of the most crucial tasks for business leaders. Innovation does not occur in isolation; it requires an environment that fosters **creativity**, supports **risk-taking**, and values diverse perspectives. A company prioritising these elements can transform into a powerhouse of ideas and solutions, driving sustained success.

At the heart of an innovative culture is the promotion of **creativity**. Leaders need to cultivate an atmosphere where questioning the status quo is welcomed, and employees are encouraged to think outside the box. Allowing employees to explore new ideas is essential for fostering creativity. For example, **Google's** famous "20% time" policy, which permits employees to dedicate a portion of their time to side projects unrelated to their main responsibilities, has led to innovations such as **Gmail** and **Google News**.

Supporting **risk-taking** is also vital in creating a culture of innovation. Innovation inherently involves experimentation and risk; not every idea will succeed. However, organisations must create an environment where failure is viewed as an opportunity to learn rather than a setback. **Amazon** is known for its willingness to embrace risk and experimentation, leading to successful innovations like the **Kindle** and **Echo** while enabling the company to learn from less successful ventures like the **Fire Phone**. This focus on learning and iteration has been key to Amazon's continued growth.

Cross-functional **collaboration** is another critical component of an innovative culture. By bringing together teams from different areas of expertise, companies can generate more creative and effective solutions. **IDEO**, a global design firm, exemplifies this approach by creating interdisciplinary teams that combine diverse skills to solve complex problems. The firm's collaborative culture has produced breakthrough innovations for clients across multiple industries.

Recognition and rewards are crucial in encouraging innovation. Leaders must acknowledge and celebrate creative efforts to reinforce the importance of innovation within the organisation. **Atlassian**, the company behind popular software such as **Jira** and **Trello**, holds "ShipIt Days," where employees work on passion projects unrelated to their usual tasks. Successful projects receive recognition, and many have been implemented into the company's offerings.

Leadership plays an integral role in fostering a culture of innovation. Leaders must model the behaviour they wish to see in their teams, such as openness to new ideas and resilience in facing challenges. Leaders like **Jeff Bezos** of Amazon exemplify this mindset, continuously pushing for innovation while encouraging a "Day 1" mentality, which focuses on maintaining agility and openness to change.

7.4 The Product Development Process

The process of turning an idea into a **market-ready product** is both exciting and complex. A structured product development process ensures that innovative ideas are transformed into viable products that meet customer needs while achieving the company's business objectives. This process typically consists of several key stages: **ideation, concept development, design, prototyping, testing**, and finally, **product launch**. Each stage is critical in its own right and plays a vital role in ensuring the product's success.

The first stage of product development is **creativity**, where ideas are generated through brainstorming sessions, market research, and customer feedback. The goal is to explore various possibilities and identify the most promising opportunities. For instance, the idea for the **Dyson vacuum cleaner** emerged from

James Dyson's frustration with existing vacuums that lost suction. He identified a common customer pain point and developed a superior solution.

Once a promising idea has been identified, the next phase is **concept development**. This involves defining the product's key features, target market, and value proposition while evaluating its technical feasibility and potential market impact. **Apple's** development of the **iPhone** is a prime example of effective concept development, as the company reimagined the mobile phone to integrate calling, music, and internet functionalities into one seamless experience.

In the design phase, the product begins to take shape. This involves creating both the **industrial design**, focusing on aesthetics and user experience, and the **engineering design**, which addresses the product's technical functionality. Prototypes are often created during this stage, allowing for early testing and refinement. The **Tesla Model S** illustrates meticulous design, merging a sleek appearance with advanced energy efficiency and high performance. Prototyping allows businesses to test usability and functionality before moving forward with full-scale production. For example, **Google** employs a "dogfooding" process, where employees use new products internally to identify potential issues before public release.

7.5 Customer-Centric Design

Focusing on the customer is paramount when designing new products in today's competitive business landscape. **Customer-**

centric design ensures that products meet the real needs of consumers, not just functional requirements. It involves understanding customers' desires, behaviours, and pain points throughout product development. Successful companies that place customers at the heart of their design are better equipped to create offerings that resonate with users, ultimately driving **customer loyalty** and long-term success.

The foundation of customer-centric design lies in understanding **customer needs**. This requires thorough market research, user testing, and data analysis to gather insights into how customers behave and what they expect from a product. **For instance, Airbnb recognised that travellers sought** unique and authentic accommodation options. By understanding this need, Airbnb designed its platform to offer diverse accommodations, significantly disrupting the hotel industry.

Customer-centric design is an iterative process requiring continuous input from users. Incorporating **customer feedback** during the development process allows businesses to refine their products and align them with market expectations. **Slack**, the workplace communication platform, utilises extensive user feedback to shape its features and interface. This approach ensures that the product evolves in ways that enhance the user experience and meet customer needs.

Empathy is crucial in customer-centric design. Product designers must consider how a product works and how it makes customers feel. Apple excels in empathetic design; its products are functional, aesthetically pleasing, and user-friendly. The company's emphasis on design simplicity and ease of use has significantly contributed to its success.

A critical aspect of customer-centric design is **user experience (UX)** design. UX design aims to make products intuitive, accessible, and enjoyable. It considers every customer interaction, from initial encounter to long-term usage. **Uber** has built its ride-sharing app with user experience in mind, making booking a ride seamless and straightforward. This focus has helped Uber become one of the most widely used ride-sharing services globally.

Personalisation is increasingly important in customer-centric design. Today's consumers expect products and services tailored to their needs. **Netflix** employs a recommendation algorithm that uses customer viewing data to suggest content, enhancing the **user experience** and driving engagement. By offering a personalised experience, Netflix ensures higher customer satisfaction and retention. Personalisation like this creates a deeper connection between the product and the user, fostering loyalty and reducing churn.

7.6 Prototyping and MVPs

Prototyping and developing **Minimum Viable Products (MVPs)** are crucial stages in the product development process. These steps allow companies to test ideas, gather feedback, and refine products before investing in full-scale production. Businesses can reduce risks, control costs, and ensure their final product meets market needs.

Prototyping brings ideas to life and helps teams explore different design concepts, test functionality, and identify potential issues early in the development cycle. Depending on the product's complexity, prototypes can range from basic mock-ups to detailed working models. For instance, Apple uses foam models during the initial design stages of its devices to experiment with different forms before refining the final design. In the automotive industry, companies like **Tesla** use working prototypes to test performance, safety, and user experience before scaling production.

The Minimum Viable Product (MVP) concept is central to the **lean startup** methodology. An MVP includes only the essential features needed to test the product with early adopters, allowing companies to validate the concept without substantial resource investment. For example, **Dropbox** used a simple video demonstration as an MVP to gauge interest and gather feedback before building the full platform, helping the company refine its offering based on real user input.

Both prototyping and MVPs are part of an **iterative design** process, where products are continuously improved based on feedback and testing. This iterative approach ensures that products evolve in response to customer needs and market conditions. Companies like **Facebook** and **Google** are known for adopting this strategy, regularly releasing updates and new features based on user data and feedback. This constant iteration helps them stay ahead of the competition and adapt to the changing demands of their user base.

7.7 Scaling Your Product

Once a product is successfully launched, the next challenge is **scaling** it to meet growing demand and expanding its reach. Scaling is not just about increasing production volume; it requires careful planning and resource management to ensure sustainable growth and that the product maintains its quality and appeal. Businesses that scale effectively can transform a successful product into a significant driver of business growth.

Optimising production processes is often the first step in scaling a product. This may involve automating tasks, investing in new technology, or streamlining workflows to improve efficiency. For example, when **Tesla** faced challenges in scaling the production of the **Model 3**, it invested heavily in automation and re-engineered its manufacturing processes. These changes allowed the company to meet production targets and reduce costs, demonstrating the importance of refining production processes during scaling.

As demand for a product grows, expanding **distribution channels** becomes crucial. This may involve forming partnerships with new retailers, entering different geographic markets, or developing direct-to-consumer sales channels. **Under Armour**, initially focused on direct sales, significantly increased its market presence by partnering with major retailers like **Dick's Sporting Goods**. This strategic expansion enabled the company to reach a broader audience and support its growth.

Strengthening the **supply chain** is essential when scaling, as increased production and distribution require robust logistical support. Companies must ensure a reliable supply of raw materials, manage inventory efficiently and optimise logistics to meet demand. For instance, **Starbucks** has invested heavily in its supply chain to consistently deliver high-quality products across its global network of stores, even as it rapidly expands.

Investing in marketing is another critical aspect of scaling. As the product reaches new markets, businesses must create awareness and attract new customers while retaining existing ones. This might include launching advertising campaigns, expanding the sales team, or leveraging digital marketing to increase visibility. **Slack**, for example, scaled its workplace communication platform by investing in targeted marketing campaigns, content marketing, and customer success initiatives to drive adoption and engagement.

Managing **customer relationships** is increasingly important as the customer base grows. Companies must maintain high service levels while scaling. This may involve expanding customer support teams, implementing Customer Relationship Management (CRM) systems, and developing self-service resources to handle inquiries efficiently. **Zendesk** successfully scaled its customer service software by expanding its support team and creating robust self-service resources, ensuring it could manage increasing inquiries without compromising service quality.

One of the biggest challenges in scaling is maintaining **product quality**. As production increases, there can be a temptation to cut corners or reduce costs, risking a decline in quality. Companies like **Lego** have maintained strict quality control processes even as they scaled their operations. By continuously monitoring product performance and customer feedback, Lego ensures that its products meet customer expectations regardless of where they are manufactured.

7.8 Intellectual Property (IP)

In today's innovation-driven economy, protecting **intellectual property (IP)** is crucial to safeguarding a company's competitive advantage. IP, including patents, trademarks, copyrights, and trade secrets, plays a vital role in protecting the products, technologies, and brands businesses develop. For companies, especially those in technology, pharmaceuticals, and entertainment, IP often represents a significant portion of their value.

Protecting IP ensures that businesses retain exclusive rights to the innovations they create, preventing competitors from copying or exploiting them. Failing to secure IP protection can lead to lost revenue, reputational damage, and a weakened market position. Companies like **Microsoft** and **Pfizer** have successfully used IP protection strategies to maintain their competitive advantages, ensuring competitors do not unfairly replicate their products and technologies.

Patents protect new inventions or technologies, granting the patent holder exclusive rights to use, sell, and license their invention for a specified period, typically 20 years from the filing date. This is particularly crucial in industries like pharmaceuticals and electronics, where substantial research and development (R&D) investments must be recouped. Pharmaceutical companies, for example, rely heavily on patent protection to maintain exclusivity over new drug formulations, allowing them to recover development costs and fund future research.

Trademarks protect brand names, logos, slogans, and other distinctive elements that identify a company's products or services. A strong trademark fosters **brand recognition** and **customer loyalty**. The **Nike "Swoosh"** and the slogan **"Just Do It"** are globally recognised trademarks contributing to the company's brand equity and competitive advantage.

Copyrights protect original works of authorship, such as books, films, music, software, and artistic works. They give creators exclusive rights to reproduce, distribute, and perform their work or to create derivative works. Like Disney, companies in the entertainment and software sectors rely heavily on copyright to protect their content. Disney's control over its intellectual properties, such as movies and characters, allows it to generate substantial revenues from licensing and merchandising.

Trade secrets, such as manufacturing processes or customer lists, protect confidential business information that gives companies a competitive edge. Unlike patents, trade secrets can remain protected indefinitely if the company keeps them confidential. A famous example is **Coca-Cola's** recipe, which has been kept as a closely guarded trade secret for over a century.

To protect IP effectively, businesses must take proactive steps, such as registering patents and trademarks with the appropriate authorities, like the **US Patent and Trademark Office (USPTO)** or the **European Patent Office (EPO)**, to secure legal protection. This grants companies the right to enforce their IP rights and take legal action against infringement. For example, **Apple** frequently files lawsuits to protect its product designs from being copied by competitors.

In addition to filing patents and trademarks, companies should monitor the market for potential infringements by conducting trademark searches, tracking competitors, and monitoring online platforms for unauthorised use of their IP. Companies like **Microsoft** actively monitor pirated software and take legal action to protect their IP rights.

Working with IP experts is critical, especially for businesses operating in multiple countries with different legal systems. Since IP laws vary widely across regions, collaborating with legal professionals ensures that a company's rights are protected in all jurisdictions where it operates.

7.9 Leveraging Data in Product Development

In today's data-driven world, using **data analytics** in product development is essential for making informed decisions, understanding customer needs, and optimising products for success. Data provides valuable insights into market trends, customer behaviour, product performance, and potential improvements, allowing businesses to reduce uncertainty and improve efficiency in product development.

The role of data in product development is multifaceted, encompassing **market research**, user behaviour analytics, A/B testing, and predictive analytics. These techniques enable businesses to gather insights and make strategic decisions throughout development. Companies like **Netflix** and **Spotify** exemplify how leveraging data has helped them create highly successful products that resonate with users.

Data-driven **market research** helps companies identify opportunities for new products or improvements to existing ones by analysing market trends, consumer preferences, and competitive landscapes. For instance, Netflix analyses viewing patterns to determine popular genres and themes, guiding its investment in original content that appeals to its audience.

Analysing **user behaviour** provides insights into the most valuable features, potential pain points, and areas for improvement. **Spotify**, for example, uses listening data to refine its recommendation algorithms and develop new features that enhance user engagement and satisfaction.

A/B testing allows companies to compare different versions of a product or feature to determine which performs better, validating design choices and optimising product performance based on user data. **Google** is well-known for extensively using

A/B testing to refine everything from search algorithms to user interface designs.

Predictive analytics use historical data and machine learning algorithms to forecast future customer behaviour and market trends. This allows businesses to anticipate customer needs and make proactive product development decisions. For instance, **Amazon** uses predictive analytics to manage inventory levels and recommend products to users, driving operational efficiency and customer satisfaction.

To maximise data value, businesses should follow best practices, such as collecting data from multiple sources, ensuring data quality, and focusing on actionable insights that lead to specific business objectives. Continuous monitoring and iteration allow companies to adapt their products based on real-time feedback, ensuring they meet evolving market needs.

7.10 Collaborative Innovation

In an interconnected global market, **collaborative innovation** has become a powerful approach for accelerating product development and leveraging external expertise. Collaborative innovation occurs when businesses, research institutions, or customers collaborate to co-create new products, services, or processes. By pooling resources, sharing knowledge, and combining diverse perspectives, companies can achieve breakthrough innovations and stay ahead of the competition.

Collaborative innovation provides companies access to new technologies, different markets, and resources that can help speed up the time to market for new products. For instance, collaborations between technology firms and universities often lead to advances in **artificial intelligence** and **biotechnology**. Such partnerships can be mutually beneficial, allowing businesses to innovate rapidly and universities to gain practical applications for their research.

A notable example of successful collaborative innovation is the partnership between **Apple** and **Nike** that resulted in the Nike+iPod Sport Kit. This product combined Nike's athletic footwear expertise with Apple's digital technology knowledge, offering a solution that resonated with fitness enthusiasts. This collaboration highlights how businesses from different sectors can create innovative products that appeal to a broader market.

Another effective form of collaborative innovation involves partnerships with **research institutions**. Companies often work with universities and research labs to tap into cutting-edge science and technology. For example, Google's collaboration with **Stanford University** has led to advancements in machine learning algorithms that underpin Google's AI-driven products and services. These collaborations often result in breakthroughs that would be challenging for a single company to achieve independently.

Co-creation with customers is another powerful strategy for collaborative innovation. Companies can gain insights into user preferences and pain points by involving customers in the development process. **LEGO Ideas**, an online platform where fans submit new LEGO set ideas, is an excellent example. The most popular submissions are turned into official products, creating a strong connection between the company and its community and driving customer engagement and loyalty.

To succeed in collaborative innovation, businesses must follow several best practices. First, clear objectives ensure all parties understand the collaboration's goals, roles, and responsibilities. Open communication is also crucial, as it fosters trust and transparency and enables the exchange of ideas. Finally, each partner should bring complementary strengths, technical expertise, market insights, or creative thinking.

7.11 Case Studies in Innovation

Innovation is a key driver of growth and transformation for market leaders, enabling them to redefine industries, create new markets, and achieve sustained success. This section presents case studies of companies that have excelled through innovation, providing valuable lessons on staying ahead in a constantly evolving business environment.

Apple has become synonymous with innovation, continually revolutionising entire industries through its unique approach to product development. Under the leadership of Steve Jobs, Apple introduced iconic products like the **iPhone**, which fundamentally changed how people communicate, work, and consume media. The iPhone's success was rooted in its sleek design, advanced technology, and user-friendly interface. Apple's ability to seamlessly integrate hardware and software set it apart from competitors and has been a key driver of its success.

Key lessons from Apple's innovation include a relentless focus on **user experience**, challenging industry norms, and a strong investment in **R&D**. By prioritising these elements, Apple has consistently delivered products that delight users and redefine industries.

Under Elon Musk's leadership, Tesla has transformed the automotive industry by mainstreaming electric vehicles (EVs). The introduction of the **Model S** in 2012 demonstrated that EVs could deliver high performance and long-range capabilities while being environmentally friendly. Tesla's focus on disruptive technology, vertical integration, and visionary leadership has enabled it to challenge traditional automotive companies and lead the shift towards sustainable transportation.

Another key player in innovation is **Amazon**, which has continually redefined e-commerce, cloud computing, and logistics. Starting as an online bookstore, Amazon expanded rapidly into other areas, using its understanding of consumer needs and technological innovation to become the world's largest online retailer. Amazon Web Services (AWS) revolutionised cloud computing by providing scalable and flexible infrastructure, becoming a key driver of Amazon's profitability.

SpaceX, also founded by Elon Musk, has revolutionised space exploration by drastically reducing costs and making space more accessible. The development of reusable rockets like the **Falcon 9** has significantly lowered the cost of space travel, making it more affordable and sustainable. SpaceX's iterative development approach and bold vision of making humanity a multi-planetary species have driven its rapid advancements in space technology.

Lastly, **Netflix** transformed from a DVD rental service to a global streaming giant by anticipating the growing demand for on-demand content. Its move into original content production with shows like **House of Cards** differentiated it from competitors and attracted millions of subscribers globally. Netflix's use of data analytics to personalise content and optimise user experience has been a significant factor in its success.

These case studies illustrate that innovation requires a clear vision, a willingness to take risks, and the ability to adapt to changing market conditions. Companies that prioritise innovation and invest in R&D are better positioned to lead their industries and achieve long-term success.

Conclusion

Innovation and **product development** are essential drivers of long-term business success, particularly in an environment characterised by rapid technological advances and shifting customer expectations. Companies prioritising innovation through incremental improvements or disruptive breakthroughs are better positioned to lead their industries and create lasting competitive advantages.

Creating a culture that encourages creativity, supports risk-taking, and fosters collaboration is crucial for generating a steady flow of innovative ideas. Successful product development requires a structured yet flexible approach that balances creativity with market demands, focusing on **customer-centric design**, leveraging data-driven insights, and adopting prototyping and MVP strategies.

Scaling a product after a successful launch presents additional challenges, but careful planning and resource management can help businesses expand operations while maintaining quality and customer satisfaction. Protecting intellectual property is also critical in safeguarding innovations from competitors.

Collaborative innovation is increasingly important in today's interconnected world. By working with external partners, businesses can access new technologies, share expertise, and accelerate innovation. Whether through partnerships with other companies, collaborations with research institutions, or co-creation with customers, collaborative innovation can drive significant advancements and help companies stay ahead of the curve.

In conclusion, the ability to innovate and bring new products to market will continue to be a defining factor in a company's success. By embracing the principles and strategies discussed in this chapter, businesses can not only stay ahead of the curve but also create products that meet the needs of today's consumers and drive future growth.

Chapter 8

Talent Management: Hiring, Developing, and Retaining the Best

8.1 - Overview

Effective talent management is crucial for organisations seeking long-term success in today's competitive business environment. Attracting, developing, and retaining top talent is more than just an HR function; it is a strategic priority that directly influences a company's ability to innovate, grow, and maintain a competitive edge. **Talent management** is more than simply filling roles; it is about creating an environment where people can thrive, contribute to the organisation's goals, and find personal and professional fulfilment.

This chapter will explore the comprehensive processes of managing the **talent lifecycle**, from attracting the right candidates to keeping them engaged and motivated within the organisation. We will delve into best practices and strategies for each stage of this journey, helping you build a high-performing workforce that drives innovation and growth. Understanding how to manage your talent pool effectively is essential for creating a resilient and successful organisation that can adapt to changing market dynamics and continue to prosper.

8.2 The Strategic Importance of Talent Management

The significance of **talent management** cannot be overstated, as it serves as a key driver for organisational success. In an era of rapid change and innovation, companies that excel in managing their human capital are better positioned to navigate challenges and seize opportunities. A well-executed **talent management** strategy aligns the skills and aspirations of employees with the company's strategic objectives, ensuring that the workforce is capable and motivated to achieve business goals.

Consider organisations like **Google**, which has built its success on a strong foundation of strategic **talent management**. By creating an environment that fosters creativity and innovation, Google attracts and retains some of the brightest minds in the tech industry. Its approach is not merely about hiring the best but creating a culture where employees feel empowered to experiment, collaborate, and challenge the status quo. This alignment between talent and strategy enables Google to consistently stay ahead of its competitors and lead the innovation market.

Another example is **Unilever**, which integrates its **talent management** practices with its broader sustainability mission. By aligning its recruitment and development strategies with its commitment to social and environmental responsibility, Unilever attracts employees who are not only skilled but also deeply motivated by the company's values. This alignment enhances employee engagement and productivity and strengthens the company's reputation as a leader in corporate responsibility.

Talent management is also essential for maintaining organisational **resilience**. Companies that can quickly adapt and respond to changes in uncertain business environments have a significant advantage. This agility is often driven by a workforce that is not only highly skilled but also capable of navigating new challenges and opportunities. For example, during the COVID-19 pandemic, companies with robust **talent management** strategies were able to rapidly pivot their operations and reskill their workforce, enabling them to continue delivering value to customers while others struggled to keep up.

In addition, effective **talent management** fosters a positive organisational culture, which is critical for attracting and retaining top talent. Companies like **Salesforce** have built strong cultures around core values such as trust, innovation, and equality. These values are deeply embedded in their **talent management** practices, helping to create an environment where employees feel supported and valued, which drives high engagement and performance.

In essence, **talent management** is a strategic necessity that affects every aspect of a business's success. Companies that excel in talent management are better equipped to achieve their immediate business goals and are more likely to sustain long-term growth and competitive advantage in a rapidly changing world.

8.3 Attracting Top Talent

Attracting **top talent** requires more than just offering a competitive salary and benefits package. It involves creating a compelling **employer brand** and fostering a workplace environment that people are eager to join. Companies that succeed in this area go beyond traditional recruitment methods by actively promoting what makes their organisation unique and why it is a great workplace. The key to attracting top talent is communicating your values, vision, and culture to potential candidates and ensuring your recruitment strategies reach the right audience. This process begins with building a strong **employer brand** and effectively showcasing it to the world.

Building a strong employer brand is essential for attracting **high-calibre candidates**. Your employer brand represents your organisation's reputation as a workplace and can significantly influence a potential employee's decision to apply. It is vital to be **authentic** in portraying what it is like to work at your company, highlighting your **company culture**, values, and vision. For example, companies like **Patagonia** have built their employer brand around their commitment to environmental sustainability, attracting individuals passionate about positively impacting the environment.

Leveraging **employee testimonials** is an effective way to enhance your employer's brand. Potential candidates often trust the experiences of current employees more than corporate messaging. Sharing stories from employees about their experiences and the opportunities they have encountered can be a powerful tool for attracting talent. This can be done through video testimonials, employee blogs, or social media content where employees share their day-to-day experiences at the company. By showcasing your employees' authentic voices, you create a more compelling and relatable image of your organisation.

Another critical element in attracting top talent is showcasing your unique **company culture**. Whether it's a collaborative environment, a focus on innovation, or a commitment to **diversity and inclusion**, highlighting what makes your culture special will help you attract candidates who are a good fit. For instance, **Zappos** has made its quirky, fun culture a central part of its employer brand. The company's focus on delivering "WOW" through service and its unique onboarding process, which includes offering new hires $2,000 to quit if they are not a cultural fit, helps attract employees who are genuinely passionate about its mission.

Effective recruitment campaigns are also crucial in attracting top talent, and a well-executed recruitment campaign reaches a broad audience. It resonates with the specific type of candidates you want to attract. Using targeted job ads on platforms like **LinkedIn**, Indeed, or specialised job boards that cater to your industry allows you to reach candidates with the specific skills and experience you seek. Social media recruitment has also become a powerful tool for reaching and engaging potential candidates. Platforms like LinkedIn, Twitter, and Instagram allow you to share job openings, highlight company culture, and provide a glimpse into what it's like to work at your organisation.

Building relationships with universities and offering **internships** can be an excellent way to attract young talent. These partnerships help you identify promising candidates early in their careers and allow you to shape their development and integrate them into your company culture. Companies like **Deloitte** have strong university recruitment programs and offer internships that often lead to full-time positions, ensuring a steady pipeline of talented graduates.

8.4 Effective Hiring Processes

Hiring the right people is one of the most critical tasks for any organisation. An effective hiring process ensures that you bring in candidates with the right skills and experience and those who align with your company's **culture and values**. A structured and well-thought-out hiring process can help you avoid common mistakes, reduce turnover, and build a high-performing team that drives your business forward. This process involves defining clear job requirements, conducting structured interviews, and making informed selection decisions.

Defining **clear job requirements** is the first step in the hiring process. Before you start recruiting, you need to clearly understand the role you're hiring for, including the necessary skills, experience, and attributes for success. A well-defined job description helps you attract the right candidates and serves as a benchmark throughout the hiring process. For example, when hiring for a leadership position, a company like **Unilever** may prioritise the candidate's ability to drive innovation, manage teams, and uphold the company's sustainability values, in addition to their technical expertise.

Conducting **structured interviews** is essential for assessing whether candidates have the skills and cultural fit needed for the role. Structured interviews involve asking each candidate the same questions, allowing for a fair comparison. Behavioural interview questions, which ask candidates to describe how they have handled situations in the past, can be particularly effective in predicting future performance. For instance, a question like "Can you describe a time when you had to overcome a significant challenge at work?" provides insight into a candidate's problem-solving abilities and resilience.

Assessment **tools** can provide additional insights into candidates' suitability for the role. These tools can include skills assessments, personality tests, and cognitive ability tests. For example, a coding test might assess a software developer's technical skills, while a personality test can help determine whether a candidate's working style aligns with your team's dynamics. Companies like **Microsoft** use a combination of technical interviews and coding assessments to evaluate software engineers, ensuring that candidates have the technical expertise and problem-solving skills required for the role.

Avoiding common **hiring mistakes** is crucial to selecting the best candidates and preventing costly turnover. One common mistake is relying too heavily on resumes, which may not fully capture a candidate's skills, motivations, and cultural fit. Dig deeper during interviews and assessments is essential to understand the candidate comprehensively. Another mistake is hiring for skills over cultural fit. While skills are important, hiring someone not aligning with your company's culture can lead to conflicts and dissatisfaction. Assessing technical competencies and cultural fit is crucial to ensure the candidate thrives in your organisation.

Making informed **selection decisions** involves weighing all the information gathered during the hiring process and choosing the candidate who best fits the role and the company. Multiple stakeholders should be involved in the decision-making process to consider different perspectives. For example, at **Google**, hiring decisions are often made by a hiring committee rather than a single manager, which helps reduce bias and ensure that the best candidates are selected.

It is also essential to regularly review and improve your hiring practices. This might include reducing the hiring time, improving candidate experience, or enhancing diversity in the candidate pool. For instance, **Facebook** has made significant efforts to improve diversity in its hiring process by setting diversity goals, training interviewers to recognise unconscious bias, and expanding recruitment efforts to reach underrepresented groups.

8.5 Onboarding and Integration

The onboarding process is crucial in setting new hires up for success. A well-structured onboarding program helps new employees integrate into the company culture, understand their roles, and become productive team members more quickly. Effective **onboarding** improves employee satisfaction and retention and lays the foundation for long-term success within the organisation. First impressions matter, and the experience new hires have in their first few weeks can significantly influence their long-term engagement and commitment to the company.

A smooth onboarding process should include **pre-boarding activities**, a structured orientation program, clear communication, and ongoing support. Pre-boarding activities might involve sending a welcome package with company-branded items, providing access to an online portal with information about the company, or scheduling informal meetings with team members. This helps build excitement and reduces first-day anxiety. For example, **Buffer**, a social media management company, sends new hires a welcome email with all the information they need for their first day and an invitation to a Slack channel to connect with their future colleagues.

Structured **orientation programs** are essential for helping new hires understand the company's mission, values, and culture and their role within the organisation. Orientation should include an introduction to key company policies, an overview of the organisational structure, and training on any tools or systems they will use. For instance, **Airbnb's** onboarding program, "Airbnb Onboarding Experience," includes sessions on the company's history, culture, and values and hands-on training on the tools and systems employees will use in their roles. This comprehensive program ensures that new hires are well-prepared to start contributing from day one.

Clear **communication** is critical during the onboarding process. New hires need to know what is expected of them, who they can turn to for support, and how their role fits into the bigger picture. Regular check-ins with managers and HR during the first few weeks can help address any questions or concerns and ensure new employees settle in well. For example, at **Salesforce**, new hires have a series of scheduled check-ins with their managers during the first 90 days to discuss their progress, address any challenges, and ensure they have the resources they need to succeed.

Ongoing **support** ensures that new employees thrive after the initial onboarding period. This might include assigning a mentor or buddy to help guide them through their first few months, providing opportunities for feedback, and offering additional training as needed. For example, **LinkedIn's** onboarding program includes a "Buddy Program," where new hires are paired with a more experienced employee who provides guidance, answers questions and helps them navigate the company's culture.

Measuring the success of your onboarding program is also important. Regularly gathering feedback from new hires about their onboarding experience can help you identify areas for improvement. For example, at **Twitter**, new hires are surveyed at the end of their first week and again after 90 days to assess their onboarding experience and gather suggestions for improvement.

8.6 Employee Development

Employee development is a crucial component of talent management that focuses on helping employees grow and achieve their full potential. Investing in employee development enhances their skills and capabilities and increases their engagement, satisfaction, and loyalty. A well-executed employee development program can drive business success by ensuring your workforce continuously improves and adapts to new challenges.

Effective **employee development** aligns individual growth with organisational goals. Employees who feel they are growing and acquiring new skills are more likely to be engaged and committed to their work. This leads to higher productivity, innovation, and job satisfaction. Moreover, employee development helps build a pipeline of future leaders within the organisation, ensuring you have the talent needed to drive long-term success.

Strategies for **employee development** include training programs, coaching and mentoring, and continuous learning opportunities. Training programs are the cornerstone of employee development and should be tailored to your organisation's and employees' needs. For example, **IBM** offers various training programs through its digital learning platform, including data science, artificial intelligence, leadership, and more courses. This ensures that employees can continuously upskill and stay ahead of industry trends.

Coaching and mentoring are powerful tools for **employee development**. Coaching involves one-on-one sessions where employees receive guidance and feedback from experienced leaders, helping them overcome challenges and develop new skills. Conversely, mentoring involves a longer-term relationship where a more experienced employee (the mentor) provides support and advice to a less experienced employee (the mentee). Companies like **General Electric (GE)** have formal mentoring programs that pair senior leaders with high-potential employees, helping them develop the skills and knowledge needed to advance in their careers.

Providing **continuous learning opportunities** is essential for keeping employees engaged and motivated. This can include access to online courses, workshops, conferences, and other learning resources. Encouraging employees to pursue professional development outside their immediate job responsibilities can lead to new ideas and innovations within the organisation. For instance, **Google's** "20% time" policy allows employees to spend 20% of their workweek on projects that interest them but are not part of their regular job. This policy has led to the development of some of Google's most successful products, including Gmail and Google News.

Employee development programs should also be aligned with the organisation's strategic goals. This ensures that the skills and knowledge employees gain will directly contribute to the company's success. For example, if your company is focused on digital transformation, your employee development programs should include training on digital skills, such as data analysis, digital marketing, and cybersecurity.

Measuring the effectiveness of **employee development** programs is crucial for continuous improvement. Regularly gathering employee feedback about their development experiences and tracking key metrics, such as employee engagement, retention, and performance, can help you identify areas for improvement. For example, **Accenture** uses a comprehensive talent analytics system to track the impact of its employee development programs, allowing the company to continuously refine its approach and ensure that it remains aligned with business objectives.

In conclusion, investing in employee development is essential for building a high-performing workforce that can drive long-term success. By providing opportunities for growth, coaching, and continuous learning, organisations can ensure that their employees remain engaged, motivated, and capable of meeting the challenges of a rapidly changing business environment.

8.7 Performance Management

Performance management is a critical element of talent management that involves setting expectations, providing feedback, and evaluating employee performance to ensure alignment with the organisation's goals. Effective performance management helps employees understand what is expected of them and provides them with the guidance and support they need to succeed. A well-structured performance management system can drive employee engagement, improve productivity, and foster a culture of **continuous improvement**.

Setting **clear expectations** is the foundation of performance management. Employees need to know what is expected of them regarding performance, behaviour, and contribution to the organisation's goals. This involves setting specific, measurable, achievable, relevant, and time-bound (SMART) goals that align with the company's objectives. For example, at **Intel**, employees work with their managers to set Objectives and Key Results (OKRs), which help track progress and ensure that everyone is working towards the same strategic goals.

Providing **regular feedback** is essential for helping employees improve and stay on track. Feedback should be timely, specific, and constructive, focusing on strengths and areas for improvement. Regular check-ins between managers and employees, often called "1:1 meetings," provide an opportunity to discuss progress, address challenges, and adjust goals as needed. For instance, **Adobe** replaced its annual performance reviews with a regular "Check-Ins" system, where managers provide ongoing feedback and support to employees throughout the year. This approach has increased employee engagement and a more agile performance management process.

Conducting **performance reviews** is an important aspect of performance management, but it should not be the only touchpoint for feedback. Formal performance reviews, typically conducted annually or semi-annually, provide an opportunity to evaluate an employee's overall performance, discuss achievements, and identify areas for development. Performance reviews must be fair, transparent, and based on objective criteria. For example, **Google** uses a peer review process where employees provide feedback on each other's performance and the manager's assessment. This 360-degree feedback approach ensures a more comprehensive evaluation of an employee's performance.

Managing **underperformance** is a challenging but necessary aspect of performance management. When an employee is not meeting expectations, it is important to address the issue promptly and constructively. This involves identifying the root causes of underperformance, providing the necessary support and resources, and setting clear improvement goals. In some cases, it may be necessary to implement a performance improvement plan (PIP), which outlines the steps the employee needs to take to improve and the consequences if they fail to meet these expectations. For instance, **Netflix** has a high-performance culture where underperforming employees are given clear feedback and opportunities to improve. Still, they are encouraged to move on if they do not meet the required standards.

Fostering a **culture of continuous improvement** is a key outcome of effective performance management. Organisations can create an environment where learning and improvement are valued by setting clear expectations, providing regular feedback, and encouraging employees to take ownership of their development. This enhances individual performance and contributes to the organisation's overall success.

8.8 Succession Planning

Succession planning is the proactive identification and development of future leaders within an organisation, ensuring continuity in key roles and a strong talent pipeline. It plays a vital role in sustaining long-term business success, as it helps ensure that the organisation remains prepared for leadership transitions or the sudden departure of key employees. Effective succession planning mitigates risks associated with leadership changes and ensures the retention of **institutional knowledge** and the consistent execution of business strategy.

Succession planning is essential because it prepares organisations for the future by identifying and grooming internal candidates who can take on key leadership positions. This reduces the need for external recruitment and ensures **continuity of leadership**. Organisations that lack a robust succession plan are more vulnerable to disruptions, particularly when critical roles are suddenly vacated. For example, **Procter & Gamble (P&G)** is renowned for its strong internal development and succession planning processes. P&G grooms future leaders through a system of rotational assignments and leadership development, ensuring the company always has a ready pool of talent to fill senior roles when needed.

Effective succession planning involves identifying key roles, assessing potential leaders, and developing a **leadership pipeline**. Identifying key roles involves focusing on positions essential to the company's success, including senior executive positions and roles requiring specialised expertise. Assessing potential leaders involves evaluating current employees who have the potential to fill these roles in the future. This assessment should include evaluating performance and potential, leadership qualities, and the ability to manage change.

Creating a leadership pipeline involves providing **high-potential employees** with the development opportunities to grow into leadership roles. This includes mentorship, leadership training, stretch assignments, and exposure to different business areas. For example, **General Electric (GE)** has a well-established leadership development program that offers its employees rotational assignments, executive coaching, and global leadership experiences, ensuring they are prepared for future leadership roles.

Aligning succession planning with the organisation's strategic goals ensures that future leaders can drive the business forward. For example, if the company is focused on digital transformation, its leadership pipeline should include individuals skilled in technology, innovation, and change management. A formal process for regularly reviewing and updating the succession plan ensures that it remains relevant and adapts to the organisation's evolving needs.

Diversity in succession planning is essential for creating a more inclusive and equitable organisation. Companies that consciously develop diverse leadership talent can benefit from a broader range of perspectives, skills, and ideas. For example, **PepsiCo** has made diversity and inclusion a core part of its succession planning efforts, ensuring that women and underrepresented minorities are included in its leadership pipeline.

Measuring succession planning's success is essential to ensuring its results. Key metrics include the percentage of leadership roles filled internally, the retention rate of high-potential employees, and the diversity of candidates in the leadership pipeline. Regularly reviewing these metrics helps the organisation adjust its approach and strengthen its talent pool.

8.9 Employee Retention Strategies

Employee retention is a key component of talent management, as high employee turnover can be costly and disruptive to business operations. Organisations that develop effective retention strategies can maintain a stable, skilled, and motivated workforce, directly impacting productivity, innovation, and overall performance. High employee retention rates also contribute to a positive company culture, where long-term employees help sustain **institutional knowledge** and mentor new hires.

Employee retention is critical because it affects operational continuity, organisational culture, and employee morale. High turnover disrupts business processes and leads to additional recruitment and training costs. On the other hand, retaining top talent ensures a high level of expertise within the workforce, fosters strong team dynamics, and promotes employee loyalty. Moreover, retention reduces the risk of losing high-performing employees to competitors, which can harm the company's competitive edge.

Successful employee retention strategies involve offering **competitive compensation**, creating a positive work environment, providing opportunities for professional growth, and recognising employee achievements. Competitive salaries, bonuses, and comprehensive benefits packages are essential for retaining top talent. Beyond financial compensation, benefits such as health insurance, retirement plans, and wellness programs can significantly impact employee satisfaction. For instance, **Google** is known for offering generous compensation packages, which include high salaries, extensive healthcare coverage, and benefits that support employee well-being, such as on-site healthcare services and free meals.

Fostering a **positive work environment** is also crucial for retention. Employees are likelier to remain with an organisation if they feel supported, engaged, and valued. This includes open communication, work-life balance, and a sense of inclusion and respect. For example, **Salesforce** has created a work culture emphasising employee well-being and social responsibility, helping retain employees by aligning their work with their values.

Providing opportunities for **growth and development** is another effective retention strategy. Employees who see clear pathways for career advancement and have access to professional development are likelier to stay with their employers. Offering leadership development programs, continuous learning opportunities, and mentorship can help retain ambitious employees looking to grow. For instance, **Accenture** offers its employees a wealth of learning and development resources, including certifications, online courses, and leadership training, encouraging retention by supporting career growth.

Recognising and **rewarding employees** for their contributions is a crucial retention strategy. Awards, promotions, bonuses, and public recognition can reinforce employees' sense of achievement and commitment to the company. For example, **Zappos** has a well-established culture of recognition, where employees are celebrated for going above and beyond, contributing to higher retention rates.

Addressing turnover involves understanding why employees leave and taking steps to address the underlying issues. This can be done through **exit interviews**, employee satisfaction surveys, and data analysis to identify trends in attrition. Based on these insights, organisations can implement targeted strategies to reduce turnover, such as enhancing benefits, improving work-life balance, or addressing leadership and management concerns.

Several companies have developed successful retention strategies. For example, **Netflix** has a culture of freedom and responsibility, allowing employees to own their work. This autonomy contributes to low turnover rates and high employee satisfaction. Similarly, **LinkedIn's** "InDay" initiative offers employees a monthly day to focus on personal growth, volunteer work, or innovative projects outside their regular responsibilities. This supports work-life balance and personal development, helping to retain talented employees.

In conclusion, retaining top talent is essential for maintaining organisational stability and performance. Organisations can retain their best people and build a high-performing, loyal workforce by offering competitive compensation, fostering a positive work environment, providing growth opportunities, and recognising employee contributions.

8.10 Diversity and Inclusion

Diversity and inclusion (D&I) are essential to a successful talent management strategy. A diverse workforce brings together people with different perspectives, experiences, and backgrounds, which fosters **innovation** and drives better decision-making. Meanwhile, inclusion ensures that all employees feel valued, respected, and empowered to contribute fully to the organisation's success, regardless of their differences. Companies prioritising diversity and inclusion outperform those that do not, benefiting from enhanced creativity, a broader talent pool, and improved employee satisfaction.

Diversity and inclusion are not just ethical imperatives but also **business imperatives**. A diverse workforce is more likely to generate innovative solutions to complex problems because it leverages various experiences and viewpoints. Furthermore, inclusive workplaces tend to have higher employee engagement and retention levels because employees feel valued and recognised for their unique contributions. Research has shown that companies with diverse leadership teams are more likely to outperform their competitors. For example, a McKinsey & Company report revealed that companies in the top quartile for racial and ethnic diversity were 35% more likely to have financial returns above their respective national industry medians.

Creating a diverse and inclusive workplace requires intentional effort and **commitment** from all levels of the organisation. Some strategies for fostering diversity include setting clear D&I goals, implementing bias training, promoting diverse leadership, and establishing employee resource groups (ERGs). Setting clear D&I goals involves defining specific, measurable objectives for increasing diversity across all levels of the business. For example, a company might aim to increase the representation of women and underrepresented minorities in leadership positions over a defined period. These goals create a clear focus for D&I efforts and foster accountability.

Implementing **bias training** is another important step in creating an inclusive workplace. Unconscious biases can significantly affect recruitment, promotion, and decision-making processes. Training employees, particularly those involved in hiring and leadership, to recognise and mitigate these biases can lead to more equitable outcomes. Companies like **Facebook** have implemented unconscious bias training to ensure equitable hiring and promotion decisions, helping to foster a more inclusive environment.

Promoting **diverse leadership** is also crucial. Representation in leadership positions can inspire and motivate employees from underrepresented groups, demonstrating that the company values diversity at all levels. For example, **Johnson & Johnson** has focused on promoting diverse leadership by developing women and minority leaders through targeted mentoring and development programs. This commitment to diversity in leadership has strengthened Johnson & Johnson's reputation as an inclusive employer.

Employee resource groups (ERGs) provide support, networking opportunities, and a sense of community for individuals with shared identities or backgrounds. ERGs are valuable resources for organisations, offering insights into the needs and concerns of diverse employees. For example, **Microsoft** has a wide range of ERGs for women, veterans, and people with disabilities. These groups help create an inclusive environment and support the development of diverse talent.

Building an **inclusive culture** goes beyond hiring a diverse workforce; it involves creating a work environment where all employees feel empowered to contribute and succeed. Promoting open communication about diversity-related issues allows employees to express their concerns, share their experiences, and suggest improvements. Leaders should create safe spaces for discussions about race, gender, and other diversity-related topics, fostering greater understanding and a culture where all voices are heard.

Implementing **inclusive policies** is another key aspect of building an inclusive culture. These policies should support diversity and inclusion, such as flexible work arrangements, parental leave, and accommodations for employees with disabilities. Such policies help create a more supportive work environment and demonstrate the company's commitment to inclusivity. For example, **Accenture** offers flexible working options and parental leave policies that support a diverse workforce, helping employees balance their personal and professional responsibilities.

Celebrating **diversity** through company-wide events, awareness days, or diversity initiatives helps promote inclusion. These activities create opportunities for employees to learn from each other and celebrate their differences. For instance, **SAP** hosts events celebrating cultural diversity and promoting gender equality, reinforcing its commitment to an inclusive workplace.

Measuring the success of D&I initiatives is crucial for understanding their impact and identifying areas for improvement. Key metrics include tracking the diversity of new hires, monitoring promotion rates among diverse employees, and conducting employee engagement surveys to assess the inclusivity of the workplace. For example, companies like **Google** publish annual diversity reports, providing data on their progress in increasing workforce diversity and fostering an inclusive environment. These reports help hold the company accountable and set new goals for improving diversity and inclusion.

Several organisations have been recognised for their commitment to D&I. For example, **Salesforce** has established itself as a leader in D&I through its comprehensive Equality Program, which includes initiatives such as equal pay assessments, inclusive hiring practices, and support for underrepresented groups. Salesforce's focus on D&I has contributed to its high employee satisfaction and reputation as a top employer for diversity.

The business case for D&I is clear: organisations that prioritise diversity and inclusion are more innovative, adaptable, and competitive. Diverse teams bring a wider range of perspectives and ideas, which can lead to more creative problem-solving and better decision-making. Inclusive organisations are also better positioned to attract and retain top talent, as employees are likelier to stay with companies where they feel valued and supported. In conclusion, diversity and inclusion are essential for building a successful and innovative organisation. Companies prioritising creating a diverse and inclusive work environment benefit from a wider range of perspectives, increased creativity, and a stronger employer brand.

8.11 Learning from Leading Employers

Learning from organisations that excel in talent management provides valuable insights and best practices for building a high-performing workforce. Leading employers have established themselves as benchmarks in hiring, employee development, retention, and diversity. By examining the strategies of these companies, organisations can adopt and adapt best practices to enhance their talent management efforts.

Leading employers excel in talent management by focusing on **employee experience**, promoting continuous learning and development, and fostering a commitment to diversity and inclusion. Creating a positive employee experience is key to attracting and retaining top talent. This includes providing a supportive work environment, fostering work-life balance, and ensuring employees feel valued and recognised. For instance, **Airbnb** has built a reputation for its strong employee experience, with initiatives focusing on employee well-being, social responsibility, and a collaborative work culture.

Promoting **continuous learning and development** is another hallmark of leading employers. These companies invest in their employees' growth by providing access to training, mentorship, and opportunities for career advancement. For example, **LinkedIn** offers its employees access to LinkedIn Learning, an online platform that provides training in various skills. This commitment to continuous learning helps LinkedIn retain top talent and maintain high employee engagement.

Commitment to **diversity and inclusion** is also a key characteristic of leading employers. They set clear D&I goals, promote diverse leadership, and implement programs that support underrepresented groups. For instance, **SAP** has been recognised for its efforts to promote gender diversity and inclusivity, with initiatives such as its Business Women's

Network and a focus on increasing female representation in leadership roles.

Several leading employers provide valuable case studies in talent management excellence. For example, **Google** is known for its innovative work environment, focusing on creating a space that fosters creativity, collaboration, and continuous learning. Google's famous perks, such as free meals, fitness centres, and flexible work arrangements, are part of a broader strategy to attract and retain top talent. In addition, Google's "20% time" policy allows employees to spend a portion of their workweek on projects of their choosing, leading to successful products like Gmail.

Similarly, **Unilever** has aligned its talent management strategy with its sustainability goals, attracting passionate employees to make a positive impact. Unilever's Sustainable Living Plan has become a key part of its employer brand, drawing in talent committed to sustainability. This alignment of business and talent management strategies has strengthened Unilever's position as an employer.

Bain & Company is another leading employer that has built its success on a people-first culture, prioritising employee development, well-being, and engagement. Bain's talent management strategy includes extensive training and mentorship programs, opportunities for international assignments, and a strong focus on work-life balance. This people-first approach has earned Bain high employee satisfaction and retention levels.

Organisations can learn several key lessons from leading employers. Aligning talent management with business strategy ensures that employees develop in ways that benefit themselves and contribute to the company's overall success. Investing in employee development enhances engagement and builds a workforce capable of driving future innovation. Fostering a **positive and inclusive work environment** helps attract and retain talent and promotes innovation and collaboration.

Conclusion

Talent management is the heart of building a resilient, innovative, and thriving organisation. As explored throughout this chapter, the strategic importance of effectively managing talent cannot be overstated. A company's ability to attract, develop, and retain top talent directly influences its capacity to innovate, remain competitive, and grow sustainably in an ever-changing business landscape.

Organisations can ensure they draw in the best candidates from the initial stages of attracting top talent through strong employer branding and effective recruitment strategies. Once hired, a structured onboarding process lays the groundwork for integrating new employees into the company culture and ensuring they feel supported and valued from day one.

As employees progress within the company, ongoing development opportunities are critical for fostering a culture of continuous learning. This enhances employees' skills and job satisfaction and ensures that the workforce is aligned with the organisation's strategic objectives. High-performing companies understand that developing employees leads to higher innovation, engagement, and overall business success.

Effective performance management helps ensure that employees consistently contribute to the company's goals while fostering a culture of continuous improvement. In tandem with a strong succession planning process, organisations can build a robust leadership pipeline, ensuring the company's long-term success through prepared and capable future leaders.

Retention strategies are vital in maintaining organisational stability, reducing costly turnover, and keeping top talent engaged. Companies that offer competitive compensation, recognise employee contributions, and provide growth opportunities are better positioned to retain their best people.

The focus on diversity and inclusion is more than just a moral or ethical obligation; it drives innovation, better decision-making, and competitive advantage. Companies prioritising creating a diverse and inclusive work environment benefit from a wider range of perspectives, increased creativity, and a stronger employer brand. By setting clear diversity and inclusion goals, fostering open communication, and promoting inclusive policies, organisations can create a workplace where all employees feel empowered to contribute their best.

Learning from leading employers provides valuable insights into building a strong talent management framework. Companies like Google, Unilever, and Bain & Company exemplify how a commitment to employee experience, continuous learning, diversity, and inclusion can drive business success. These organisations are benchmarks for attracting, developing, and retaining top talent while fostering a positive and supportive work environment.

Ultimately, talent management is about managing people and unleashing the workforce's full potential to drive organisational success. Companies that master talent management understand that their people are their greatest asset. Organisations can remain competitive, adaptable, and ready to meet future challenges by investing in their employees' growth, development, and well-being.

Companies must remain committed to refining and improving their talent management practices as the business landscape evolves. By doing so, they can build a workforce equipped to meet today's challenges and seize tomorrow's opportunities.

Talent management is a strategic cornerstone of any organisation's success. By applying the principles and best practices outlined in this chapter, companies can cultivate a high-performing workforce, drive innovation, and achieve sustained business success. The future belongs to organisations that understand the power of their people and invest in their growth, development, and well-being.

Chapter 9

Corporate Culture and Values: Crafting a Cohesive Identity

9.1 Overview

Corporate culture and values are the bedrock of any organisation, shaping its internal dynamics and influencing how it is perceived externally. These elements guide employee behaviour, inform decision-making, and establish the organisation's public image. A strong, cohesive culture aligns with the company's strategic goals, creating a unified workforce committed to achieving shared objectives. This chapter delves into defining, developing, and sustaining a corporate culture that resonates with employees, customers, and stakeholders. We will explore the tangible impact of culture on performance and behaviour and discuss strategies for maintaining cultural integrity as businesses evolve. Through real-world examples, we will present a practical framework for building a cohesive identity that drives organisational success.

9.2 The Power of Corporate Culture

Corporate culture extends beyond mission statements or slogans, embodied in employees' daily actions and attitudes. A strong culture is crucial for achieving organisational objectives, as it permeates every aspect of operations, from employee relationships to innovation strategies and problem-solving approaches. When employees are aligned with the company's

core values and objectives, they are more likely to exhibit behaviours that contribute positively to business outcomes.

The impact of corporate culture on both behaviour and performance is profound. Leaders must actively shape a culture that encourages the behaviours necessary for organisational success. Employees who internalise the company's values are more inclined to act in ways that support its goals. For instance, a company prioritising customer service will see employees go the extra mile to meet customer expectations. At the same time, an organisation that values innovation will foster an environment where employees feel empowered to take risks and think creatively.

Southwest Airlines exemplifies the power of a strong corporate culture. With its emphasis on customer service, teamwork, and creating a fun work environment, Southwest has cultivated a culture that enhances employee satisfaction and reduces turnover. This positive internal dynamic translates into profitability and customer loyalty, setting Southwest apart in a highly competitive industry.

Moreover, a robust corporate culture shapes an organisation's external reputation. Companies with positive cultures attract top talent and foster strong customer loyalty. For example, **Patagonia's** commitment to environmental sustainability has attracted employees who share these values and built a loyal customer base that resonates with its principles. In contrast, a toxic culture can be detrimental, leading to disengaged employees, high turnover, and reputational damage, as seen in **Uber's** cultural challenges under former CEO Travis Kalanick.

Ultimately, corporate culture is a critical driver of organisational behaviour and performance. A positive culture fosters employee engagement, loyalty, and a strong public image, while a negative culture can undermine organisational success. Cultivating and maintaining a positive corporate culture is essential for companies striving for long-term success.

9.3 Defining Your Company's Core Values

Core values are the guiding principles that shape an organisation's operations and decision-making processes. They are the foundation of corporate culture and influence how the company interacts with employees, customers, and stakeholders. Establishing and articulating these values is crucial for creating a cohesive organisational identity that aligns with strategic business objectives.

Defining core values begins with deeply understanding the organisation's identity and purpose. Engaging key stakeholders, including employees, leaders, and customers, can help identify values that truly reflect what the company stands for. These values must be genuine, embodying the organisation's most important beliefs and principles. Authenticity is crucial; employees and customers quickly recognise when core values are mere buzzwords or marketing slogans. For example, **Zappos** has built its culture around values such as "Deliver WOW

Through Service" and "Create Fun and a Little Weirdness," which are evident in its daily operations and customer interactions.

Core values must also be **actionable**. They should translate into specific organisational practices and behaviours. If innovation is a core value, for example, it should be evident in how the company encourages creativity, rewards new ideas, and supports continuous learning. These values must be operationalised to be meaningful and actionable for employees in their everyday work.

Involving employees in defining core values ensures that these values resonate across the organisation. Employees are more likely to embrace values they have helped shape. **Netflix**, for instance, involves its employees in developing its "Freedom and Responsibility" culture, which emphasises autonomy, trust, and accountability. This collaborative approach helps embed the values deeply within the company and influences daily behaviour.

Core values must also align with the organisation's strategic goals. They should support the company's mission and drive the behaviours needed to achieve strategic objectives. For example, a company prioritising rapid growth may adopt "agility" and "customer focus" to ensure responsiveness to market changes while maintaining high service standards.

Effective **communication** is essential for embedding core values within the organisation. Leaders must go beyond listing values in handbooks or websites; they should regularly communicate them and recognise employees who embody them. For instance, **Starbucks** reinforces its values through "Partners of the Quarter," highlighting employees who exemplify its commitment to community and customer service.

In conclusion, defining core values is fundamental to building a strong corporate culture. These values must be authentic, actionable, and aligned with the organisation's strategic objectives. By involving employees in the process and communicating the values effectively, leaders can create a cohesive identity that shapes behaviour, supports business goals, and enhances the organisation's reputation.

9.4 Leadership's Role in Culture Building

Leadership plays a pivotal role in developing and sustaining corporate culture. Leaders' actions, decisions, and behaviours set the tone for the entire organisation, influencing how employees perceive and engage with the company's culture. Effective leaders do more than articulate the organisation's vision and values; they embody these principles in their daily interactions and act as role models for employees at all levels.

One of the most critical responsibilities of leadership is to champion **the organisation's culture**. This means consistently communicating the company's core values and ensuring these values are reflected in all aspects of the business, from strategic planning to daily operations. When leaders demonstrate a genuine passion for the organisation's culture, they inspire employees to align their behaviours with these values, fostering a sense of commitment and purpose throughout the company.

Leading by example is essential for employees to embrace the organisation's values. Leaders must model the behaviours they expect from their teams, whether they focus on innovation, dedication to customer service, or a commitment to ethical practices. **Satya Nadella**, Microsoft's CEO, exemplifies this approach. He transformed Microsoft's culture by promoting a growth mindset, collaboration, and inclusivity, significantly reshaping its internal environment and driving its resurgence as a technology leader.

For corporate culture to thrive, it must be treated as a **strategic priority**. This means integrating cultural initiatives into the organisation's broader business strategy and ensuring that culture is considered in every major decision. Leaders should regularly assess the state of the company's culture and make necessary adjustments to ensure it remains aligned with its evolving goals. For example, Tony Hsieh, the late CEO of Zappos, made culture central to the company's strategy by prioritising employee happiness and fostering a unique corporate culture, contributing significantly to Zappos' business success.

Trust is the foundation of a strong corporate culture, and leaders play a crucial role in building and maintaining that trust. Employees must believe their leaders act in the organisation's and its people's best interests. Achieving this requires transparency, integrity, and open communication. Leaders who are forthright about challenges, involve employees in decision-making, and follow through on commitments foster a culture of trust. **Mary Barra**, CEO of General Motors, exemplified this approach when she steered the company through the ignition switch recall crisis with a leadership style characterised by transparency and accountability.

Leaders must also cultivate a culture of **accountability**. This means holding themselves and their teams responsible for upholding the organisation's values and meeting objectives. Addressing issues such as unethical behaviour or underperformance swiftly and fairly reinforces the importance of accountability within the organisation. **Reed Hastings**, CEO of Netflix, has built a high-performance culture by setting clear expectations and making difficult decisions, such as parting ways with employees who do not meet the company's standards.

Another key leadership responsibility is empowering employees to contribute actively to the corporate culture. Leaders should encourage open dialogue, provide opportunities for feedback, and recognise employees who exemplify the company's values. For instance, **Airbnb** co-founders Brian Chesky and Joe Gebbia regularly seek feedback and involve employees in decisions that shape the company's culture, fostering a sense of ownership and belonging.

In summary, leadership is fundamental to developing and sustaining a strong corporate culture. Leaders must champion the company's values, lead by example, prioritise culture as part of the business strategy, build trust, and promote accountability. By empowering employees to shape the culture, leaders can create a cohesive and resilient organisational environment that supports long-term success.

9.5 Communicating Culture

Effective communication is vital for embedding and sustaining a strong corporate culture. Defined values and missions are not enough. These principles must be continuously communicated to employees, customers, and stakeholders to shape how the culture is perceived and lived within the organisation. Symbols, stories, rituals, and consistent messaging help reinforce a company's cultural identity and ensure employees understand and embrace it.

Symbols serve as visual representations of a company's culture and values. These can range from logos and branding to office design and specific language used within the organisation. Symbols create a cohesive identity and serve as constant reminders of the company's core values. For instance, the **office design** can reflect a company's cultural values. Open-plan offices with collaborative spaces suggest a culture of transparency and teamwork, while private offices may indicate a more hierarchical or formal environment. **Google's offices**, known for their playful and creative layout, mirror its culture of innovation and collaboration, fostering an environment that supports creativity.

Similarly, a company's **branding and logos** are significant cultural symbols that convey the organisation's identity to both internal and external audiences. **Apple's minimalist logo** and product designs reflect its culture of simplicity and innovation, reinforcing its identity as a leader in design and technology. These visual symbols are not merely decorative but powerful reinforcements of the company's values and mission.

Stories are among the most effective tools for communicating and reinforcing an organisation's culture. These narratives embody its values and inspire employees, whether they describe the company's founding, celebrate major achievements, or highlight challenges overcome. Founding stories often serve as cultural cornerstones, representing the principles that continue to drive the organisation. For example, the story of **Hewlett-Packard's garage beginnings** symbolises innovation and perseverance, setting a lasting standard for the company's entrepreneurial spirit.

Hero stories also play a crucial role in reinforcing cultural values. Celebrating individuals who embody the company's principles reinforces the importance of these values across the organisation. For instance, **Nordstrom** frequently highlights stories of employees going above and beyond in customer service, reinforcing its customer-centric culture. Such stories are shared in meetings, newsletters, and other communication channels, ensuring that the cultural values are understood and appreciated throughout the organisation.

Rituals, or regular activities and ceremonies within a company, help create a sense of shared identity and strengthen cultural bonds. These rituals can range from company-wide meetings to celebrations of achievements and milestones. For example, **Salesforce's all-hands meetings** are a regular ritual where leadership communicates updates, celebrates successes, and reinforces the company's values. This practice supports Salesforce's "Ohana" culture, promoting a sense of family and employee unity.

Celebrating **milestones** such as product launches or company anniversaries can also serve as cultural rituals, reinforcing a sense of shared success and purpose. **HubSpot**, for example, celebrates employees who best embody the company's values with its annual "Culture Code" awards. These rituals recognise individual contributions and reinforce the company's cultural standards and expectations.

For cultural communication to be effective, it must be consistent across all channels. Inconsistent messages can lead to confusion and undermine cultural initiatives. Consistency in internal and external communication ensures that employees and stakeholders clearly understand the company's values. **Internal communications**, such as regular updates from leadership, are crucial for keeping the company's values and mission at the forefront of employees' minds. For instance, **Jeff Bezos' regular letters to shareholders** consistently highlight Amazon's "Day 1" mentality, emphasising the importance of maintaining a startup-like mindset even as the company grows.

External communications also play a key role in shaping the perception of corporate culture. How a company presents itself to the public can reinforce its cultural values and enhance its reputation. For example, **Patagonia's consistent messaging** about environmental sustainability across its marketing, social media, and corporate initiatives reinforces its commitment to these values and strengthens its internal and external identity.

In conclusion, effectively communicating corporate culture involves symbols, stories, rituals, and consistent messaging. By embedding these cultural communication tools into the organisation's fabric, leaders can ensure that employees understand, embrace, and live the company's values. This fosters a cohesive and aligned organisational culture that supports long-term success.

9.6 Aligning Culture with Strategy

Corporate culture and business strategy are closely intertwined, and alignment is crucial for achieving organisational success. When culture and strategy are in harmony, the organisation operates more efficiently, with employees motivated to achieve goals that reflect the company's values. Conversely, misalignment between culture and strategy can hinder performance and make it difficult to achieve business objectives.

An organisation's culture acts as its **operating system**, guiding how decisions are made, how employees interact, and how work is completed. When culture and strategy are aligned, the organisation operates cohesively, with employees working towards shared goals that align with the company's values. A well-aligned culture can be a powerful enabler of strategic success. For example, a company focused on innovation benefits from a culture encouraging creativity, risk-taking, and continuous learning. In contrast, a company focused on operational efficiency needs a culture that values process improvement, attention to detail, and results-driven performance.

Tesla is a prime example of how aligning culture with strategy can lead to remarkable success. Tesla's strategy is based on disruptive innovation in the automotive and energy sectors. Its culture, in turn, reflects a focus on boldness, experimentation, and a relentless pursuit of excellence, all essential to achieving its ambitious strategic objectives. This alignment has enabled Tesla to remain a market leader in electric vehicles and sustainable energy solutions.

Maintaining cultural alignment during periods of change, such as mergers, acquisitions, or shifts in strategy, is particularly challenging but essential. As companies grow or evolve, ensuring that the culture remains aligned with the new strategic direction is crucial for maintaining employee engagement and organisational cohesion. Leaders must communicate the strategic vision clearly and explain how the culture will support this new direction. For example, when **IBM** shifted its focus from hardware to cloud computing and artificial intelligence, leadership took deliberate steps to communicate the new strategic vision and align the culture with innovation and agility.

Involving employees in aligning culture with strategy is vital for gaining buy-in and reducing resistance to change. Gathering feedback, involving employees in decision-making, and encouraging them to contribute ideas for cultural transformation are effective strategies for fostering engagement. When **Procter**

& Gamble underwent a major restructuring, leadership engaged employees at all levels to ensure that the company's culture of innovation and consumer focus remained intact.

One of the most effective ways to align culture with strategy is by linking **incentives and rewards** to strategic objectives. Recognising and rewarding behaviours that support the company's goals reinforces the importance of cultural alignment. For example, **Salesforce** ties its incentive structure to customer success, ensuring that employees are meeting sales targets and helping customers achieve their goals, thus supporting the company's customer-centric culture.

Regularly assessing and adjusting cultural alignment is an ongoing process. Leaders should conduct **cultural assessments** to evaluate whether the company's culture continues to support its strategic objectives. For instance, **Intel** regularly conducts assessments to evaluate whether its culture supports its strategic focus on innovation and operational excellence. Maintaining flexibility and adapting the culture to meet new challenges, whether entering new markets, adopting new technologies, or responding to changing customer expectations, is essential for sustaining alignment over time.

In conclusion, aligning culture with strategy is essential for achieving long-term organisational success. A well-aligned culture enables the company to execute its strategic objectives, fosters employee engagement, and improves the organisation's ability to adapt to changes in the business environment. Leaders must regularly assess and adjust cultural alignment to ensure continued success.

9.7 Cultural Transformation

Cultural transformation involves a fundamental shift in an organisation's culture, often driven by new strategic priorities, changes in the business environment, or the need to address deeply rooted issues. While cultural transformation can be challenging, ensuring the organisation remains competitive, adaptable, and aligned with its strategic goals is sometimes necessary. Navigating cultural change successfully requires a clear vision, strong leadership, and a structured approach to change management.

Cultural transformation is necessary when there is a significant **misalignment** between the organisation's culture and strategic objectives. This misalignment can result in poor performance, low employee engagement, or an inability to innovate and respond to changing market conditions. Mergers, acquisitions, leadership changes, or shifts in the organisation's mission or values often trigger the need for cultural transformation. For example, **Kodak**, despite being a pioneer in digital photography, failed to transform its culture from one focused on traditional film to digital innovation, leading to its decline.

Successfully navigating cultural transformation requires a **systematic approach**. The first step is defining the desired culture and articulating how it aligns with the organisation's strategic objectives. Leaders must communicate this vision clearly, explaining why the transformation is necessary and how it will benefit the organisation. Engaging leadership and key stakeholders is crucial for gaining broad support. Leaders must champion the change, model the desired behaviours, and engage managers and other influencers to ensure organisational alignment.

Before implementing changes, it is crucial to assess the current culture to understand the gap between the existing state and the desired future state. This can be done through employee surveys, focus groups, and cultural audits. Understanding the strengths and weaknesses of the current culture provides a baseline for measuring progress and identifying areas needing the most attention. Developing a comprehensive change management plan is essential for a successful cultural transformation. This plan should outline clear objectives, timelines, and milestones, detailing specific actions to shift the culture.

Managing **resistance to change** is a natural part of any transformation process. Employees may be reluctant to let go of familiar working methods, especially if they are comfortable with the existing culture. Effective change management requires acknowledging and addressing these concerns through open communication, involvement, and support. For instance, leaders should be transparent about the reasons for the cultural transformation, involve employees in decision-making, and provide resources to help them navigate the change.

Ensuring that cultural transformation is **sustainable** requires a long-term commitment from leadership and a continuous focus on reinforcing the new culture. This involves embedding the new values and behaviours into the organisation's systems, processes, and policies. Ongoing communication is essential to keep the new values and behaviours at the forefront of employees' minds. Leaders should regularly assess how well employees embrace the new culture and track progress towards achieving the desired outcomes.

In conclusion, cultural transformation is a complex but necessary process for organisations that must adapt to new strategic priorities or address deep-rooted cultural challenges. By following a structured approach to change management, engaging leadership and employees, and ensuring that the new culture is embedded into the organisation's systems and processes, leaders can navigate cultural transformation successfully and position their organisation for long-term success.

9.8 Engaging Employees

Employee engagement is critical in fostering a strong corporate culture and driving organisational success. Engaged employees are more productive and committed to their work and more likely to contribute positively to the company's culture and overall business performance. Building a culture of engagement requires a multifaceted approach that addresses employees' diverse needs and motivations while aligning them with the organisation's values and strategic objectives.

Employee engagement goes beyond mere job satisfaction. It involves a deep **emotional connection** between employees and the organisation, where individuals feel valued, motivated, and understood. This emotional bond leads to higher productivity, lower turnover, and increased innovation. Research has consistently shown that companies with high levels of employee engagement outperform their competitors in profitability, productivity, and customer satisfaction. When employees feel connected to the company's mission and values, they are more likely to take initiative, offer innovative ideas, and go the extra mile to achieve their goals.

Engagement is also a powerful tool for reducing **turnover**. Engaged employees are less likely to leave the organisation, reducing the costs associated with recruiting, training, and onboarding new employees. A strong sense of belonging and alignment with the company's culture significantly increases employee retention. For instance, companies like **Southwest Airlines** and **Google** have consistently high engagement and retention rates, contributing to their long-term success and stability in highly competitive industries.

Building a culture of engagement requires a comprehensive approach that includes providing opportunities for growth, fostering a sense of purpose, encouraging open communication, and recognising employee contributions. Employees are more engaged when they understand how their work contributes to their mission and goals. Leaders should regularly communicate the company's vision and values, reinforcing how each employee's role supports these objectives. For example, at

Patagonia, employees are deeply engaged because they believe in the company's mission of environmental sustainability, and they see how their daily work contributes to this larger purpose.

Providing opportunities for **growth and development** is another key driver of engagement. Employees feel more connected and committed when they see clear personal and professional growth pathways. Offering training, mentorship, and career advancement opportunities can significantly increase engagement. Companies like **LinkedIn** and **Salesforce** invest heavily in continuous learning and development programmes, ensuring employees have the resources and support to advance their careers and develop new skills.

Open communication is crucial for building trust and engagement within the organisation. Employees should feel comfortable sharing their ideas, concerns, and feedback; leaders should actively listen and respond to this input. This two-way communication fosters a sense of ownership and belonging. At **Microsoft**, for example, employee resource groups provide platforms for open dialogue on various issues, contributing to a more inclusive and engaged workforce.

Recognising and rewarding employee contributions is also essential for fostering engagement. Employees who feel appreciated and recognised for their efforts are likelier to remain motivated and committed to their work. Recognition can take many forms, from formal awards and bonuses to informal praise and public acknowledgements. **Zappos** is known for its culture of recognition, where employees are celebrated for going above and beyond in delivering exceptional customer service, reinforcing the company's core values and enhancing engagement.

Creating a **supportive and inclusive work environment** is fundamental to employee engagement. Employees who feel they belong, are respected and have the resources they need to succeed are likelier to stay engaged. Inclusive practices such as flexible work arrangements, diversity initiatives, and employee support programmes contribute to a positive work environment. **Unilever's Agile Working initiative**, which allows employees to work flexibly from various locations, has significantly boosted engagement by enabling employees to balance their work and personal lives more effectively.

Successful organisations implement specific initiatives to strengthen engagement and ensure employees feel connected to the company's culture. For example, **LinkedIn's "InDays"** allows employees to dedicate one month to personal development, volunteer work, or creative projects, fostering work-life balance and continuous learning. Similarly, **Unilever's Agile Working initiative** supports flexible work arrangements, enhancing employee satisfaction and engagement by promoting a balance between work and personal commitments.

Regularly assessing employee engagement is critical to understanding initiatives' effectiveness and identifying improvement areas. **Employee surveys, feedback loops, and engagement metrics** provide valuable insights into how engaged the workforce is and where further efforts are needed.

Companies like **Amazon** use annual engagement surveys to gather feedback on various aspects of the employee experience, including culture, leadership, and work-life balance. These insights help leaders make informed decisions to enhance engagement and address any areas of concern.

Tracking engagement metrics such as turnover, absenteeism, and productivity can provide additional insights. High turnover or absenteeism rates may indicate underlying engagement issues that must be addressed. Acting on feedback is crucial; collecting data is only the first step. Leaders must communicate the results, outline actions to address concerns and provide regular updates on progress. This transparency builds trust and shows employees that their voices are heard and valued.

In conclusion, employee engagement is a key driver of organisational success. By fostering a sense of purpose, providing growth opportunities, encouraging open communication, recognising contributions, and creating a supportive work environment, leaders can cultivate a culture of engagement that enhances performance, reduces turnover, and strengthens the company's culture.

9.9 Measuring Cultural Health

Assessing the health of an organisation's culture is essential for understanding how well it aligns with strategic goals and how employees perceive it. Regularly measuring cultural health helps leaders identify areas for improvement, track progress, and ensure that the culture remains a powerful enabler of organisational success. Tools such as employee surveys, feedback loops, and cultural audits provide valuable insights into the state of the culture and help guide actions to strengthen it.

Understanding the health of an organisation's culture is critical to maintaining a **positive and productive work environment**. A healthy culture drives employee engagement, supports performance, and enhances the ability to attract and retain top talent. Conversely, a weak or unhealthy culture can lead to disengagement, high turnover, and damage to the company's reputation. Companies with strong, healthy cultures often enjoy a competitive advantage. A positive culture can improve the organisation's brand, elevate employee morale, and increase customer loyalty. For example, **Southwest Airlines** is known for its strong customer service culture and high employee satisfaction, contributing to its long-standing success in a highly competitive industry.

Several tools and methods can be employed to assess the health of a company's culture. **Employee surveys** are among the most common tools for measuring cultural health. They provide insights into how employees perceive the company's culture, how aligned they feel with its values, and how engaged they are in their roles. Surveys can be tailored to specific aspects of culture, such as communication, leadership, work-life balance, and diversity and inclusion. For instance, **Google's annual "Googlegeist" survey** gathers feedback on various aspects of its culture, including innovation, collaboration, and employee well-being. The results are used to identify areas for improvement and track progress over time.

Feedback loops involve regularly gathering and acting on employee feedback to foster continuous cultural improvement. This can be achieved through regular check-ins, focus groups, or suggestion boxes. **Facebook**, for example, has implemented a feedback loop system where employees can provide anonymous feedback on the company's culture and leadership. Management then reviews this feedback to make necessary adjustments and improvements.

Cultural audits are comprehensive assessments of an organisation's culture, often conducted by external consultants. These audits typically involve interviews, focus groups, and surveys to evaluate the alignment between the company's stated values and the actual behaviours of its employees. The results of a cultural audit can provide a detailed analysis of the culture's strengths and weaknesses, offering recommendations for improvement. For example, **Deloitte** offers cultural audit services that help organisations assess their health and identify areas for enhancement, supporting long-term cultural alignment and effectiveness.

Collecting data on cultural health is just the first step; interpreting this data and taking action based on the findings is key. Leaders should identify trends, recognise areas of strength and weakness, and implement targeted initiatives to address concerns. For example, suppose survey results indicate that employees feel disconnected from the company's mission. In that case, leaders might develop programmes to communicate their strategic vision better and how employees' roles contribute to achieving it.

Recognising areas of strength is equally important. Organisations should highlight where the culture is thriving, such as high alignment with core values or effective collaboration, while acknowledging areas that need improvement. Implementing targeted initiatives based on these insights can help strengthen the culture and address specific issues. For instance, if feedback indicates a need for better work-life balance, an organisation might introduce flexible work schedules or wellness programmes to address the issue.

In conclusion, measuring cultural health is crucial for maintaining a positive and productive work environment that aligns with an organisation's strategic goals. Using tools such as employee surveys, feedback loops, and cultural audits, leaders can gain valuable insights into their culture's state and identify areas for improvement. Acting on this data and consistently monitoring cultural health helps ensure the organisation's culture remains strong and aligned with its objectives.

9.10 Case Studies of Strong Cultures

Examining real-world examples of organisations that have successfully built and sustained strong cultures offers valuable insights into the strategies and practices contributing to cultural success. These companies have defined and embedded their values into every aspect of their operations, creating resilient and cohesive organisations that thrive even in competitive markets. This section explores several companies that have excelled in building and sustaining strong cultures and the lessons that can be learned from their experiences.

Patagonia is widely recognised for its strong culture rooted in **environmental sustainability** and **social responsibility**. The company's mission statement, "We are in business to save our home planet," reflects its deep commitment to protecting the environment, and this mission is evident in every aspect of its culture and operations. Patagonia encourages its employees to participate in environmental initiatives and offers paid time off for volunteering. Additionally, the company integrates sustainability into its product development processes, using eco-friendly materials and promoting responsible consumption.

The key lesson from Patagonia's culture is the importance of **authenticity and alignment**. The company's values are not merely words on paper but are lived out in its daily practices, attracting employees and customers who share them. This strong alignment between the company's mission, values, and actions creates a sense of purpose and loyalty among employees and customers. This demonstrates that a clear and authentic cultural identity can be a powerful driver of business success.

Netflix offers another compelling example of how a unique corporate culture can drive success. Netflix's culture is built on the principles of **freedom and responsibility**, which empower employees to make decisions, take risks, and innovate without being constrained by bureaucratic processes. This culture has been a key driver of Netflix's rapid growth and its ability to compete in the dynamic entertainment industry. The company hires top talent and allows them to pursue projects they believe will add value while holding them accountable for results.

The lesson from Netflix's approach is the power of **trust and empowerment**. By giving employees the freedom to experiment and the responsibility to deliver results, Netflix has created an environment where creativity and innovation thrive. This culture of autonomy and accountability has enabled Netflix to stay ahead of competitors and rapidly adapt to changes in the market, highlighting the importance of fostering a high-performance culture that aligns with strategic goals.

Zappos, the online shoe and clothing retailer, is famous for its **customer-centric culture** and commitment to delivering "WOW" experiences. Zappos has built a reputation for exceptional customer service by empowering its employees to go above and beyond to meet customer needs. This commitment to service is deeply embedded in the company's culture, as reflected in its core values, such as "Deliver WOW Through Service" and "Create Fun and a Little Weirdness." Zappos' unique onboarding process and emphasis on employee happiness have fostered a positive and engaging work environment.

The key takeaway from Zappos' culture is the value of **customer experience and employee engagement**. Zappos has differentiated itself in a competitive market by aligning its culture with customer service goals and prioritising employee well-being. This example illustrates the power of a culture that delivers outstanding customer experiences and fosters employee loyalty and satisfaction.

Salesforce, a global leader in customer relationship management (CRM) software, is known for its **Ohana culture**, which means "family" in Hawaiian. This culture emphasises trust, customer success, innovation, and equality, creating a supportive and inclusive environment for its employees. Salesforce's core values are reflected in its business practices, leadership, and employee engagement initiatives. The company encourages its employees to participate in community service through its 1-1-1 model, which dedicates 1% of its equity, product, and employee time to charitable causes.

The lesson from Salesforce's culture is the importance of a **values-driven approach** that extends beyond business operations to community impact. Salesforce's commitment to trust, innovation, and equality has fostered business success and created a positive work environment. This case demonstrates how a strong, values-based culture can drive employee engagement and brand reputation while supporting broader societal goals.

Google is renowned for its culture of **innovation, creativity, and continuous learning**, which has made it one of the most successful companies in the world. The company encourages employees to take on ambitious projects, experiment with new ideas, and collaborate across teams. Google's "20% time" policy, which allows employees to spend part of their time on projects outside their core responsibilities, has led to the development of some of its most successful products, including Gmail and Google News.

Google's culture illustrates the importance of **fostering innovation and collaboration**. By creating an environment where employees are encouraged to explore new ideas and take risks, Google has cultivated a culture of creativity and breakthrough innovation. This example shows that organisations can achieve long-term success by promoting a culture that supports experimentation, collaboration, and continuous learning.

These case studies demonstrate that building and sustaining a strong culture requires a clear set of values, a commitment to employee engagement, and alignment with strategic goals. Patagonia, Netflix, Zappos, Salesforce, and Google have successfully embedded their cultures into every aspect of their operations, creating cohesive and resilient organisations that thrive in competitive markets. Leaders can apply the lessons learned from these companies to create a strong and sustainable culture that drives organisational success.

9.11 Sustaining Culture During Growth and Change

Maintaining a strong and cohesive culture during periods of growth or significant change is one of the most challenging tasks for any organisation. As companies expand, merge, or adapt to new market conditions, sustaining the integrity of their culture can become increasingly difficult. However, a strong culture can also serve as a stabilising force, guiding the organisation through these transitions. This section explores strategies for maintaining cultural integrity during growth and change and tips on staying true to core values while adapting to new challenges.

Growth, mergers, acquisitions, and changes in strategic direction can all put significant pressure on a company's culture. As an organisation grows, it may become more difficult to maintain the close-knit, family-like atmosphere that characterised its early stages. New employees may struggle to embrace the company's values, and the influx of new ideas and practices can lead to **cultural drift**. This occurs when the original values and behaviours that define a company's culture become diluted or overshadowed by new influences. For example, as **Facebook** rapidly expanded its workforce, it faced challenges maintaining its original "hacker" culture and sense of mission.

Mergers and acquisitions often involve bringing together companies with distinct cultures, creating potential conflicts and challenges in integrating different values and practices. The merger of **Disney and Pixar** is an example of successful cultural integration, where both companies maintained their unique creative cultures while benefiting from the merger's synergies. The challenge lies in creating a cohesive new culture that preserves the best elements of each while fostering a shared sense of identity.

To maintain the integrity of a company's culture during periods of growth and change, leaders must take proactive steps to reinforce the organisation's values, engage employees, and ensure cultural alignment. One effective strategy is to **reinforce core values** consistently. This involves regularly communicating the values to employees, integrating them into decision-making processes, and recognising and rewarding behaviours aligning with them. For instance, **Amazon** has maintained its customer-centric culture even as it has grown into one of the world's largest companies. The company's leadership consistently reinforces the importance of customer obsession, a value deeply embedded in Amazon's decision-making processes.

Another crucial strategy is onboarding and integrating new employees. As new employees join the organisation, it is essential to ensure that they are fully integrated into the company's culture. Comprehensive onboarding programmes introducing new hires to the company's values, mission, and cultural practices are critical. **Airbnb** has developed a robust onboarding programme that includes sessions on the company's history, culture, and values, ensuring that new employees understand and embrace the culture from their first day.

Engaging employees during periods of change is also vital. Leaders should involve employees in decision-making, solicit feedback, and provide support and resources to help them navigate the transition. At **Salesforce**, during periods of rapid growth and change, the company engages employees through regular communication, town hall meetings, and feedback loops, ensuring that everyone remains aligned with the company's mission and values.

Transparency and communication are essential during times of growth and change. Leaders should regularly update employees on the progress of changes, explain the rationale behind decisions, and address any concerns or questions. This builds trust and ensures employees remain aligned with the company's culture. Under **Satya Nadella's leadership**,

Microsoft has maintained a culture of transparency and open communication, which has been instrumental in aligning the company's culture with its new strategic direction.

While maintaining the integrity of the company's culture during growth and change is challenging, it is equally important to remain true to the organisation's core values. However, this does not mean that the culture should remain static. Instead, the culture should evolve to remain consistent with the company's values while embracing new opportunities and challenges. Successful companies balance preserving their cultural traditions and embracing innovation. This might involve maintaining certain rituals, symbols, and practices that define the company's culture while being open to new ideas and approaches that align with the company's values.

As companies grow and evolve, they must stay true to their core values and adapt to new challenges. For example, **IBM** successfully shifted its culture from focusing on hardware to software and services, aligning its culture with its new strategic priorities. This adaptability has allowed IBM to remain relevant in a rapidly changing industry, demonstrating the importance of cultural evolution in response to strategic shifts.

Examining companies that have successfully maintained their culture during periods of growth and change provides valuable insights into best practices for other organisations. **Google** has managed to sustain its culture of innovation and creativity even as it has grown into one of the world's largest technology companies. The company has achieved this by continuously reinforcing its core values, fostering collaboration and openness, and allowing employees to pursue new ideas. Google's "20% time" policy, which allows employees to spend part of their time on projects outside their core responsibilities, has been key in sustaining the company's culture of innovation.

The merger of **Disney and Pixar** offers another example of successful cultural integration during a merger. Both companies were known for their strong creative cultures, and the challenge was to integrate these cultures while preserving each company's unique strengths. The key to their success was maintaining open communication, respecting each company's cultural identity, and creating a new culture that combined the best elements of both.

Salesforce's Ohana culture has also been maintained successfully during rapid growth and expansion. The company has achieved this by continuously reinforcing its core values, engaging employees through regular communication and feedback, and ensuring that new employees are fully integrated into the culture through comprehensive onboarding programmes.

In conclusion, sustaining a strong and cohesive culture during periods of growth and change requires proactive leadership, continuous reinforcement of core values, and effective communication and engagement with employees. By staying true to the company's core values while adapting to new challenges, leaders can ensure that the culture remains a stabilising force that guides the organisation through transitions and supports long-term success. The experiences of companies like Google, Disney, and Salesforce provide valuable lessons on maintaining cultural integrity while navigating growth and change.

Conclusion

In today's dynamic and competitive business environment, a strong and cohesive **corporate culture** is not just a nice-to-have but a critical component of an organisation's success. Throughout this chapter, we have explored the significant impact of culture and values on every aspect of an organisation, from employee engagement and performance to customer satisfaction and brand reputation. A well-defined and deeply embedded culture guides employees' actions and behaviours with the organisation's strategic goals and fosters an environment where people and businesses can thrive.

Crafting a cohesive corporate culture begins with clearly articulating the organisation's **core values**. These values should reflect the organisation's identity and purpose and be consistently demonstrated through leadership behaviour and organisational practices. An authentic and aligned culture with the company's mission resonates more strongly with employees, customers, and stakeholders, creating a sense of unity and purpose. It is not enough to state these values; they must be integrated into every decision and action to become meaningful.

Leadership plays a pivotal role in building and sustaining corporate culture. Leaders must communicate and embody the organisation's vision and values through their actions. When leaders are seen as true champions of the culture, they inspire employees to align their behaviours with the company's values, fostering a sense of commitment and engagement. Furthermore, leaders must ensure that culture is treated as a strategic priority, integrated into business planning, and reinforced through systems and processes.

Effective communication is another cornerstone of a strong corporate culture. Regular, transparent, consistent messaging ensures employees understand and embrace the company's values. Symbols, stories, and rituals can be powerful tools for reinforcing culture, creating shared experiences, and building a cohesive organisational identity. Additionally, maintaining alignment between culture and strategy is essential for long-term success. When culture and strategy are in harmony, employees are more motivated and focused on achieving the organisation's goals, driving performance and innovation.

As organisations grow and evolve, sustaining a strong culture becomes more challenging. Periods of rapid growth, mergers, acquisitions, and changes in strategic direction can all test a company's culture's resilience. Leaders must proactively manage these transitions by reinforcing core values, engaging employees, and ensuring cultural alignment. Successful organisations balance maintaining their cultural traditions with embracing new ideas and practices that align with their evolving strategic priorities.

The case studies of companies like Patagonia, Netflix, Zappos, Salesforce, and Google highlight the diverse ways in which strong cultures can be built and sustained. These organisations have defined clear and authentic values and embedded them deeply into their operations, creating environments where employees feel empowered, engaged, and aligned with the company's mission. Their experiences offer valuable lessons for any organisation seeking to strengthen its culture and achieve long-term success.

In conclusion, a resilient and cohesive corporate culture is the foundation upon which organisations can build enduring success. By prioritising culture, involving employees in its evolution, and ensuring that it remains aligned with strategic objectives, leaders can create an environment where people are motivated to perform at their best and where the organisation can adapt and thrive in a constantly changing business landscape. As your organisation grows and faces new challenges, let your corporate culture be the North Star that guides every decision and action, ensuring that your identity remains strong, cohesive, and aligned with your vision for the future.

Chapter 10

Effective Communication: Inside and Outside the Company

10.1 Overview

Effective **communication** is a critical foundation for successful leadership and business management. Whether guiding a team through a strategic transformation, presenting complex ideas to potential investors, or managing a public relations crisis, the ability to communicate with **clarity**, **consistency**, and **precision** often determines success or failure. In today's highly interconnected business environment, clear communication allows leaders to build strong relationships, articulate their vision effectively, and navigate internal and external communication complexities. This chapter outlines essential skills and strategies that aspiring leaders and entrepreneurs must master for effective communication within and outside their organisations. By understanding key principles supported by real-world examples, readers will be better equipped to foster collaboration, maintain transparency, and address the challenges presented by the fast-paced nature of modern communication channels.

10.2 Foundations of Effective Communication

Effective communication involves more than just exchanging information. It requires ensuring that the message is understood and achieves the intended outcome. Three core principles,

clarity, **consistency**, and **context**, are essential to mastering effective communication.

Clarity is fundamental to successful communication. Without it, messages are likely to be misunderstood, resulting in confusion and misalignment. Achieving clarity means being concise, avoiding unnecessary jargon, and tailoring the message to the audience's level of understanding. For example, explaining complex financial concepts to non-financial stakeholders is crucial to simplify the information through analogies or visual aids to ensure comprehension. Jeff Bezos, founder of Amazon, famously banned PowerPoint presentations in meetings, preferring narrative memos to promote clarity of thought and communicate complex concepts in a straightforward and actionable manner. **Consistency** is equally important. Maintaining a consistent message across all platforms, whether internal emails, public statements, or marketing efforts, helps build stakeholder trust and credibility. Inconsistent communication can lead to confusion, undermine trust, and damage the organisation's reputation. Apple is an excellent example of maintaining consistency in communication. The company's commitment to **simplicity** and **innovation** is reflected not only in its products but also in its messaging. Whether in marketing campaigns or customer service interactions, Apple consistently reinforces its brand values, cultivating a loyal customer base.

Context refers to the surrounding circumstances that shape communication, including timing, audience, and the medium used. Considering the context ensures that the message is appropriate and relevant. For instance, a leader must be mindful of the team's emotional state when addressing employees after a major organisational change. Delivering the message in a tone that acknowledges concerns while offering reassurance is critical. During the 2008 financial crisis, Starbucks CEO Howard Schultz effectively used context in his communications, emphasising the company's commitment to community and ethical business practices, which helped maintain morale and customer loyalty.

In conclusion, clarity, consistency, and context are the foundations of effective communication. Leaders who ensure their messages are clear, aligned with organisational goals, and contextually appropriate are more likely to build trust, foster alignment, and achieve desired outcomes.

10.3 Internal Communication Strategies

Internal communication is the backbone of any organisation. It ensures that teams remain connected and aligned with shared goals and fosters a culture of collaboration and inclusivity. Effective internal communication helps leaders manage expectations, inspire employees, and maintain operational efficiency, even during change or uncertainty. To achieve this, leaders must adopt strategies that promote transparency, encourage open dialogue, and ensure a seamless flow of information across all organisational levels.

Transparency is crucial in internal communication. When leaders are open and honest with their teams, it fosters **trust** and accountability. Sharing successes and challenges and explaining the reasoning behind key decisions helps employees feel valued and involved in the organisation's direction. Buffer, a social media management company, exemplifies transparency by sharing nearly every aspect of its business, including salaries and decision-making processes. This radical transparency has helped Buffer build a strong, trust-based culture where employees feel empowered and aligned with the company's mission.

Open dialogue is another cornerstone of effective internal communication. Leaders must create an environment where employees feel comfortable sharing ideas, raising concerns, and offering feedback. Such two-way communication fosters innovation and keeps leaders connected to their teams' pulse. Google's "TGIF" (Thank God It is Friday) meetings allow employees to ask questions directly to senior leadership, fostering transparency and ensuring employees feel heard. This open line of communication helps the company stay innovative and responsive to employee needs.

Choosing appropriate communication channels is essential in today's digital workplace. Leaders must select tools appropriate for the message and the audience to ensure effective communication. Options range from emails and messaging apps to video conferencing and collaborative platforms. For example, while emails are suitable for formal announcements, messaging platforms like Slack are ideal for quick updates and team coordination. Video conferencing tools like Zoom have become invaluable for face-to-face interactions in remote or hybrid work environments.

Cross-functional collaboration is key to breaking down silos and promoting effective communication within large organisations. Teams may work in isolation without such collaboration, leading to miscommunication and duplicated efforts. Encouraging collaboration across departments helps ensure that the organisation is working toward common goals. Pixar's "dailies" meetings bring animators, directors, and producers together to review and critique work, ensuring alignment and fostering collaboration, contributing to the company's reputation for producing innovative, high-quality animated films.

Internal communication strategies that promote transparency, encourage open dialogue, select appropriate channels, and foster cross-functional collaboration are essential for organisational success. Leaders who adopt these strategies are better positioned to build a cohesive, aligned workforce that can effectively achieve organisational goals.

10.4 Public Speaking and Presentation Skills

Leaders must often inspire, influence, and communicate their vision to diverse audiences, including employees, investors, customers, and the media. Public speaking and presentation skills are indispensable for delivering compelling messages, engaging audiences, and making a lasting impact. A leader's ability to communicate confidently and persuasively can determine the success of their message.

Engaging the audience is one of the most critical aspects of public speaking. A successful speaker must connect with their audience intellectually and emotionally to maintain their attention and make a lasting impression. Techniques such as **storytelling**, rhetorical devices, and visual aids can make presentations more relatable and memorable. Steve Jobs, co-founder of Apple, was renowned for his mastery of storytelling. During his 2007 iPhone launch presentation, Jobs framed the introduction of the product as the beginning of a technological revolution, captivating his audience and making the presentation unforgettable.

Clarity in communication is equally important. A well-structured presentation, with simple language and clear points, ensures the audience can easily follow and retain the message. Presenters who overwhelm their audience with too much information risk diluting the impact of their message. Brené Brown's TED Talk, "The Power of Vulnerability", exemplifies clarity. Her ability to distil complex ideas into accessible insights has made her one of the most effective communicators in her field.

Confidence and body language play a significant role in how a speaker is perceived. Confidence conveys credibility, while effective body language, including eye contact, posture, and gestures, helps reinforce the speaker's message and engage the audience. Michelle Obama, former First Lady of the United States, is known for her confident and engaging public speaking style. Her steady eye contact and purposeful gestures amplify her message and help her connect with audiences worldwide.

Handling questions and challenges during a presentation is essential for enhancing a speaker's credibility. Thoughtfully responding to questions or challenges reinforces the speaker's expertise and helps clarify points that may have been misunderstood. Warren Buffett, CEO of Berkshire Hathaway, is recognised for his calm and witty handling of questions during shareholder meetings. His ability to clarify complex points while offering additional insights serves as a model for effective question management.

Preparation and practice are crucial even for experienced public speakers. Rehearsing allows speakers to refine both their content and delivery, ensuring they are well-prepared to engage with their audience effectively. Sir Richard Branson, founder of the Virgin Group, attributes much of his public speaking success to thorough preparation. Despite his charisma, Branson emphasises the importance of practising to ensure that his messages are delivered clearly and confidently.

In conclusion, public speaking and presentation skills are essential tools for leaders. Leaders can significantly enhance their communication impact by engaging the audience, delivering clear messages, projecting confidence, handling questions adeptly, and thoroughly preparing.

10.5 Crisis Communication

Communication during a crisis is perhaps the most critical test of leadership. Whether dealing with a product recall, public relations disaster, or internal scandal, how an organisation communicates during a crisis can make or break its reputation. The key principles of crisis communication include **speed**, **transparency**, **empathy**, and **consistency**.

Speed is essential in crisis communication. In the digital age, news spreads rapidly, and delays in responding to a crisis can lead to speculation, misinformation, and losing control over the narrative. Organisations must act swiftly to provide accurate information and contain the situation before it escalates. Johnson & Johnson's response to the 1982 Tylenol poisonings is a classic example of speed in crisis communication. The company immediately recalled 31 million bottles of Tylenol and issued public warnings, protecting consumers and restoring trust in the brand.

Transparency is vital in managing crises. Attempting to cover up or minimise the impact of a crisis can result in a loss of credibility and exacerbate reputational damage. Leaders must communicate openly, acknowledge mistakes, and update regularly to keep stakeholders informed. Toyota faced a significant recall crisis in 2010 due to unintended vehicle acceleration. Although the initial response was slow, the company took full responsibility and worked closely with regulators to resolve the issue. This transparency helped Toyota rebuild public trust over time.

Empathy plays an important role in crisis communication. Crises often generate emotional responses from stakeholders, and acknowledging the impact on those affected can help maintain loyalty and trust. In 2011, after a renter ransacked a guest's home, Airbnb CEO Brian Chesky issued a heartfelt apology and implemented new safety measures. This empathetic response helped restore trust in the platform and reassured hosts and guests that Airbnb was committed to their safety.

Consistency in messaging is crucial during a crisis. Organisations must maintain consistent communication across all channels when multiple stakeholders seek information to avoid confusion and misinterpretation. BP's inconsistent and often contradictory communication during the 2010 Deepwater Horizon oil spill led to public distrust and worsened the situation. A coordinated communication strategy could have mitigated some of the damage.

Preparation is essential for effective crisis management. Organisations should outline roles, responsibilities, and strategies for addressing crises in a crisis communication plan. Regularly reviewing and updating this plan ensures the organisation is prepared for potential crises. Starbucks, for example, maintains a detailed crisis communication plan with pre-prepared statements and designated spokespersons, enabling the company to navigate multiple crises effectively.

In conclusion, crisis communication is a vital skill for leaders. By acting swiftly, being transparent, demonstrating empathy, maintaining consistency, and being prepared, organisations can mitigate the negative effects of a crisis and protect their reputations.

10.6 Media Relations

Building positive relationships with the media is a crucial part of an organisation's communication strategy. Media relations involve managing how the company is portrayed in the press, generating favourable coverage, and effectively responding to media inquiries. A well-executed media relations strategy can enhance a company's reputation, increase its visibility, and shape public perception.

Building media relationships is the foundation of successful media relations. Establishing trust and credibility with key journalists can result in more favourable coverage and create opportunities for the company to share its story. Nike, for example, has built strong media relationships by providing journalists with access to executives, offering exclusive stories, and maintaining transparency. This approach has helped Nike secure positive coverage, even during challenging times.

Crafting effective press releases is essential for engaging the media. A well-written press release should give journalists the information they need to write a compelling story. Tesla's press release announcing the launch of its Model S electric car highlighted the vehicle's innovative features, environmental benefits, and performance capabilities. Accompanied by quotes from CEO Elon Musk, the release generated significant media attention and coverage.

Handling media inquiries requires responding promptly, providing accurate information, and staying on message. Apple is known for its controlled media relations strategy. The company rarely responds to rumours, and when it engages with the media, its statements are carefully crafted to align with its broader communication strategy.

Managing media during a crisis is particularly challenging as media attention increases dramatically. Ensuring that the company's story is accurately represented becomes paramount. Volkswagen's slow and disorganised response during the emissions scandal allowed negative narratives to dominate the media. The company later issued public apologies and implemented corrective measures, but the delayed response highlighted the importance of managing media relations effectively during a crisis.

Proactively seeking positive coverage involves pitching stories, organising press events, or arranging interviews highlighting the company's successes and innovations. Unilever has successfully used media relations to promote its sustainability initiatives. By engaging with the media and showcasing its commitment to corporate social responsibility, Unilever has enhanced its reputation and attracted ethically conscious consumers.

Media training for spokespersons ensures that company representatives are prepared for interviews, know how to stay on message, and are equipped to handle difficult questions confidently. Well-trained spokespeople can effectively represent the company and enhance its credibility. Microsoft offers media training to its executives, ensuring they are well-prepared for public appearances. This training includes mock interviews and message development, which helps Microsoft's leaders communicate effectively with the media.

In conclusion, media relations are crucial to any organisation's communication strategy. Organisations can shape public perception and enhance their reputation by building strong relationships with journalists, crafting effective press releases, responding to media inquiries strategically, and managing the media during crises.

10.7 Digital Communication

In today's digital age, communication strategies must extend beyond traditional media to include online platforms, social media, and digital content. Digital communication provides powerful tools for reaching a global audience, engaging with customers in real-time, and shaping a company's online presence. However, it also presents challenges, such as the need for rapid responses and the risk of negative feedback spreading quickly.

Social media is central to modern communication strategies. Platforms like Twitter, LinkedIn, Facebook, and Instagram allow companies to engage directly with customers, share updates, and build brand awareness. Managing social media effectively requires a strategic approach that aligns with the company's broader communication goals. Wendy's fast-food chain has garnered attention for its witty and engaging social media presence, particularly on Twitter. Wendy's uses humour and timely responses to connect with its audience, generate buzz, and reinforce its brand identity.

Content creation and curation are critical elements of digital communication. Providing valuable, relevant content, such as blog posts, videos, infographics, and podcasts, helps establish the company as a thought leader and fosters engagement with its audience. HubSpot, a leader in inbound marketing, has built its brand by offering high-quality content that helps businesses grow. HubSpot's blog, webinars, and free resources provide practical advice that attracts and engages its target audience.

Managing digital presence involves monitoring online conversations, responding to reviews, and ensuring consistent communication across all digital platforms. JetBlue Airways is known for its customer-centric approach to social media. The airline actively monitors social platforms and often responds to real-time feedback and complaints, enhancing its reputation for excellent customer service.

Crisis management in the digital space can be particularly challenging as negative feedback can go viral quickly. Companies must be prepared to respond rapidly to viral complaints or negative reviews to minimise damage to their reputation. In 2017, United Airlines faced a public relations crisis when a passenger was forcibly removed from an overbooked flight. The incident went viral on social media, and United's slow response exacerbated the situation. The company eventually apologised, but the delay underscored the importance of swift digital crisis management.

The power of digital analytics lies in its ability to provide invaluable insights into audience behaviour and the effectiveness of digital communication strategies. Analysing data from social media platforms, websites, and digital campaigns helps companies make informed, data-driven decisions. Netflix uses sophisticated digital analytics to track viewer preferences, optimise content recommendations, and personalise the user experience. This data-driven approach informs Netflix's communication strategies and enhances customer satisfaction.

Engaging with online communities is a powerful way to build customer loyalty and deepen relationships with the brand. Companies that create platforms for customer interaction through forums, live chats, or webinars can strengthen connections with their audience. LEGO, for instance, has cultivated a vibrant online community through its LEGO Ideas platform, where fans can submit design ideas for new LEGO sets. This community-driven approach fosters loyalty and generates innovative product ideas.

In summary, digital communication is a critical component of modern communication strategies. Companies that build strong social media presences, create valuable content, manage their online reputations, respond swiftly to crises, and use digital analytics effectively will enhance their visibility and reputation in the digital world.

10.8 Stakeholder Engagement

Effective communication with stakeholders, including investors, partners, customers, employees, and the community, is essential for building strong relationships and ensuring long-term success. Stakeholder engagement involves keeping stakeholders informed, addressing their concerns, and involving them in decision-making processes. By doing so, organisations can foster trust and collaboration, benefiting all parties.

Building trust through communication is the cornerstone of successful stakeholder engagement. Stakeholders must feel that their interests are being considered and their input valued. Transparent, regular communication helps build this trust and ensures that relationships remain strong. Unilever has made stakeholder engagement a core aspect of its business strategy. By consistently communicating with its stakeholders about its sustainability efforts and business performance, Unilever has built strong relationships and maintained its reputation as a leader in corporate responsibility.

Involving stakeholders in decision-making can increase their commitment to the organisation's success. Whether through advisory boards, stakeholder committees, or consultations, including stakeholders in key decisions fosters collaboration and trust. Patagonia actively involves its stakeholders, particularly on environmental sustainability issues. By consulting with employees, customers, and environmental groups, Patagonia ensures its actions align with its stakeholders' values, strengthening its reputation and customer relationships.

Tailoring communication to stakeholders is crucial as different groups have different needs, interests, and levels of understanding. Customising messages for each group ensures effective and relevant communication. Tesla, for example, tailors its communication to suit different stakeholder groups. Investors receive detailed financial reports, while customers are engaged with messages about innovation and sustainability. This targeted approach ensures that each stakeholder group's unique needs are addressed.

Listening to stakeholder feedback is essential for understanding their concerns and improving organisational practices. Actively seeking feedback through surveys, focus groups, or meetings allows organisations to demonstrate that they value stakeholder input. Starbucks encourages customer feedback through its "My Starbucks Idea" platform, where customers can submit ideas for new products or services. The company has implemented several customer suggestions, demonstrating its commitment to listening to stakeholders and maintaining an open dialogue.

Communicating during organisational change requires special attention. Transparent communication is essential to managing expectations and maintaining trust with stakeholders. During GE's 2018 restructuring, leadership prioritised stakeholder communication by providing regular updates and explaining the rationale behind the changes. This transparent approach helped maintain stakeholder confidence during a challenging period of organisational transition.

Measuring stakeholder engagement is important for ensuring communication strategies work as intended. Regular assessments, such as surveys or performance metrics, help organisations refine their approaches to better meet stakeholder needs. BP uses a stakeholder engagement framework that regularly assesses stakeholder satisfaction and communication effectiveness. This approach allows the company to improve its engagement strategies and continuously foster strong stakeholder relationships.

In conclusion, effective stakeholder engagement is essential for building trust and fostering collaboration. By tailoring communication, involving stakeholders in decision-making, listening to feedback, and maintaining transparency during times of change, organisations can strengthen their relationships with stakeholders and align their interests with the organisation's goals.

10.9 Brand Communication

Brand communication goes beyond traditional marketing. It involves crafting a consistent and compelling message that aligns with the company's identity and resonates with its target audience. Effective brand communication ensures that every interaction reinforces the company's values, mission, and personality through advertising, social media, or customer service. By developing strong brand communication strategies, companies can differentiate themselves in a competitive market and foster lasting connections with consumers.

Brand consistency is vital for building recognition, trust, and loyalty. When communication is consistent across all platforms, the brand's identity is clear, and every interaction reinforces the same core message. Coca-Cola exemplifies brand consistency. The company's iconic red and white colour scheme, classic logo, and messaging around happiness and togetherness have remained unchanged for decades. This consistency has helped Coca-Cola become one of the world's most recognisable brands.

Crafting a compelling brand narrative helps differentiate a brand from its competitors and creates an emotional connection with the audience. A strong narrative tells the brand's story, its origins, values, and vision for the future in a way that resonates with consumers and makes the brand memorable. Nike's brand narrative is built around athletic achievement and empowerment. The company's "Just Do It" slogan and advertising campaigns often feature stories of athletes overcoming adversity, creating an emotional connection with consumers and reinforcing Nike's brand identity.

Aligning brand communication with values is increasingly important as consumers seek brands that are transparent about their values and take a stand on social, environmental, or ethical issues. Aligning brand communication with these values is essential for authenticity and trust. Ben & Jerry's has built its brand on social justice and environmental activism. The company's commitment to causes such as climate change and racial justice is evident in its marketing, product development, and public statements, strengthening Ben & Jerry's connection with like-minded consumers.

Storytelling in brand communication allows companies to connect with their audience more deeply. By sharing stories that reflect the brand's values and mission, companies can make their messages more engaging and memorable. Airbnb's "Made Possible by Hosts" campaign highlights its users' unique experiences, reinforcing the brand's message of connection and belonging through authentic, real-life stories.

Maintaining consistency across channels is essential for a cohesive brand image. Whether through the company's website, social media, or customer service, every interaction must reflect the brand's identity and values. Apple is an excellent example of brand consistency across all touchpoints. Every element reinforces Apple's focus on innovation, quality, and user-centric design, from its product design and retail store aesthetics to its advertising and customer service.

Global brands must adapt their communication to different markets. Messaging should reflect cultural differences and resonate with local consumers without compromising the brand's core values. McDonald's successfully adapts its brand communication to different global markets. In India, for instance, McDonald's offers a range of vegetarian options and uses culturally relevant messaging while maintaining its core identity as a family-friendly, affordable fast-food chain.

In conclusion, effective brand communication delivers a consistent and compelling message that aligns with the company's identity and resonates with its target audience. Companies can build stronger brands and forge lasting consumer relationships by maintaining brand consistency, crafting a strong narrative, aligning communication with values, and adapting to different markets.

10.10 Listening Skills

Active listening is one of effective communication's most critical yet frequently overlooked aspects. It involves hearing the words spoken, understanding the message, interpreting the underlying emotions, and responding to acknowledge the speaker's perspective. For leaders and entrepreneurs, strong listening skills are essential for building trust, fostering collaboration, and making informed decisions.

Building trust through listening is crucial. When leaders actively listen to employees, customers, or stakeholders, they signal that their input is valued and that their concerns are taken seriously. Building trust through listening helps create meaningful connections and promotes a positive organisational culture. Indra Nooyi, the former CEO of PepsiCo, was known for conducting "listening tours." During these tours, she met with employees at all levels to hear their ideas and feedback, building trust and engagement within the organisation.

Empathy in listening involves understanding the words spoken and the emotions behind them. Leaders who listen with empathy create a deeper connection with their audience and ensure the speaker feels understood. Oprah Winfrey's success as a talk show host and media mogul can be largely attributed to her empathetic listening skills. By genuinely listening to her guests and creating a safe space for them to share their stories, Oprah built deep trust with her interviewees and the audience.

Listening to understand rather than respond promotes more meaningful communication. Many people listen with the primary goal of formulating a response, but true listening involves fully understanding the speaker's message before reacting. Satya Nadella, Microsoft's CEO, is praised for his listening-focused leadership style. Nadella prioritises understanding the perspectives of his employees and customers before making decisions, fostering a more inclusive and innovative culture at Microsoft.

Asking thoughtful questions enhances active listening by encouraging the speaker to elaborate and provide further insight. Thoughtful questions also show that the listener is engaged and seeking to fully understand the speaker's message. Apple's CEO, Tim Cook, is known for asking insightful questions during meetings, helping uncover new perspectives, and ensuring that all viewpoints are considered during decision-making.

Non-verbal listening skills, such as eye contact, facial expressions, and attentive posture, are as important as verbal communication. These cues demonstrate engagement and reinforce that the speaker's message is being taken seriously. Sheryl Sandberg, Facebook's COO, is known for her strong nonverbal listening skills. Her focused body language and consistent eye contact during meetings signal that she fully engages with the conversation and values the speaker's input.

In conclusion, active listening is a critical leadership skill. By building trust, listening with empathy, asking clarifying questions, and using non-verbal cues effectively, leaders can improve communication and foster stronger relationships within their organisations.

10.11 Case Studies in Communication Excellence

Studying real-world examples of companies and leaders who have excelled in communication provides valuable insights into the strategies and practices that lead to success. These case studies highlight the importance of clarity, consistency, empathy, and strategic thinking in communication. By examining how different organisations have handled communication challenges, leaders can learn practical lessons to apply in their organisations.

Starbucks and crisis communication: In 2018, Starbucks faced a major crisis when two Black men were arrested at a Philadelphia store while waiting for a friend, leading to accusations of racial profiling. The incident quickly went viral, sparking outrage and calls for boycotts. Starbucks CEO Kevin Johnson responded swiftly by issuing a public apology, meeting with the men involved, and pledging to close all Starbucks stores for racial bias training. The company's proactive and empathetic response helped restore public trust. By addressing the issue head-on and taking concrete actions, Starbucks mitigated the crisis and avoided long-term damage to its brand.

Coca-Cola and brand communication: Coca-Cola has long been known for its mastery of brand communication, consistently reinforcing its core values of happiness, togetherness, and refreshment. One of its most iconic campaigns, "Share a Coke," demonstrated the power of personalised brand communication. The 2011 campaign replaced the Coca-Cola logo on bottles and cans with popular first names, encouraging consumers to "share a Coke" with friends and family. Supported by social media engagement, the campaign was a huge success, increasing sales, brand engagement, and social media buzz, showcasing the power of a well-crafted, personalised brand message.

Patagonia and stakeholder engagement: Patagonia has built its brand around environmental sustainability and stakeholder engagement. The company actively involves its stakeholders in decision-making, ensuring its actions align with its values. One of Patagonia's standout initiatives is the "Worn Wear" program, which encourages customers to repair and reuse their products rather than buy new ones. This initiative is part of Patagonia's broader commitment to environmental sustainability and aligns with its stakeholder values. Patagonia's commitment to stakeholder engagement has helped the company build a loyal customer base and a reputation as a leader in corporate responsibility.

Microsoft and internal communication: Under CEO Satya Nadella, Microsoft has undergone a cultural transformation driven by a renewed focus on internal communication. Nadella's emphasis on empathy, collaboration, and continuous learning has reshaped Microsoft's internal culture, fostering innovation and employee engagement. Nadella prioritises open communication and transparency, regularly holds town hall meetings, and promotes a culture of inclusion and continuous learning. Microsoft's internal communication strategy has improved employee engagement, collaboration, and innovation, contributing to the company's significant business success.

Tesla and media relations: Tesla, led by CEO Elon Musk, has adopted an unconventional approach to media relations. Rather than relying on traditional media channels, Musk frequently bypasses them and communicates directly with the public through social media platforms like Twitter. Musk uses Twitter to communicate directly with the public, shaping the narrative around Tesla's products and vision for the future. Tesla's media strategy has helped the company generate significant attention and position itself as a leader in the electric vehicle market. However, Musk's unfiltered communication style has also led to controversy, highlighting the risks of direct engagement without media mediation.

Conclusion

Mastering effective communication is essential for leadership and business success. As demonstrated throughout this chapter, the ability to communicate with clarity, consistency, and empathy can significantly influence an organisation's trajectory. Whether communicating internally or with external stakeholders, effective communication builds trust, fosters collaboration, and creates a shared vision that propels the organisation toward its goals. Leaders who adopt the strategies discussed in this chapter will be well-equipped to navigate the complexities of modern communication. From clear internal communication practices that promote transparency and collaboration to adept crisis management strategies that protect a company's reputation, effective communication is at the heart of strong leadership.

The real-world case studies presented in this chapter highlight the tangible impact of communication excellence. Whether through Starbucks' swift and empathetic crisis response, Coca-Cola's consistent brand messaging, Patagonia's commitment to stakeholder engagement, Microsoft's transformation through internal communication, or Tesla's innovative media relations strategy, these examples provide valuable lessons for any aspiring leader. Ultimately, communication lies at the core of every successful organisation. Leaders and entrepreneurs who invest in developing their communication skills will be better equipped to inspire their teams, influence their markets, and lead their companies to sustained success. By mastering the principles and strategies of effective communication, leaders can avoid common pitfalls and create lasting, positive impacts in their organisations and beyond.

Chapter 11

Navigating Global Markets: Expansion and Localisation Strategies

11.1 Overview

Expanding into **global markets** presents businesses with extraordinary opportunities but also significant challenges. For ambitious leaders, the allure of international growth is often counterbalanced by the complexities of navigating diverse **cultural**, **economic**, and **regulatory** environments. Successful expansion requires understanding how to adapt business models to local contexts while building effective cross-border teams. This chapter explores the key strategies needed for global growth, including **market analysis**, cultural adaptation, managing international supply chains, and mitigating financial risks. Leaders who grasp these elements can achieve remarkable growth and establish a strong global presence.

The **timing** of expansion is crucial. Moving too early can strain resources, and waiting too long might result in missed opportunities. Before entering new markets, companies must assess their internal readiness, including financial stability and operational capacity. Simultaneously, evaluating the **market readiness** involves analysing the target region's economic conditions and competitive landscape. This dual assessment ensures that companies are well-prepared to navigate the complexities of international markets.

Businesses often pursue global expansion for strategic reasons, such as escaping domestic market saturation or tapping into growth opportunities in emerging economies. For example, IKEA expanded into China to access a large consumer base and reduce its dependence on the European market. Companies may also seek new markets to access scarce resources or talent in their home countries. Understanding the strategic motivations behind global expansion is essential for making informed decisions that align with long-term business goals.

In summary, while global expansion offers substantial rewards, it also poses significant challenges that require careful planning and strategic foresight. Companies must be clear about their motivations, assess their readiness, and choose their timing wisely to ensure success in international markets.

11.2 Market Analysis and Selection

Selecting the right markets is critical for any business looking to expand globally. Comprehensive **market analysis** helps identify the most promising opportunities while avoiding markets with insurmountable challenges. This process involves using various analytical tools and methodologies to evaluate potential markets and align them with the company's strategic goals.

Identifying potential markets begins with analysing economic size, growth prospects, and consumer behaviour. For instance, **Netflix** expanded into India after recognising its large population, growing middle class, and increasing internet penetration. However, this decision was not made lightly; it was based on extensive research into local content preferences and regulatory landscapes. Such **data-driven** decisions are critical for identifying markets with the best potential for success.

PESTEL (Political, Economic, Social, Technological, Environmental, and Legal factors) and **SWOT** (Strengths, Weaknesses, Opportunities, and Threats) analyses are invaluable in evaluating external and internal factors that could impact business operations. For example, a PESTEL analysis can highlight potential regulatory hurdles or economic instability in a market. In contrast, a SWOT analysis can help companies assess their internal capabilities relative to market opportunities.

Once potential markets are identified, companies must assess their size, growth rate, and profitability. **Tesla**, for instance, carefully evaluated the growing demand for electric vehicles in China alongside government incentives and the competitive landscape before entering the market. This comprehensive evaluation provided a clear picture of the market's potential and helped shape Tesla's entry strategy.

A thorough market analysis also includes assessing **risks** such as political instability or currency fluctuations. For example, when **Nike** entered Brazil, it faced complex tax laws and bureaucratic challenges. However, by partnering with local distributors and adapting its supply chain strategy, Nike overcame these obstacles and established a strong regional presence.

In conclusion, selecting the right markets for global expansion requires a systematic approach to considering opportunities and risks. Using tools like PESTEL and SWOT, companies can make informed decisions and position themselves for success in international markets.

11.3 Cultural Sensitivity and Adaptation

Cultural sensitivity is crucial for successful global expansion. Companies that fail to understand and respect local cultures risk alienating consumers and facing operational challenges. To thrive in international markets, businesses must adapt their **products**, **services**, and **marketing strategies** to align with local cultural norms and consumer preferences.

Understanding **cultural differences** is the first step in this process. Unique cultural norms, values, and consumer behaviours shape each market. For instance, **McDonald's** successfully adapted its menu in India by introducing vegetarian options like the McAloo Tikki and removing beef products. This cultural adaptation allowed McDonald's to connect with local consumers and establish a strong market presence.

Beyond understanding cultural differences, companies must **localise their products** and services to meet the needs of local consumers. This might involve altering product features, packaging, or even business models. For example, **Airbnb** adapted its platform for the Japanese market by aligning with the country's unique regulatory environment and cultural norms around hospitality. These adjustments enabled Airbnb to grow its presence in Japan.

Marketing strategies also need to be tailored to reflect local cultural sensibilities. **Coca-Cola** has a long history of adapting its campaigns to local markets. In China, for example, Coca-Cola's "Taste the Feeling" campaign was modified to emphasise themes of family and togetherness, resonating with local cultural values. This localisation strategy helped Coca-Cola strengthen its brand appeal in the Chinese market.

Training and sensitising teams to cultural differences are essential. **Cross-cultural training** can prevent misunderstandings and help build stronger relationships with local employees and partners. For instance, **HSBC** invests heavily in cross-cultural training for its employees, ensuring they can navigate diverse cultural environments effectively.

Examples of cultural missteps, such as **Walmart's** failed entry into Germany, highlight the importance of cultural sensitivity. Walmart's attempt to impose American-style retail practices in a market that was not receptive to them led to significant losses and an eventual exit. This case underscores the need for companies to be culturally adaptable and responsive to local consumer expectations.

In summary, cultural sensitivity and adaptation are vital for global success. Companies can build stronger connections with consumers and avoid costly mistakes by understanding local cultures, localising products and services, and tailoring marketing strategies.

11.4 Building a Global Team

Building a global team is fundamental to successful international expansion. The ability to recruit, manage, and integrate a diverse workforce across multiple countries can significantly influence the success of global operations. This requires a strategic approach prioritising cultural sensitivity, clear communication, and strong leadership.

The first step in building a global team is recruiting individuals with the necessary skills and cultural adaptability. **Google**, for example, hires local experts in its international offices, allowing the company to tailor its services more effectively to regional markets. This strategy ensures that Google deeply understands local market dynamics and consumer needs.

Navigating **cultural differences** within a global team is essential. Leaders must create an inclusive environment that respects these differences while fostering a sense of unity. **Unilever** strongly emphasises cultural diversity within its global teams, promoting cross-cultural collaboration as a core element of its leadership development programmes.

Creating a cohesive global team requires a shared sense of purpose and alignment with the company's mission and values. This can be challenging when team members are spread across different time zones and cultural contexts. Regular communication through video conferencing and collaboration platforms can help bridge geographical gaps and keep team members connected.

Cross-cultural training equips team members with the knowledge and skills to work effectively globally. **IBM's** extensive cross-cultural training programmes help employees navigate the complexities of international business, promoting collaboration and innovation across its global teams.

Managing remote and distributed teams requires a different approach from traditional co-located teams. Leaders must establish clear communication protocols, set expectations, and provide the tools for effective remote collaboration. **Automattic**, the company behind WordPress, operates as a fully distributed company with employees in over 70 countries. Its strong communication culture and transparent practices enable its global teams to collaborate effectively across time zones and cultures.

Consistent leadership is crucial for maintaining alignment and cohesion within a global team. **GE's** global leadership team is renowned for its commitment to clear expectations and open communication, ensuring that team members work towards the same goals regardless of location.

Building and managing a global team requires a strategic approach prioritising cultural sensitivity, clear communication, and strong leadership. Companies that recruit diverse talent, foster cross-cultural understanding, and support remote collaboration can create cohesive global teams that drive international success.

11.5 International Supply Chains

Managing international supply chains is a complex yet critical aspect of global expansion. As businesses expand across borders, they must address logistical challenges, comply with varying regulations, and mitigate the risks associated with global supply chains. This section explores strategies for ensuring efficiency, minimising risks, and maintaining compliance in international supply chains.

International supply chains often involve multiple layers of complexity, including transportation, customs clearance, and distribution across different countries. **Zara**, the fast-fashion retailer, is known for its highly efficient supply chain, which allows it to deliver new products to stores within weeks of design. This rapid turnaround is achieved through centralised production, advanced logistics, and a well-coordinated global distribution network.

Compliance and regulation are significant challenges in managing international supply chains. Companies must ensure their operations comply with local laws and regulations, including customs procedures, import/export controls, and environmental standards. **Apple**, for example, has developed a robust compliance programme to manage its complex global supply chain, ensuring that its suppliers meet local regulatory requirements and adhere to the company's ethical standards.

Global supply chains are exposed to numerous risks, including **political instability**, natural disasters, and fluctuations in currency exchange rates. Companies must develop strategies to mitigate these risks and ensure the continuity of their supply chains. Diversifying suppliers, building redundancy into the supply chain, and investing in risk management tools can all help reduce exposure to risks. **Toyota** has implemented a multi-tiered risk management strategy, including maintaining close relationships with suppliers and developing contingency plans for potential disruptions.

Sustainability is an increasingly important aspect of global supply chains. Companies are now expected to reduce the environmental impact of their operations, ensure fair labour practices, and source materials responsibly. **Unilever** has made sustainability a central pillar of its supply chain strategy, with initiatives focused on reducing carbon emissions, improving water efficiency, and promoting ethical sourcing. These efforts have enhanced Unilever's sustainability credentials and strengthened its brand reputation.

Technology plays a crucial role in optimising global supply chains. Advanced analytics, automation, and real-time tracking systems can help companies reduce costs and respond more quickly to changes in demand or supply. **Amazon**, for instance, has pioneered technology in its global supply chain, employing sophisticated algorithms, robotics, and data analytics to streamline operations and ensure rapid delivery times.

Building strong supplier relationships is essential for ensuring the smooth functioning of international supply chains. Companies must work closely with suppliers to ensure quality, reliability, and compliance with ethical standards. **Nestlé**, for example, has developed long-term partnerships with its suppliers, particularly in the agricultural sector, to ensure a consistent supply of high-quality raw materials. Nestlé's supplier relationship management includes regular audits, training programmes, and initiatives to support sustainable farming practices.

Managing international supply chains requires a strategic approach that addresses logistical challenges, compliance requirements, risk management, sustainability, and technology. By building strong supplier relationships and leveraging technological advancements, companies can create efficient and resilient supply chains that support global expansion.

11.6 Global Marketing Strategies

Effective global marketing is crucial for building **brand recognition**, driving sales, and establishing a strong presence in international markets. However, marketing across different cultures, languages, and economic environments presents unique challenges. This section explores strategies for tailoring marketing messages and campaigns to diverse global audiences while highlighting successful global marketing initiatives.

One of the key challenges in global marketing is ensuring that a brand's **message** resonates with diverse audiences while maintaining consistency across markets. This requires a deep understanding of local cultural norms, values, and consumer behaviour. For instance, **Nike** tailors its marketing campaigns to reflect different regions' cultural values and aspirations. In China, Nike's campaigns often focus on themes of perseverance and hard work, resonating with local cultural values. Meanwhile, in the United States, Nike's marketing tends to emphasise individual achievement and self-expression. Nike strengthens its brand identity globally by adapting its messages to suit each market.

Marketing strategies, including pricing, distribution channels, and promotional tactics, must also be adapted to the economic conditions of each market. When **Procter & Gamble (P&G)** entered emerging markets such as India, it adjusted its product sizes and pricing to suit the lower purchasing power of local consumers. P&G also invested in localised marketing campaigns and promotions to build brand awareness, helping the company establish a foothold in these price-sensitive markets.

Localisation goes beyond translating marketing materials into the local language; it requires adapting content to reflect local customs and preferences. This might include using local celebrities in advertising campaigns, referencing cultural events, or adjusting product names and packaging. **Coca-Cola** is a master of content localisation, often developing country-specific campaigns that reflect local traditions and festivals. For instance, during the Chinese New Year, Coca-Cola's marketing frequently incorporates symbols of luck and prosperity deeply rooted in

Chinese culture. This localised approach has helped Coca-Cola build a strong emotional connection with consumers in China.

The rise of digital and social media platforms has transformed global marketing strategies. Companies must now navigate a complex landscape of digital channels, each with its own audience demographics and cultural nuances. **L'Oréal** has successfully leveraged social media to expand its presence in Asia. The company uses platforms like WeChat and Weibo in China to engage consumers through influencer partnerships, live-streaming events, and interactive campaigns. This digital-first approach has been instrumental in driving brand awareness and sales in the region.

While localisation is important, maintaining **global brand consistency** is equally crucial. Companies must strike a balance between adapting to local markets and preserving the essence of their brand. **Apple** has mastered this balance by maintaining a consistent brand image focused on innovation, simplicity, and premium quality while tailoring its marketing strategies to reflect the needs and preferences of local markets. This approach ensures that Apple's global brand identity remains strong, even as it resonates with diverse consumer segments.

To ensure the success of global marketing efforts, companies must regularly measure the effectiveness of their campaigns across different markets. This involves tracking key performance indicators (KPIs) such as brand awareness, customer engagement, sales growth, and return on investment (ROI). Companies should also gather feedback from local teams and consumers to refine their strategies and improve future campaigns. **Unilever** employs a robust system for measuring the impact of its global marketing campaigns, using data analytics and consumer insights to continuously optimise its marketing efforts and drive growth in international markets.

In conclusion, effective global marketing requires a strategic approach that balances localisation with brand consistency. By tailoring marketing messages, adapting to local economic contexts, and leveraging digital and social media platforms, companies can successfully navigate the complexities of global markets and build strong, recognisable brands worldwide.

11.7 Currency Risks and Financial Management

Navigating **currency risks** and managing financial operations in international markets is critical for the success of global expansion. Fluctuations in exchange rates, tax law variations, and differences in financial regulations can pose significant challenges for companies operating across borders. This section explores strategies for managing currency risks, optimising financial operations, and ensuring compliance with international financial regulations.

Currency risk, also known as **exchange rate risk**, arises from fluctuations in the value of one currency relative to another. These fluctuations can impact the profitability of international operations, especially when revenues are earned in one currency and expenses are incurred in another. For example, a company that exports goods from the United States to Europe and receives payments in euros may face losses if the euro depreciates against the dollar. To mitigate this risk, businesses must closely monitor exchange rate trends and implement strategies to minimise potential losses.

One of the most common strategies for managing currency risk is **hedging**, which involves using financial instruments to protect against adverse currency movements. Companies can use forward contracts, options, or currency swaps to lock in exchange rates for future transactions, reducing uncertainty and stabilising cash flows. For instance, **General Electric (GE)** uses hedging extensively to manage its exposure to currency fluctuations across its global operations. By hedging a significant portion of its foreign currency transactions, GE can protect its earnings from the volatility of exchange rates.

Effective cash management is essential for maintaining liquidity and minimising financial risks in international markets. This involves optimising the flow of funds across different regions, managing working capital efficiently, and ensuring access to sufficient credit facilities. **Caterpillar**, a global construction and mining equipment leader, has implemented a sophisticated cash management system that centralises its global cash operations, reduces transaction costs, and optimises working capital. This approach has enabled Caterpillar to maintain financial stability and support its global expansion efforts.

Navigating **international taxation** and regulatory compliance is a complex area that requires careful management. Companies must understand different tax regimes, avoid double taxation, and ensure compliance with local laws and regulations. This may involve structuring international operations to take advantage of tax treaties, transfer pricing rules, and incentives offered by certain jurisdictions. For example, **Google** has faced scrutiny over its tax practices, particularly its use of the "Double Irish" and "Dutch Sandwich" tax structures to minimise global tax liabilities. While controversial, these strategies highlight the importance of understanding and managing international tax obligations to optimise financial performance.

In addition to currency risks, businesses must manage other financial risks associated with global operations, such as credit, interest rate, and liquidity risks. This involves implementing robust risk management frameworks, diversifying funding sources, and maintaining a strong balance sheet. **A multinational conglomerate, Siemens** has developed a comprehensive financial risk management programme that includes scenario analysis, stress testing, and contingency planning. Siemens' proactive approach enables the company to identify potential risks early and take steps to mitigate them.

Technology plays a critical role in managing financial operations in international markets. Companies can use financial management software, treasury management systems, and data analytics to gain real-time visibility into their global financial position, monitor currency movements, and optimise cash flows. **Microsoft**, for example, has invested heavily in financial technology infrastructure, allowing it to efficiently manage its complex global financial operations and quickly respond to changes in the economic environment.

Managing currency risks and financial operations in international markets requires a strategic approach that includes hedging, optimising cash management, ensuring tax compliance, mitigating financial risks, and leveraging technology. By implementing these strategies, companies can protect their profitability, maintain financial stability, and support their global expansion efforts.

11.8 Legal and Regulatory Compliance

Expanding into global markets introduces a range of **legal** and **regulatory** challenges. Companies must navigate complex international laws, regulations, and standards to ensure compliance and avoid legal risks. This section guides understanding and complying with international laws, protecting intellectual property, and managing legal risks in global operations.

Every country has a legal framework that governs business operations, including **corporate governance**, labour laws, environmental regulations, and trade practices. Companies must familiarise themselves with the legal requirements in each market they enter to ensure compliance. For example, **Volkswagen's emissions scandal** in the United States, which resulted in billions of dollars in fines and legal settlements, highlights the importance of understanding and complying with local regulations.

Protecting **intellectual property (IP)** is a critical concern for companies operating in international markets. IP laws vary significantly between countries, and businesses must take steps to secure patents, trademarks, copyrights, and trade secrets in each market to safeguard their innovations and brand assets. **Pfizer's** robust IP protection strategy involves filing patents in multiple jurisdictions and closely monitoring potential infringements. This approach has been key to protecting Pfizer's pharmaceutical innovations and maintaining its competitive advantage in global markets.

Understanding international **trade agreements** and tariffs is essential for global operations. Companies must assess the implications of trade agreements, such as NAFTA or the EU's trade policies, and adjust their strategies accordingly. Tariffs and trade barriers can affect pricing, supply chains, and market access. **Harley-Davidson**, for instance, faced challenges when the European Union imposed tariffs on American motorcycles in response to U.S. trade policies. Harley-Davidson shifted some of its production to international facilities, allowing the company to avoid tariffs and maintain competitiveness in the European market.

Compliance with **local business laws**, such as licensing requirements, antitrust regulations, and consumer protection laws, is crucial for operating legally in international markets. Companies must ensure their business practices align with local regulations to avoid fines, legal disputes, and reputational damage. **Uber**, for example, has faced numerous legal challenges related to its business model in various countries, including worker classification, safety regulations, and competition laws.

These challenges illustrate the importance of adapting business practices to meet local legal requirements.

Companies operating in international markets must also comply with **anti-corruption laws**, such as the U.S. Foreign Corrupt Practices Act (FCPA) and the UK Bribery Act. These laws prohibit bribery and other forms of corruption in business dealings and impose strict penalties for violations. Businesses must implement comprehensive compliance programmes to prevent unethical practices and ensure all employees and partners adhere to ethical standards. **After facing a major bribery scandal, Siemens** implemented a rigorous anti-corruption programme that includes extensive compliance training, internal audits, and a zero-tolerance policy for corruption. This programme has helped Siemens rebuild its reputation and ensure compliance with international anti-corruption laws.

Legal risks in global operations can arise from various factors, including contractual disputes, regulatory changes, and litigation. Companies must implement risk management strategies to identify, assess, and mitigate these risks. Seeking legal counsel, conducting regular compliance audits, and establishing contingency plans are key steps in managing legal risks. **Coca-Cola's legal risk management framework** includes close collaboration with legal experts, proactive monitoring of regulatory changes, and a comprehensive contract management process. This framework helps Coca-Cola navigate legal risks and maintain compliance across its global operations.

Legal and regulatory compliance is critical to the success of global expansion. Businesses must understand and navigate the legal landscape of each market, protect their intellectual property, comply with trade agreements, and manage legal risks. By implementing robust compliance programmes and staying informed about legal developments, companies can avoid legal pitfalls and operate successfully in international markets.

11.9 Case Studies of Successful Global Expansion

Examining case studies of companies that have successfully expanded into global markets offers valuable insights for aspiring leaders. This section explores each global venture's strategies, challenges, and outcomes, demonstrating the importance of strategic planning and adaptability in international expansion.

IKEA's Expansion into India showcases how the Swedish furniture giant successfully entered a complex and competitive market. Known for its flat-pack furniture and minimalist design, IKEA faced unique challenges in India, where consumer preference leaned towards ready-made furniture. To overcome this, IKEA adapted its business model by introducing an in-home assembly service, a departure from its usual DIY approach. The company also adjusted its product range to include smaller, space-saving furniture tailored to the needs of urban Indian households. This flexibility, coupled with IKEA's commitment to local sourcing, enabled the company to navigate India's complex regulatory environment and gain a strong foothold in the market.

Another notable example is **Netflix's Global Expansion**. The streaming giant has penetrated over 190 countries by adopting a strategy focused on local content and platform adaptation. In Spain, for instance, Netflix produced *La Casa de Papel* (Money Heist), which became a global sensation. In India, Netflix created original content like *Sacred Games*, building a loyal following. This strategy of investing in local productions and adapting its platform to local languages and payment systems has been crucial in overcoming regulatory hurdles and competing with established local players. Netflix's global success demonstrates the importance of understanding and catering to local preferences.

Toyota's Success in the United States highlights the importance of quality and reliability in capturing a new market. Competing against established American car manufacturers like Ford and General Motors, Toyota positioned itself as a leader in affordable, fuel-efficient, and low-maintenance vehicles. Models such as the Toyota Camry and Corolla became best-sellers, largely due to their appeal to American consumers who valued these attributes. Toyota also invested heavily in local manufacturing to reduce costs and avoid import tariffs, further cementing its presence in the U.S. market. This commitment to quality and customer satisfaction helped Toyota become one of the top-selling car brands in the United States.

Unilever's Expansion into Emerging Markets demonstrates the potential of local adaptation in achieving global success. The British-Dutch multinational focused on understanding the unique needs of consumers in regions such as Asia, Africa, and

Latin America. Unilever tailored its product offerings by introducing smaller, affordable sachets of products like shampoo and detergent, making them accessible to low-income consumers. The company also invested in local production facilities and distribution networks to support its growth. This strategy has boosted Unilever's sales in emerging markets and strengthened its reputation for social responsibility and sustainability.

Airbnb's Expansion into China is a case study of overcoming significant challenges in one of the world's largest and most competitive markets. With local rivals like Tujia and Xiaozhu, Airbnb adopted a localisation strategy, rebranding itself as "Aibiying," which translates to "welcome each other with love" in Mandarin. The company also partnered with local businesses and integrated popular Chinese payment systems like Alipay and WeChat Pay. Despite regulatory challenges and intense competition, Airbnb's efforts to adapt its platform and marketing to Chinese consumers have helped it establish a presence in this key market.

These case studies illustrate that successful global expansion requires a deep understanding of local markets, strategic adaptability, and a willingness to invest in long-term growth. Companies like IKEA, Netflix, Toyota, Unilever, and Airbnb have demonstrated that, with the right approach, businesses can navigate the complexities of global markets and achieve significant success.

11.10 Exiting a Market

Not all global expansion efforts result in success, and there are times when businesses must decide to exit a market. Whether due to financial losses, regulatory challenges, or changes in strategic priorities, exiting a market requires careful planning and execution to minimise losses and protect the company's reputation. This section explores strategies for withdrawing from a market and managing the impact of an exit.

Recognising the need to exit a market is the first step. Prolonged financial losses, insurmountable regulatory hurdles, or shifts in strategic focus may drive this decision. For example, **Best Buy** decided to exit the European market in 2013 after struggling to compete with local retailers and facing high operating costs. The company determined that its resources would be better allocated to strengthening its core markets in North America. This strategic withdrawal allowed Best Buy to refocus on more profitable areas of its business.

Once the decision to exit has been made, companies must develop a comprehensive **exit strategy**. This strategy should outline the steps to be taken, the timeline, and the responsibilities of key stakeholders. For instance, **Dunkin' Donuts** exited the Russian market in 2020 by gradually closing its stores, compensating employees, and ensuring all legal obligations were met. This careful planning minimised stakeholder impact and preserved the company's reputation in other markets.

Exiting a market can be costly, but businesses can take steps to **minimise financial losses**. This might involve selling off assets, negotiating with suppliers and landlords, and repatriating funds. Sometimes, companies may choose to sell their operations to a local competitor or partner. **Walgreens**, for example, sold its pharmacy operations in China to a local firm, allowing the company to recoup some of its investment and ensure a smoother exit. This approach can help businesses mitigate losses and maintain good relationships in the market.

A poorly managed exit can damage a company's brand and reputation. Businesses must communicate transparently with all stakeholders, including employees, customers, and partners, to explain the reasons for exit and the steps to mitigate its impact. When exiting the Southeast Asian market, **Uber** communicated openly about its decision to sell its operations to local competitor Grab, emphasising its strategic rationale. This transparency helped maintain trust with its global customer base and highlighted the importance of clear communication during a market exit.

Maintaining **positive relationships with stakeholders** after exiting a market can be crucial for future opportunities. Companies must ensure they fulfil all contractual obligations, treat employees fairly, and leave the market on good terms. When exiting the European market, **General Motors (GM)** worked closely with its employees, dealers, and suppliers to ensure a smooth transition and maintain positive relationships for future collaborations. This approach demonstrated GM's commitment to ethical business practices and its respect for its stakeholders.

Finally, businesses should take the time to **reflect on the reasons for the exit** and the lessons learned from the experience. This analysis can provide valuable insights that inform future global expansion efforts and help avoid similar pitfalls. For instance, **Marks & Spencer** exited several international markets in the early 2000s, including France and Germany, after struggling with profitability. The company's review of its international strategy led to a more focused and disciplined approach to global expansion in subsequent years, ensuring better outcomes in its remaining and future markets.

Exiting a market is a challenging but sometimes necessary decision. By recognising the need to exit, developing a comprehensive strategy, minimising financial losses, managing brand impact, maintaining stakeholder relationships, and learning from the experience, companies can navigate the complexities of a market exit and position themselves for future success.

Conclusion

Navigating global markets is a multi-faceted journey that requires a careful balance between seizing opportunities and mitigating challenges. As this chapter has demonstrated, the allure of international expansion comes with the need for strategic foresight, cultural sensitivity, and operational adaptability. Companies that succeed globally invest time and resources to understand local markets, adapt their products and services, and build culturally aware teams. They also leverage technology, ensure compliance with complex legal and regulatory environments, and develop robust strategies for managing financial and operational risks.

Global expansion is not a one-size-fits-all venture; each market presents its own set of opportunities and obstacles. The case studies presented in this chapter, from IKEA's careful adaptation in India to Netflix's local content strategy, illustrate that success in global markets often depends on a company's ability to adapt to local conditions while maintaining a consistent global brand identity. Equally important is knowing when to exit a market, as this decision can be as strategic as entering one.

For leaders and entrepreneurs, the path to global success is paved with continuous learning, adaptation, and innovation. As you consider your journey into global markets, the insights from this chapter should help guide you through the complexities and capitalise on the opportunities that lie ahead. With thoughtful planning and execution, your business can expand its reach and build a resilient and thriving global presence.

Chapter 12

Corporate Responsibility and Ethics: Building a Sustainable Future

12.1 – Overview

In today's complex and interconnected business world, **corporate responsibility** and **ethics** are no longer optional considerations; they have become integral to how companies operate and succeed. Businesses prioritising ethical leadership and embracing **corporate social responsibility (CSR)** contribute positively to society and the environment, build stronger brands, attract and retain top talent, and foster long-term sustainability and profitability. This chapter explores the multifaceted aspects of CSR and ethical business practices, shedding light on how these elements can be strategically integrated into business models to create value for the company and its stakeholders. By understanding these principles, future leaders and entrepreneurs can develop businesses that thrive financially and make a lasting, positive impact on the world.

12.2 - The Importance of Corporate Social Responsibility (CSR)

Corporate Social Responsibility (CSR) has emerged as a critical component of modern business strategy. Companies that embed **responsible practices** into their core operations are better positioned to navigate challenges and seize opportunities. CSR goes beyond philanthropy; it requires companies to align their strategies with societal expectations and environmental sustainability. By enhancing their brand reputation, fostering loyalty among consumers and employees, and achieving a competitive edge, businesses can see the strategic benefits of CSR that inspire and motivate future leaders and entrepreneurs.

The Role of Business in Society: Businesses wield significant influence over societal development through their products, services, and operational practices. As global issues such as **climate change**, **social inequality**, and **resource scarcity** become more urgent, businesses are increasingly expected to address these challenges proactively. Companies are now seen as pivotal players in advancing societal well-being, protecting the environment, and promoting ethical labour practices throughout their supply chains.

Long-Term Success and CSR: Implementing CSR strategies involves fulfilling moral obligations and making sound business sense. Companies that integrate CSR into their operations often experience improved financial performance. A prominent example is **Patagonia**, which has built its brand on a commitment to environmental sustainability. This focus has secured a loyal customer base and positioned Patagonia as a leader in sustainable business practices, driving growth and profitability. Similarly, companies like TOMS, which donates a pair of shoes for every pair sold, and Microsoft, which invests in education and digital inclusion, are also successful examples of CSR in action.

The Shift from Shareholder to Stakeholder Capitalism: The traditional focus on **maximising shareholder value** is evolving towards a broader **stakeholder capitalism** model, where businesses consider the interests of all stakeholders, including employees, customers, suppliers, and the communities they operate in. This shift reflects a growing recognition that long-term business success is intertwined with the health and stability of the broader society and environment. Companies like **IKEA** and **Unilever** exemplify this approach by integrating social and environmental goals into their business strategies.

Impact on Brand and Reputation: Engaging in CSR can significantly enhance a company's **brand** and **reputation**. Consumers today are more inclined to support brands aligning with their values. Similarly, employees are more likely to be engaged and committed to companies that are committed to ethical practices. For instance, **Unilever** has embedded sustainability into its core strategy through its Sustainable Living Plan, which aims to reduce its environmental impact while increasing its social contribution. This has strengthened its brand and contributed to its global success.

The Business Case for CSR: While the ethical imperatives of CSR are clear, the business case is equally compelling. Companies investing in CSR initiatives can save costs through improved **energy efficiency**, reduced waste, and better resource management. Additionally, CSR can drive **innovation** as businesses develop new products and services that address social and environmental challenges. **Tesla** is a prime example of a company whose commitment to renewable energy and electric vehicles has driven its growth and reshaped the automotive industry.

In conclusion, **CSR** is both a moral responsibility and a business strategic opportunity. Companies embracing CSR can create shared value, meaning societal and business needs are interdependent. By addressing societal issues through their core business activities, companies can enhance their reputations and ensure long-term success. The transition towards stakeholder capitalism highlights the need for businesses to evaluate the broader impacts of their actions on society and the environment.

12.3 - Ethical Leadership

Ethical leadership is not just a concept but a powerful tool for fostering a culture of integrity and responsibility within an organisation. Leaders set the tone for their company's values and behaviours, influencing how employees make decisions and interact with stakeholders. Ethical leadership, which extends beyond compliance with laws and regulations, involves doing what is right, even in difficult choices. This reassures the audience of the positive impact of ethical leadership, instilling confidence in its effectiveness.

Setting the Tone from the Top: The behaviour and values of a company's leadership have a profound impact on its ethical culture. Leaders who demonstrate integrity, **transparency**, and a strong commitment to ethical principles inspire their teams to uphold these values. For instance, ethical leadership was crucial during the Tylenol crisis in 1982 when Johnson & Johnson prioritised customer safety over financial losses by recalling millions of bottles of Tylenol. This decision, though costly, ultimately reinforced the company's reputation and consumer trust.

Navigating Ethical Dilemmas: Leaders frequently encounter complex ethical dilemmas where competing interests must be balanced. Ethical decision-making requires considering the long-term implications of actions and prioritising the greater good over short-term gains. A well-known example is Merck's decision to distribute Mectizan for free to combat river blindness in developing countries despite no immediate financial benefit. This decision, driven by a commitment to social good, has had a lasting positive impact on millions of lives.

The Role of Values in Ethical Leadership: Ethical leadership is not just about making decisions but about being guided by a clear and consistent set of values, such as integrity, fairness, and respect. Leaders must ensure these values are not just words on a page but are integrated into the company's policies and practices. Companies like Starbucks are known for their commitment to ethical sourcing and community involvement, values consistently reinforced by their leadership and reflected in their business practices. This stress on the role of values in ethical leadership inspires the audience and provides a clear guide for their future actions.

Building an Ethical Culture: Cultivating an ethical culture involves more than just implementing policies. It requires creating an environment where employees feel empowered to voice concerns, where ethical behaviour is rewarded, and where there is a genuine commitment to doing what is right. **Salesforce** exemplifies this approach by promoting a culture of trust, transparency, and equality, encouraging employees to act ethically and responsibly.

Challenges of Ethical Leadership: Ethical leadership is not without its challenges. Leaders may face pressure to compromise on ethical standards for short-term gains or encounter resistance from stakeholders prioritising profit over integrity. Overcoming these challenges requires courage and a steadfast commitment to ethical principles. For instance, when Kenneth Frazier, CEO of Merck, resigned from President Trump's manufacturing council in 2017 in protest of the President's response to the violence in Charlottesville, his decision, guided by his ethical convictions, demonstrated the importance of standing by one's values despite potential backlash. Other challenges include navigating cultural differences in global operations, managing conflicts of interest, and balancing the needs of various stakeholders.

Ethical **leadership** is crucial for building a sustainable and respected business. By setting an ethical tone, navigating dilemmas with integrity, and fostering an ethical culture, leaders can ensure that their organisations remain aligned with their values and societal responsibilities.

12.4 - Sustainability Practices

Sustainability is a cornerstone of corporate responsibility, focusing on the long-term impact of business activities on the environment and society. As awareness of environmental issues grows, companies are increasingly expected to adopt sustainable practices that reduce their **carbon footprint**, conserve resources, and promote environmental stewardship.

The Business Case for Sustainability: Embracing sustainability benefits the environment and business performance. Companies prioritising sustainability can reduce costs, enhance their brand reputation, and drive innovation. For example, **IKEA** has integrated sustainability into its core business strategy, using renewable energy, responsibly sourcing materials, and designing products that can be easily recycled. This focus has helped IKEA attract eco-conscious consumers and position itself as a leader in sustainable retail.

Strategies for Reducing Carbon Footprint: Reducing a company's carbon footprint is a key aspect of sustainability. Businesses can achieve this by adopting energy-efficient technologies, switching to renewable energy, and improving supply chain efficiency. **Google**, for instance, has achieved carbon neutrality through investments in renewable energy and energy-efficient practices across its data centres and offices. This commitment has not only benefited the environment but has also enhanced Google's brand as a sustainable company.

Promoting Circular Economy Practices: The circular economy challenges the traditional linear model of production and consumption. Companies can promote sustainability and resource efficiency by designing products that are easier to repair, recycle, or refurbish. **Dell** has implemented circular economy practices by incorporating recycled materials into its products and offering recycling programs for its electronics. This focus on sustainability has reduced waste and opened new business opportunities.

Sustainability Reporting and Accountability: Transparency is essential to sustainability efforts. Companies must report their environmental impact and progress towards sustainability goals through recognised frameworks such as the Global Reporting Initiative (GRI). **Unilever** has been a leader in sustainability reporting, providing detailed information on its environmental and social performance. This transparency has built trust with stakeholders and demonstrated Unilever's commitment to sustainability.

Examples of Companies Leading in Sustainability: Many companies have set high standards for sustainability. **Patagonia**, for instance, is renowned for its commitment to environmental and social responsibility. It uses recycled materials in its products, donates a portion of its sales to environmental causes, and encourages customers to repair and reuse their clothing. Similarly, **Tesla** has revolutionised the automotive industry with its focus on electric vehicles and renewable energy, driving growth and establishing itself as a leader in transitioning to a low-carbon economy.

Sustainability is essential to corporate responsibility, benefiting both businesses and the environment. By adopting sustainable practices, companies can reduce their environmental impact, drive innovation, and build a strong, positive brand reputation.

12.5 - Social Impact

Corporate social responsibility extends beyond environmental sustainability to encompass a company's broader social impact. Businesses can create positive change through **philanthropy**, community engagement, and inclusive business practices. This section explores how companies can maximise their social impact and contribute to society's well-being.

The Role of Business in Society: Companies play a crucial role in the communities they serve and are responsible for contributing positively to society. This includes addressing social challenges, supporting local economies, and promoting social equity. Companies that actively work to improve society can build stronger relationships with stakeholders and enhance their brand reputation. **Ben & Jerry's** is an example of a company that has consistently aligned its business practices with social values, advocating for social justice and environmental sustainability.

Philanthropy and Corporate Giving: Philanthropy is one of the most direct ways companies make a positive social impact. Corporate giving can include donations to charities, sponsorship of community projects, or support of employee volunteer programs. **Through its Philanthropies program, Microsoft** provides grants, software donations, and technology training to underserved communities, demonstrating its commitment to social responsibility and community engagement.

Community Engagement and Development: Beyond philanthropy, businesses can engage with local communities to support economic development, education, and health. Community engagement involves working closely with local stakeholders to identify challenges and develop initiatives to address them. **Nestlé** has implemented its Creating Shared Value (CSV) approach, which focuses on improving the well-being of the communities where it operates through initiatives like providing clean water and supporting local farmers.

Inclusive Business Practices: Inclusive business practices create opportunities for underserved or marginalised groups, promoting social mobility and economic inclusion. **Grameen Bank** has pioneered such practices by offering microloans to low-income individuals, particularly women in developing countries. This approach has empowered millions to start businesses and improve their livelihoods, demonstrating the power of inclusive business models.

Measuring Social Impact: To ensure the effectiveness of their social impact initiatives, companies must measure and report on their outcomes. This involves setting clear goals, tracking progress, and evaluating the impact of their efforts. **The Body Shop** has implemented a robust system for measuring its social impact, focusing on human rights, fair trade, and environmental sustainability. This transparency has built trust with stakeholders and reinforced its commitment to social responsibility.

By maximising their social impact, businesses can contribute to societal well-being and build stronger, more resilient organisations.

12.6 - Stakeholder Engagement

Effective stakeholder engagement is essential for balancing the diverse interests of customers, employees, investors, and the community. It involves understanding stakeholder needs, building trust, and fostering collaboration to achieve mutual goals. This section explores strategies for engaging with stakeholders in a way that promotes transparency, accountability, and long-term success.

The Importance of Stakeholder Engagement: In today's interconnected world, businesses are accountable not only to their shareholders but also to a broader range of stakeholders, including employees, customers, suppliers, and the communities they operate in. Engaging with these stakeholders is crucial for building trust, managing risks, and aligning business practices with societal expectations. **Nestlé**, with its Creating Shared Value approach, actively engages stakeholders to address social and environmental challenges while driving business success.

Strategies for Effective Stakeholder Engagement: Effective stakeholder engagement requires a strategic approach that includes identifying key stakeholders, understanding their needs and concerns, and establishing open communication channels. Companies like **Unilever** have implemented comprehensive stakeholder engagement strategies involving regular consultations with various stakeholders, including NGOs, governments, and consumers. This engagement has strengthened relationships and built trust.

Balancing Competing Interests: Balancing the competing interests of different stakeholder groups can be challenging. For example, investors' needs for financial returns may conflict with employees' interests in fair wages. Ethical leaders must navigate these competing interests by making decisions considering the long-term impact on all stakeholders. **Patagonia** has successfully balanced stakeholder interests by prioritising environmental sustainability and social responsibility, demonstrating that achieving social and economic goals is possible.

Stakeholder Communication and Transparency: Transparency is key to effective stakeholder engagement. Companies must communicate openly and honestly with stakeholders about their goals, challenges, and progress. **Starbucks** regularly publishes reports on its sustainability initiatives and community engagement efforts, demonstrating its commitment to transparency and reinforcing its reputation as a socially responsible company.

Building Long-Term Relationships: Building strong, long-term relationships with stakeholders requires ongoing dialogue, collaboration, and partnership. **Toyota** has fostered long-term partnerships with its suppliers, employees, and communities, emphasising mutual respect and continuous improvement. This approach has helped Toyota build a resilient and sustainable business.

Stakeholder engagement is crucial for building trust, managing risks, and achieving long-term success. Businesses can effectively engage stakeholders to align their practices with societal expectations and create shared value.

12.7 - Transparency and Reporting

Transparency and reporting are fundamental to corporate social responsibility. They enable businesses to build trust with their stakeholders and demonstrate accountability for their social and environmental impact. This section delves into the importance of transparency in CSR efforts and guides effective reporting of CSR activities and outcomes.

The Role of Transparency in CSR: Transparency forms the foundation of trust between a company and its stakeholders. By being open about CSR initiatives, companies provide stakeholders with the information they need to evaluate the company's performance and make informed decisions. **Danone** regularly publishes detailed reports on its sustainability efforts, covering environmental impact and social initiatives. This commitment to transparency has strengthened its reputation and built a solid relationship of trust with stakeholders.

Reporting CSR Activities and Outcomes: Effective CSR reporting involves more than just listing activities; it requires providing meaningful data on the impact of those activities and progress towards set goals. **Marks & Spencer** is recognised for its comprehensive CSR reporting, detailing its Plan A sustainability programme, which covers a wide range of social and environmental metrics. This transparency helps stakeholders understand the company's efforts and areas for improvement.

Ensuring Honesty and Impact in Reporting: Companies should provide balanced and accurate information to avoid "greenwashing", the practice of exaggerating or misrepresenting CSR achievements. **Novo Nordisk** has been commended for its transparent and honest reporting on sustainability efforts, including third-party verification of its data. This approach enhances credibility and builds trust with stakeholders.

Using Reporting Frameworks and Standards: Adopting frameworks such as the Global Reporting Initiative (GRI) or the Sustainability Accounting Standards Board (SASB) ensures consistency and comparability in CSR reporting. **L'Oréal** uses the GRI framework to provide stakeholders with a comprehensive and standardised view of its CSR performance, aligning its reporting with industry best practices.

The Benefits of Transparent Reporting: Transparent CSR reporting brings numerous benefits, including enhanced reputation, strengthened stakeholder relationships, and positive financial performance. Companies like **Microsoft** and **Procter & Gamble** have seen positive impacts on their brand reputation and investor relations through transparent reporting on their social and environmental impact.

By adopting transparent and honest reporting practices, companies can build trust, demonstrate accountability, and enhance their reputation as responsible corporate citizens.

12.8 - Ethical Supply Chain Management

Ethical supply chain management ensures fairness, sustainability, and integrity throughout the supply chain. As global supply chains become more complex, companies must actively manage risks, vet suppliers carefully, and ensure alignment with their ethical standards.

The Importance of Ethical Supply Chains: A company's supply chain reflects its values and commitment to ethical business practices. Ensuring suppliers operate responsibly is vital for protecting a company's reputation and mitigating risks. **Apple**, for example, has developed a Supplier Code of Conduct and regularly audits its suppliers to ensure compliance with its ethical standards.

Vetting Suppliers and Managing Risks: Vetting suppliers involves conducting due diligence on labour practices, environmental impact, and regulatory compliance. **Nike**, which faced criticism in the 1990s for unethical labour practices, has since developed a rigorous supplier vetting process and established a Code of Conduct outlining its requirements for fair labour practices and environmental responsibility.

Promoting Sustainability in the Supply Chain: Businesses must work with suppliers to minimise environmental impact. **Unilever** has implemented the Sustainable Agriculture Code, which sets strict standards for sustainable farming practices across its supply chain. This collaboration has enhanced

Unilever's environmental performance and reduced its overall impact.

Building Strong Supplier Relationships: Strong supplier relationships are essential for ethical supply chain management. **Walmart** has developed long-term partnerships with its suppliers through its Sustainability Index, measuring products' environmental and social impact throughout the supply chain. This approach has improved sustainability practices and fostered a more responsible supply chain.

Transparency and Accountability in the Supply Chain is key to ethical supply chain management. Companies should share information about their supply chain practices, including supplier locations and audit results. **Patagonia** provides detailed information about its suppliers, demonstrating its commitment to transparency and ethical business practices.

Ethical supply chain management is crucial for building a responsible and sustainable business. By vetting suppliers, promoting sustainability, and fostering transparency, companies can ensure their supply chains reflect their ethical values.

12.9 - Crisis Management and Ethical Dilemmas

Crisis management and ethical dilemmas are inevitable challenges for businesses. Handling these situations can significantly impact a company's reputation and success. This section examines strategies for managing crises while maintaining ethical standards, with case studies of companies facing and overcoming ethical challenges.

The Role of Ethics in Crisis Management: During a crisis, the pressure to act quickly can sometimes lead to ethical lapses. However, maintaining ethical standards is crucial for preserving a company's reputation and stakeholder trust. For example, during the Tylenol crisis in 1982, **Johnson & Johnson** prioritised consumer safety over financial losses by recalling millions of bottles of Tylenol. This decision reinforced its reputation and demonstrated the importance of ethical crisis management.

Navigating Ethical Dilemmas: Ethical dilemmas occur when conflicting values or interests complicate determining the best action. For example, **Volkswagen** faced a significant ethical dilemma when it was discovered that the company had installed software to cheat emissions tests. This decision, driven by a desire to meet regulatory standards without compromising performance, led to a global scandal, highlighting the importance of making ethical decisions even when faced with difficult trade-offs.

Strategies for Ethical Crisis Management: To manage a crisis ethically, companies should adopt transparency, take responsibility, and prioritise stakeholders. **BP**'s response to the Deepwater Horizon oil spill in 2010 was criticised for a lack of transparency, which harmed its reputation. In contrast, **Toyota**'s proactive approach during its 2010 recall crisis helped restore consumer confidence.

Case Studies of Ethical Crisis Management: Companies like **Starbucks** and **Samsung** have effectively managed crises while upholding ethical standards. Starbucks addressed accusations of racial profiling with transparency and commitment to improvement, while Samsung prioritised consumer safety during the Galaxy Note 7 crisis, conducting a thorough investigation and recalling affected devices.

Managing crises ethically is essential for preserving reputation and stakeholder trust. Companies can navigate crises effectively and uphold ethical standards by maintaining transparency, taking responsibility, and prioritising stakeholders.

12.10 - Conclusion

Corporate responsibility and ethics are essential for businesses to thrive in today's complex, interconnected world. Companies can build financially successful, socially responsible, and environmentally sustainable businesses by embracing corporate social responsibility, fostering ethical leadership, adopting sustainable practices, engaging with stakeholders, and managing crises with integrity.

Throughout this chapter, we have explored the significance of CSR, the role of ethical leadership, the importance of sustainability practices, and the need for effective stakeholder engagement. We have also examined strategies for managing ethical supply chains and navigating crises with integrity. The case studies demonstrate that companies can rise to these challenges and emerge stronger by committing to ethical and responsible business practices.

In an increasingly interconnected world, businesses must recognise their impact on society and the environment. By doing so, they can build resilient, trustworthy, and sustainable businesses that contribute positively to the global community.

Chapter 13

Risk Management: Anticipating and Mitigating Threats

13.1 Overview

Risk management is essential for organisations aiming for **long-term success** in today's unpredictable business landscape. The ability to **anticipate, assess, and mitigate risks** is crucial in determining whether a business can thrive in a competitive market or fall victim to unforeseen challenges. This chapter provides a comprehensive guide to understanding and managing various business risks. Covering aspects such as **financial risks**, **operational disruptions**, **reputational threats**, and **crisis management**, it offers tools and strategies designed to safeguard businesses from potential threats. Through practical insights and real-world case studies, readers will gain the knowledge needed to build a robust risk management framework that protects the business and enhances its **resilience** and **agility** in uncertainty.

13.2 Understanding Risk Management

Risk management is a structured process involving identifying, assessing, and prioritising risks, followed by coordinated efforts to reduce, monitor, and control the impact of these risks. It enables organisations to make informed decisions that protect the business while allowing them to take advantage of opportunities that carry some risk. Companies face various risks: strategic, operational, financial, compliance, and reputational. **Strategic risks** arise from external factors affecting a business's direction, such as market conditions or technological advancements. **Operational risks** involve internal processes and systems, including supply chain disruptions and equipment failures. **Financial risks** relate to market fluctuations, credit challenges, or foreign exchange volatility. **Compliance risks** emerge from failing to meet legal or regulatory obligations, while **reputational risks** are associated with negative perceptions that can damage customer trust.

Anticipating risks is crucial for ensuring **business continuity** and long-term success. By identifying potential threats early, organisations can devise strategies to mitigate them before they materialise, significantly reducing the likelihood of negative outcomes. This forward-looking approach helps businesses navigate uncertainty with greater confidence and control, ultimately positioning them for sustained success.

13.3 Identifying Risks

Identifying risks is the most critical step in effective **risk management**. Without a clear understanding of potential threats, businesses cannot develop appropriate mitigation strategies. Various tools and techniques, such as **risk assessments**, **audits**, and **scenario planning**, are used to identify risks comprehensively. **Risk assessments** involve systematically identifying and evaluating potential risks by gathering information about a business's operations and objectives. **Internal or external audits** thoroughly examine a company's processes, systems, and controls, highlighting potential vulnerabilities. **Scenario planning** involves creating hypothetical situations based on identified risks and analysing how the business would respond to them. This technique is particularly useful for preparing for **strategic** and **operational** risks, such as economic downturns, supply chain disruptions, or regulatory changes.

Engaging the entire organisation in risk identification is also essential. Involving employees at all levels ensures a broader range of risks is identified and fosters an organisational culture attuned to potential threats. Leaders should promote a **risk-aware culture** where employees feel empowered to speak up about risks they encounter daily. This can be achieved through regular training, open communication, and a commitment to transparency.

For example, a retail company might conduct a risk assessment of its supply chain by involving procurement, logistics, and operations employees. The company can identify risks such as dependency on a single supplier, transportation delays, and fluctuating raw material costs. With this comprehensive understanding, the business can develop strategies to diversify suppliers, improve inventory management, and negotiate better contracts, reducing overall risk exposure.

In summary, identifying risks requires a systematic approach and the involvement of the entire organisation. Utilising risk assessments, audits, and scenario planning allows businesses to address potential threats and take steps to mitigate them proactively.

13.4 Assessing Risks

Once risks have been identified, the next step is to **assess** them. Risk assessment involves evaluating each identified risk's potential **impact** and **likelihood**, enabling businesses to prioritise efforts and allocate resources effectively. This process can be approached from both **quantitative** and **qualitative** perspectives.

Quantitative risk assessment uses numerical data and statistical models to evaluate risks, particularly for financial and operational threats. For example, a company might use a value-at-risk (VaR) model to estimate potential losses under different market conditions. In contrast, **qualitative risk assessment** relies on subjective criteria such as expert judgment and intuition to evaluate risks, often using a risk matrix to assess the severity and likelihood of reputational or compliance risks.

After assessing the risks, businesses must prioritise them based on their potential impact and likelihood. This prioritisation helps focus on managing the most critical threats. **High-impact, high-likelihood risks** should be addressed immediately, while **low-impact, low-likelihood risks** may require less attention. A practical tool for this process is a **risk matrix**, which plots risks on a grid according to their impact and likelihood, assigning a score or rank to each risk.

For instance, a manufacturing company might identify risks such as supply chain disruptions, equipment failures, and regulatory changes. Quantitative analysis might show that equipment failures have a high potential impact but a low likelihood, whereas supply chain disruptions have a moderate impact but a higher likelihood. Based on this assessment, the company would prioritise managing supply chain disruptions, followed by equipment failures and regulatory changes.

In conclusion, risk assessment is a crucial step that enables businesses to evaluate each risk's potential impact and likelihood. By using quantitative and qualitative methods and effectively prioritising risks, organisations can allocate resources to mitigate the most critical threats and safeguard their operations.

13.5 Strategies for Risk Mitigation

After identifying and assessing risks, businesses must develop strategies to **mitigate** them. Risk mitigation involves taking proactive steps to reduce the likelihood or impact of identified risks, ensuring the organisation is better prepared to manage potential threats. Various strategies, such as **prevention**, **reduction**, **transfer**, and **avoidance**, can be employed depending on the nature of the risk.

Prevention strategies aim to eliminate or avoid risks before they materialise. For example, a financial services firm might implement **advanced cybersecurity measures** like firewalls, encryption, and multi-factor authentication to prevent data breaches. By addressing vulnerabilities proactively, the firm significantly reduces the likelihood of a cyberattack and protects sensitive customer data.

Reduction strategies focus on minimising the impact of risks that cannot be entirely prevented. A manufacturing company, for instance, might invest in **backup generators** and redundant systems to mitigate the impact of power outages. Although the risk of power outages cannot be eliminated, these measures ensure that operations can continue with minimal disruption.

Transfer strategies involve shifting the financial burden of a risk to a third party, typically through insurance or outsourcing. For example, a construction company may purchase **liability insurance** to cover potential accidents on the job site. By transferring this risk to an insurance provider, the company can shield itself from the financial repercussions of accidents or claims.

In some cases, **avoidance strategies** are the best option, involving decisions that eliminate the risk by not engaging in activities that create it. For instance, a business may choose not to enter a new market if the political or economic risks are too high. By avoiding the market entirely, the business eliminates the potential for financial loss due to instability.

Case studies provide valuable insights into effective risk mitigation. For example, Toyota's **lean manufacturing system** incorporates risk mitigation strategies such as just-in-time (JIT) inventory management and continuous improvement (Kaizen).

These practices enable Toyota to reduce operational risks and enhance its ability to respond to supply chain disruptions. Similarly, Coca-Cola has faced operational and reputational risks regarding water usage in regions with water scarcity. The company implemented a comprehensive water stewardship program to address these risks, including reducing water use, improving efficiency, and replenishing water in local communities.

In summary, risk mitigation is a crucial component of risk management. By employing strategies such as prevention, reduction, transfer, and avoidance, businesses can reduce their exposure to potential threats. Real-world examples from companies like Toyota and Coca-Cola demonstrate how effective mitigation strategies contribute to long-term success and resilience.

13.6 Financial Risks

Financial risks pose some of the most significant threats to a business, directly impacting its financial health and sustainability. These risks include **market fluctuations**, **credit risk**, and **liquidity challenges**. Managing these risks requires a deep understanding of the financial landscape and the implementation of effective strategies to maintain financial stability during uncertain times.

Market risk refers to the potential for financial loss due to changes in market conditions such as interest rates, currency exchange rates, or stock prices. For instance, a company that relies heavily on exports might face increased costs if its local currency strengthens, making its products more expensive for foreign buyers. **Credit risk** arises when a borrower or counterparty fails to meet their financial obligations, particularly relevant for businesses extending credit to customers. A supplier, for example, may face credit risk if a major customer defaults on payment.

Liquidity risk occurs when a business cannot meet short-term financial obligations due to a lack of cash or liquid assets. This situation might arise if the company experiences a sudden revenue drop or an unexpected expense increase. **Interest rate risk** involves fluctuations in interest rates that can affect borrowing costs or the return on investments. For example, a company with variable-rate debt may face higher interest expenses if rates rise unexpectedly.

Businesses can employ several strategies to manage these financial risks. Hedging involves using financial instruments like derivatives to offset potential losses from market fluctuations. For instance, a company might use currency futures to hedge against exchange rate risks that could affect its international revenue. **Diversification** spreads investments or business activities across different markets, sectors, or asset classes to reduce exposure to a single risk. For instance, a company might diversify its product line or invest in different geographic markets to mitigate the impact of downturns in any area.

Maintaining **adequate liquidity** is crucial for managing liquidity risk. Businesses can achieve this by maintaining healthy cash reserves, securing lines of credit, or closely managing working capital. To manage **credit risk**, businesses should implement strict credit policies, conduct thorough credit assessments, and regularly monitor outstanding receivables. Interest rate risk can be mitigated using fixed-rate debt to lock in borrowing costs or employing interest rate swaps.

A case study of General Electric (GE) illustrates effective financial risk management. During the 2008 financial crisis, GE faced significant risks within its financial services division, GE Capital. To manage these risks, GE reduced its reliance on GE Capital, increased liquidity, and diversified its business portfolio. The company also used **hedging strategies** to manage currency and interest rate risks, helping stabilise its financial position during the crisis.

Managing financial risks is critical to a business's long-term sustainability. Hedging, diversifying, and maintaining liquidity can safeguard a business's financial health even in uncertain times.

13.7 Operational Risks

Operational risks are inherent to any business's day-to-day functioning. They can arise from **process inefficiencies**, **technology failures**, **supply chain disruptions**, or **human errors**. Managing these risks effectively is crucial for ensuring smooth operations and maintaining business continuity.

Process inefficiencies are often the result of delays or errors in production, logistics, or service delivery, leading to increased costs and reduced productivity. For example, a poorly managed production line can result in defective products, waste, and customer dissatisfaction. **Technology failures**, including system outages, software bugs, and cybersecurity threats, are another significant source of operational risk. A cyberattack, for instance, could disrupt operations and compromise sensitive data, severely impacting business functions.

Supply chain disruptions are a common operational risk resulting from natural disasters, transportation delays, or supplier failures. They can lead to shortages, increased costs, and production delays. Human **errors**, such as incorrect data entry, miscommunication, or accidents, can have serious consequences, particularly in healthcare, manufacturing, and finance industries.

Businesses should focus on process optimisation, technology risk management, and supply chain resilience to manage these risks. Process optimisation involves regularly reviewing and improving workflows to reduce inefficiencies. This can be achieved through **automation**, **lean management principles**, and **process mapping tools** to identify and eliminate bottlenecks. To manage **technology risks**, businesses should invest in a robust IT infrastructure, conduct regular audits, and implement strong cybersecurity measures. Backup systems and **disaster recovery plans** are essential for ensuring continuity in a system failure.

Building a **resilient supply chain** is also critical. This requires diversifying suppliers, maintaining safety stock, and developing contingency plans for potential disruptions. Strong relationships with key suppliers can also help mitigate risks. For example, a company might create a **business continuity plan (BCP)** that outlines how operations will continue during disruptions. This plan should identify critical functions, processes, and resources necessary to maintain these functions in a crisis.

Toyota is a prime example of effective operational risk management. The company's approach includes optimising processes, building supply chain resilience, and investing in workforce training. Toyota's **just-in-time (JIT)** inventory system reduces waste while ensuring a stable supply chain and its strong relationships with suppliers ensure efficient production flow.

In summary, managing operational risks is essential for maintaining efficient business operations. By optimising processes, managing technology risks, and building supply chain resilience, businesses can reduce the likelihood and impact of operational disruptions, ensuring smoother and more efficient operations.

13.8 Reputational Risks

Reputational risk arises when negative publicity, customer complaints, regulatory violations, or unethical behaviour damage a company's reputation. A tarnished reputation can have far-reaching consequences, affecting **customer trust**, **investor confidence**, and **employee morale**. Safeguarding a company's reputation is essential for maintaining its competitive position and long-term success.

Several sources contribute to reputational risks, including **negative publicity**, **customer complaints**, **regulatory violations**, and **unethical behaviour**. Negative media coverage, for example, can damage a company's reputation, whether the criticism is warranted or not. This might result from product recalls, environmental incidents, or legal disputes. Similarly, poor product quality or service can lead to customer dissatisfaction, resulting in negative word-of-mouth or online reviews that can quickly go viral.

Regulatory violations can also pose significant reputational risks. Failing to comply with legal or regulatory requirements can lead to fines, legal action, and damage to a company's public image. For example, a company using unethical labour practices might face public backlash and regulatory scrutiny. Unethical behaviour, including fraud, corruption, or discrimination, can severely impact a company's reputation. Customers, employees, and investors expect companies to operate with integrity, and breaches of ethical standards can result in a significant loss of trust.

To manage reputational risks effectively, businesses should engage in **proactive reputation management** and be prepared for crises with a clear communication plan. Proactive reputation management involves regular monitoring of public perception, media coverage, and online sentiment. Early identification of potential reputational risks allows businesses to take corrective action before issues escalate. **Crisis communication** is also crucial in managing public perception during a reputational crisis. This requires transparency, responsibility, and clear communication with stakeholders.

Building a strong corporate culture prioritising ethical behaviour, transparency, and accountability is another effective strategy for managing reputational risks. Encouraging employees to uphold ethical standards and report concerns is vital to this approach. Regular engagement with stakeholders, including customers, employees, investors, and the community, also helps build trust and manage reputational risks.

A notable example of effective crisis management is Johnson & Johnson's response to the **Tylenol crisis** 1982. After several people died from cyanide-laced Tylenol capsules, the company prioritised customer safety over financial loss by recalling 31 million bottles of Tylenol. Although costly, this decision demonstrated Johnson & Johnson's commitment to its customers and helped rebuild trust in the brand.

Rebuilding a damaged reputation requires a long-term commitment to **transparency**, **accountability**, and continuous improvement. Businesses should publicly acknowledge any mistakes or wrongdoing, take corrective actions to address the cause of the issue, and engage in open communication with stakeholders. This approach helps rebuild trust and demonstrates a commitment to ethical and responsible business practices.

In conclusion, reputational risks can significantly impact a business, affecting customer trust, investor confidence, and employee morale. However, companies can protect and enhance their reputations by proactively managing public perception, fostering a strong corporate culture, and responding effectively during crises. Johnson & Johnson's response to the Tylenol crisis illustrates the importance of transparency and accountability in managing reputational risks.

13.9 Crisis Management Planning

Crisis management planning is essential for preparing for unexpected events that could disrupt business operations, damage a company's reputation, or threaten financial stability. A well-developed crisis management plan (CMP) ensures businesses can respond effectively to crises, minimising damage and maintaining continuity. Preparing for unexpected events requires a structured approach that includes **risk assessment**, scenario planning, and developing response strategies.

A CMP should establish a **crisis management team (CMT)** comprising representatives from key operations, communications, legal, HR, and IT departments. Each member must have a clear role during a crisis to ensure coordinated and effective action. **Risk assessment** is another critical component of the CMP, involving the identification of potential crises such as natural disasters, cyber-attacks, or product recalls. **Scenario planning** helps develop detailed response plans that outline necessary steps, resources required, and the roles of the CMT.

Effective **crisis communication** is vital during any crisis. The CMP should include a communication plan that specifies how information will be relayed to stakeholders such as employees, customers, investors, and the media. Identifying key messages, communication channels, and spokespersons ensures consistent and transparent communication. A **business continuity plan (BCP)** is also crucial for outlining how a business will continue operations during and after a crisis. The BCP should identify critical functions and processes and provide instructions for maintaining these functions during disruptions.

Conducting regular drills and simulations is essential to ensure the CMP's effectiveness. These exercises allow the CMT to practice their roles and identify gaps in the plan. **Tabletop exercises** are discussion-based simulations that enable the CMT to walk through crisis response procedures in a low-pressure environment. **On the other hand, full-scale drills** simulate a crisis in real-time, involving active participation from employees and stakeholders.

The CMP should be regularly reviewed and updated to reflect changes in the business environment, organisational structure, or potential risks. Updating contact information, revising procedures, or incorporating new technologies ensures the CMP remains relevant and effective.

An excellent example of effective crisis management is Starbucks' response to the **2018 incident** involving the arrest of two Black men at a Philadelphia store. The incident led to widespread accusations of racial profiling. Starbucks responded by activating its CMP, which included public apologies, company-wide closures for racial bias training, and community dialogue.

The company's swift and transparent response helped manage the crisis effectively and rebuild customer trust.

In conclusion, crisis management planning ensures businesses can respond effectively to unexpected events. By developing a comprehensive CMP, conducting regular drills, and continuously reviewing and updating the plan, businesses can minimise the impact of crises and maintain continuity. Starbucks' response to the 2018 incident highlights the importance of a robust CMP in managing and recovering from crises.

13.10 Insurance and Risk Transfer

Insurance is a vital tool for transferring risk and protecting businesses from the financial impact of unexpected events. While not all risks can be eliminated, insurance allows companies to transfer the financial burden to a third party, ensuring they can recover from losses and continue operations. Insurance is particularly useful for managing risks with a low likelihood but high potential impact, such as natural disasters or major property damage.

Several types of insurance coverage are essential for businesses. **Property insurance** covers physical assets like buildings, equipment, and inventory against risks such as fire, theft, or natural disasters. **Liability insurance** protects businesses from legal liabilities arising from accidents, injuries, or damages caused to third parties. **Business interruption insurance** covers loss of income and additional expenses incurred when a business cannot operate due to a covered event, helping maintain cash flow during downtime. In today's digital world,

cyber insurance has become critical, covering losses related to cyberattacks, data breaches, and other digital risks.

Selecting the right insurance policies requires careful consideration. Businesses should begin by assessing their risks, considering the nature of their operations, the value of their assets, and potential legal liabilities. Working with a trusted **insurance broker** can provide expert advice and help businesses find policies that best meet their needs. Regularly reviewing policies and updating coverage ensures the business is protected as its operations evolve.

A construction industry case study highlights insurance's role in managing risks. Construction companies often rely on a combination of insurance and risk transfer agreements to protect themselves from various risks, such as job site accidents or project delays. For example, a company might purchase general liability insurance while requiring subcontractors to carry their liability insurance, effectively distributing the risk.

In conclusion, insurance is a critical tool for transferring risk and protecting businesses from the financial impact of unexpected events. By selecting the appropriate coverage and working with a trusted broker, businesses can ensure they are adequately protected from various risks. The construction industry example highlights the importance of a comprehensive risk management approach that includes insurance and contractual risk transfer agreements.

13.11 Case Studies in Effective Risk Management

Real-world case studies offer valuable insights into how businesses successfully manage risks and navigate challenges. These examples illustrate the importance of proactive risk management and provide lessons that aspiring leaders and entrepreneurs can apply in their organisations.

Apple's **supply chain risk management** is an excellent example of effective risk management. With a global supply chain that involves numerous suppliers and manufacturers across various countries, Apple faces significant supply chain risks, such as disruptions from natural disasters, geopolitical events, and supplier failures. To mitigate these risks, Apple has diversified its suppliers, maintained strong relationships, and engaged in scenario planning to develop contingency plans.

JPMorgan Chase, one of the world's largest financial institutions, faces various financial risks. The company's approach to **financial risk management** includes a strong risk governance structure, advanced risk modelling techniques, and strict credit risk management practices. By adopting a proactive and disciplined approach to risk management, JPMorgan Chase has successfully navigated financial market volatility.

Toyota's response to the **2011 Tohoku Earthquake** in Japan is another compelling case study. The disaster caused significant disruptions to Toyota's supply chain and production facilities. However, Toyota's rapid crisis response, supply chain resilience, and business continuity planning allowed the company to recover quickly and resume operations. Toyota's experience underscores the importance of preparedness and resilience in managing operational risks.

Unilever's approach to **reputational risk management** highlights the importance of sustainability and transparency. The company's Sustainable Living Plan sets ambitious goals for reducing its environmental footprint and improving its social impact. By embedding sustainability into its core business strategy, Unilever has strengthened its reputation as a responsible and ethical company.

Finally, Microsoft's **cybersecurity risk management** is a testament to the importance of advanced threat detection, a zero-trust security model, and a robust incident response plan. Microsoft's approach has allowed the company to protect its systems and data from evolving cyber threats, demonstrating the importance of prioritising cybersecurity in risk management.

These case studies demonstrate the critical role of effective risk management in ensuring business success. Companies like Apple, JPMorgan Chase, Toyota, Unilever, and Microsoft have shown that proactive risk management protects businesses from potential threats and provides a competitive advantage in a volatile environment.

Conclusion

Risk management is an essential aspect of modern business strategy. It enables organisations to anticipate, assess, and mitigate threats, protecting their operations, reputation, and financial stability. The case studies presented throughout this chapter illustrate how businesses can effectively manage various risks, from financial uncertainties to operational disruptions and reputational threats.

By adopting proactive and strategic approaches to risk management, businesses can safeguard themselves from unforeseen challenges and position themselves for long-term success. Effective risk management is key to building resilient and agile organisations capable of thriving in uncertainty, whether managing supply chain risks, financial uncertainties, or cybersecurity threats.

For aspiring leaders and entrepreneurs, these real-world examples offer valuable lessons in building robust risk management frameworks that protect the business and enhance its resilience and agility in a rapidly changing world. By integrating risk management into their core operations and decision-making processes, businesses can navigate the complexities of the modern business environment and secure a sustainable future.

Chapter 14

Navigating Economic Cycles and Market Changes

14.1 Overview

Economic **cycles** and **market changes** are integral to the global business environment, and no company is immune to their effects. Whether a business operates during economic **prosperity** or faces the difficulties of an economic **downturn**, its ability to navigate these fluctuations often determines its long-term survival and success. This chapter explores the different aspects of economic cycles, outlining strategies to survive during downturns and thrive during growth periods. Furthermore, we will examine methods businesses can employ to predict **market changes**, develop **recession-proof strategies**, capitalise on opportunities during expansion, and maintain **financial stability** during uncertain times.

We will also highlight the role of **innovation** in stimulating progress during difficult economic periods and why managing **costs** and **efficiency** becomes crucial in such scenarios. In addition, this chapter will discuss the importance of sustaining **employee morale** and retention in times of economic instability. Drawing on real-world examples and historical insights, this chapter aims to equip readers with practical tools to effectively navigate the economic cycles and market shifts that all businesses inevitably encounter.

14.2 Economic Cycles Overview

Economic or **business cycles** are natural and recurring phenomena in the economy. They represent fluctuating levels of **economic activity** over time and generally include phases of **growth** (expansion) followed by periods of **decline** (contraction). Business leaders and entrepreneurs need to understand the different phases of these cycles as they directly influence business strategies, decision-making processes, and **financial performance**.

Economic cycles are typically divided into four main phases: **expansion**, **peak**, **contraction**, and **trough**. Each of these phases presents unique challenges and opportunities for businesses. During the **expansion** During this phase, which is characterised by rising economic activity, key indicators such as GDP, employment levels, and consumer spending increase. Businesses in this phase often experience growing demand for their products and services, leading to higher revenues and profits. Companies typically invest in growth during this period, expanding operations, launching new products, and hiring more staff to meet increased demand. However, this phase requires careful financial planning to avoid overextending resources.

The **peak** represents the highest point of economic activity. At this stage, growth rates slow, and the economy may exhibit signs of overheating, such as rising **inflation** and inflated asset prices. Businesses might face increased costs, tighter labour markets, and potential supply chain constraints. While profits remain high during the peak, companies must be cautious and prepare for an impending downturn.

After the peak, the economy enters a **contraction** phase, often marked by declining economic activity, reduced consumer spending, and rising unemployment. This phase, which can be classified as a **recession** when prolonged, poses significant challenges as demand for goods and services shrinks, leading to lower revenues. Companies in this phase usually resort to cost-cutting measures, staff reductions, and improved survival efficiency.

The **trough** is the lowest point in the economic cycle, where economic activity stabilises and begins to recover. Businesses can observe early signs of improvement, such as increased consumer confidence, stabilising prices, and modest upticks in demand. Companies that survive the contraction phase can refocus on growth as the economy recovers.

Understanding the economy's cyclical nature enables businesses to plan strategically and adjust their operations based on the current economic environment. Anticipating different phases allows companies to take advantage of opportunities during expansions and shield themselves from the negative effects of downturns.

A notable example of the impact of economic cycles on businesses is the **tech boom** of the 1990s, driven largely by technological advances and the rise of the internet. This period witnessed rapid expansion in the tech industry, with many companies experiencing unprecedented growth. However, the dot-com bubble burst in the early 2000s, resulting in a significant market contraction. Many companies that over-leveraged themselves during the boom faced severe financial difficulties, while those that adopted a balanced approach were better equipped to withstand the downturn.

14.3 Predicting Market Trends

One of the critical tasks for business leaders is the ability to predict **market trends** and make informed decisions based on these predictions. While predicting the future with complete accuracy is impossible, several tools and indicators provide valuable insights into upcoming market changes. By analysing these indicators, businesses can better adapt to market shifts and mitigate potential risks.

Key tools and indicators for predicting market trends include **economic indicators**, **market sentiment**, and **technological trends**. Economic indicators, such as GDP growth rates, unemployment rates, inflation rates, and consumer confidence indices, provide crucial insights into the economy's current state. For instance, rising consumer confidence and declining unemployment rates often signal an economic expansion, while increasing unemployment and falling GDP growth may suggest an impending downturn. Monitoring these indicators helps businesses anticipate changes in market conditions and adjust their strategies accordingly.

Market sentiment refers to the overall attitude of investors, businesses, and consumers towards the economy or a specific market. This sentiment can be gauged through stock market performance, surveys, and media coverage. A bullish stock market with positive media coverage may indicate optimism, while bearish sentiment marked by declining stock prices and negative news coverage suggests caution. Staying ahead of **technological advancements** can also give businesses a competitive edge, as these developments frequently drive market changes.

Understanding competitors' actions provides insights into potential market trends. Businesses can identify broader industry trends by analysing competitors' product launches, marketing strategies, and growth initiatives. Additionally, **industry reports** and **research** provide detailed analyses of market dynamics, consumer behaviour, and emerging trends.

Economic data can be a powerful tool for making strategic business decisions when correctly interpreted. For instance, a company in the consumer goods sector may monitor trends in **disposable income** to gauge potential demand for its products. If data suggest disposable income rises, the company might consider launching higher-end products or expanding its market presence. Conversely, if disposable income declines, the company may focus on offering more affordable products or enhancing operational efficiency to maintain profitability.

A notable example of successful market trend prediction is **Netflix**'s transformation from a DVD rental service to a streaming platform. In the early 2000s, Netflix recognised the growing trend towards digital content consumption and the potential of internet streaming technology. By investing in streaming infrastructure and securing content licensing deals, Netflix was able to pivot its business model, ultimately revolutionising the entertainment industry and capturing a significant share of the growing streaming market.

Accurately predicting market trends requires combining economic analysis, industry expertise, and an understanding of technological advancements and competitive dynamics. Leveraging these tools and indicators enables businesses to anticipate market changes better and make informed decisions that position them for long-term success.

14.4 Recession-Proofing Your Business

Economic downturns are an inevitable part of the business cycle, and while they pose challenges, well-prepared businesses can weather the storm and, in some cases, emerge stronger. **Recession-proofing** a business involves implementing strategies designed to protect the company from the adverse impacts of a downturn, including reduced consumer spending, tighter credit conditions, and increased uncertainty.

Strategies for recession-proofing include **cost-cutting** and efficiency improvements, diversifying revenue streams, and focusing on core strengths. Managing costs becomes crucial during a recession. Businesses should review their expenses and identify areas where costs can be reduced without compromising product quality or customer satisfaction. This could include renegotiating supplier contracts or streamlining operations.

For instance, during the 2008 financial crisis, **Ford Motor Company** implemented a comprehensive cost-cutting strategy, including workforce reductions and closing underperforming plants. This proactive approach allowed Ford to survive without requiring a government bailout, setting it apart from many competitors.

Diversifying revenue sources is another key strategy for reducing risk and ensuring stability during a recession. Expanding into new markets or introducing new product lines can help mitigate the impact of downturns. **Procter & Gamble**, for example, has diversified its portfolio by offering both premium and value brands, allowing it to maintain market share even as consumers tighten their budgets.

Concentrating on core strengths and competitive advantages is vital during tough economic times. Scaling back non-core activities and divesting underperforming assets can help businesses navigate challenges. After the 2001 recession, IBM refocused on its strengths in enterprise services by divesting its PC business, ultimately reinforcing its market position.

Strengthening customer relationships becomes even more essential during a recession. Businesses should prioritise customer service, offer value-added services, and maintain open lines of communication. During the COVID-19 pandemic, many retailers enhanced customer service by implementing contactless delivery options and flexible return policies, fostering loyalty.

Building financial resilience is crucial for surviving a recession. Maintaining healthy cash flow, reducing debt, and building reserves to cushion against revenue declines are essential strategies. Apple's robust cash reserves were key during the 2008 financial crisis, enabling continued investment in research and development that ultimately led to the successful launch of the iPhone 3G.

Companies that have navigated recessions successfully often share common characteristics, such as a focus on **innovation**, agility, and strong leadership. During the 2008 crisis, Starbucks implemented a turnaround strategy focused on improving operational efficiency and enhancing customer experiences, allowing it to emerge stronger.

Recession-proofing requires a proactive and strategic approach. By cutting costs, diversifying revenue streams, focusing on core strengths, and building financial resilience, businesses can protect themselves from the negative impacts of economic downturns and position themselves for long-term success.

14.5 Capitalising on Economic Growth

While preparing for economic downturns is essential, businesses must also be ready to take advantage of opportunities that arise during periods of **economic growth**. Economic expansions allow businesses to invest in operations, innovate, and expand their market presence. This section explores strategies for capitalising on economic growth and identifying growth opportunities in a favourable economic environment.

Strategies for capitalising on growth include investing in **expansion**, innovating and launching new products, and strengthening market presence. During periods of economic growth, businesses should consider expanding their operations by opening new locations or entering new markets. Amazon's rapid expansion during the 2010s exemplifies this approach, as the company invested heavily in fulfilment centres and product offerings in response to increased consumer demand.

Economic growth also provides an ideal environment for **innovation** and product development. With increased consumer confidence and spending, businesses can seize positive market conditions to launch new products or services. Innovation drives revenue growth and helps companies stay competitive in a changing market.

For example, during the economic expansion of the 1990s, **Microsoft** capitalised on the growing personal computer market by launching Windows 95. The success of Windows 95, coupled with rising demand for personal computers, helped Microsoft dominate the software industry.

Strengthening market presence is also vital during economic growth. Businesses can use targeted marketing and branding to enhance visibility and attract new customers. **Coca-Cola** has consistently capitalised on periods of economic growth by investing in marketing and branding initiatives to strengthen its global market presence.

Mergers and Acquisitions (M&A) often increase during periods of economic growth as businesses seek to expand their capabilities, enter new markets, or gain a competitive edge. M&A can provide the resources and scale to capitalise on growth opportunities. However, thorough due diligence is essential to ensure acquisitions align with the company's strategic goals.

For example, Disney's 2006 acquisition of Pixar is a prime illustration of a successful merger during economic growth. By acquiring Pixar, Disney gained access to advanced animation technology, revitalising its animation division and driving significant revenue growth through blockbuster films.

Leveraging technology and digital transformation is another opportunity during economic growth. Investing in technology initiatives can enhance operational efficiency, reduce costs, and improve customer experiences. For instance, during the economic expansion after the 2008 financial crisis, financial institutions like **JPMorgan Chase** invested in digital transformation to improve operations and customer engagement.

To capitalise on economic growth, businesses must identify emerging market opportunities. This requires staying attuned to **industry trends**, consumer behaviour, and competitive dynamics. Regular assessments of market positions and exploration of new growth opportunities through product innovation or strategic partnerships are crucial.

However, while economic growth presents expansion opportunities, businesses must remain mindful of the risks associated with rapid growth. Overexpansion, excessive debt, and neglecting core operations can lead to financial instability and operational challenges. Balancing growth initiatives with prudent risk management practices is critical to ensure sustainable expansion.

14.6 Financial Planning for Volatility

Economic **volatility** is an inevitable aspect of the business environment, and companies must be prepared to navigate fluctuations in market conditions, interest rates, and currency exchange rates. Effective financial planning is crucial for maintaining stability and ensuring the business can weather economic uncertainty. This section explores strategies for managing financial volatility, including maintaining **cash flow**, reducing debt, and building financial reserves.

Strategies for financial planning in volatile times include maintaining healthy cash flow, reducing debt, and building reserves. Cash flow is the lifeblood of any business, and maintaining positive cash flow is essential for navigating economic volatility. Businesses should regularly monitor their cash flow, identify potential shortfalls, and implement measures to ensure sufficient liquidity to meet their obligations.

For instance, during the 2008 financial crisis, many companies faced cash flow challenges due to declining sales and tighter credit conditions. Companies like **Procter & Gamble**, with strong cash flow management practices, continued to invest in innovation and marketing, allowing them to maintain market share during the downturn.

Reducing debt and managing leverage are also vital. High debt levels can pose significant risks during periods of economic volatility, as businesses may struggle to meet debt obligations if revenues decline. Companies should focus on reducing debt, managing leverage, and improving their debt-to-equity ratio to ensure financial stability.

After the dot-com bubble burst in the early 2000s, many technology companies faced financial difficulties due to excessive debt. However, companies like **Apple**, which maintained low debt levels, weathered the storm and continued investing in growth opportunities.

Building financial reserves provides a cushion that helps businesses navigate economic volatility and unexpected challenges. By setting aside a portion of profits during periods of growth, companies can build a financial buffer to cover expenses or manage risks during downturns.

For example, **Warren Buffett**'s Berkshire Hathaway is known for its conservative financial management and substantial cash reserves. This approach allowed the company to exploit investment opportunities during economic downturns, such as acquiring undervalued assets.

Scenario planning and stress testing are valuable tools for assessing the potential impact of economic volatility on a business. By exploring different scenarios, businesses can identify vulnerabilities and develop contingency plans. For instance, banks in the Eurozone were required to undergo stress tests during the European debt crisis to assess their resilience to adverse economic conditions.

Practical tips for managing financial volatility include monitoring key financial metrics, implementing cost control measures, and maintaining access to credit. Regularly tracking metrics such as cash flow, debt levels, profitability, and liquidity ratios is essential for identifying potential risks early.

14.7 Innovation During Downturns

While economic downturns pose significant challenges, they can also present unique opportunities for **innovation** and the development of new business models. In tough times, businesses are often forced to think creatively, streamline operations, and find new ways to deliver customer value. This section explores how economic downturns can foster innovation and provides examples of companies that have thrived by innovating during challenging periods.

Opportunities for innovation during downturns include developing **cost-effective solutions** that meet the needs of budget-conscious consumers. Companies that deliver high value at a lower cost will likely capture market share and build customer loyalty during downturns. For example, during the 2008 financial crisis, **Airbnb** emerged as a cost-effective alternative to traditional hotels, offering affordable lodging options that disrupted the hospitality industry.

Business model innovation is another key aspect. Downturns prompt businesses to rethink their existing models and explore new revenue streams or delivery methods. Netflix's shift from a DVD rental service to a streaming platform during the economic downturn of the late 2000s exemplifies this trend. Recognising the growing demand for digital content, Netflix embraced a subscription-based model, transforming its business into a dominant player in the entertainment industry.

Leveraging technology is crucial during downturns, as it drives businesses to adopt new technologies that improve efficiency, reduce costs, and enhance customer experiences. During the early 2000s recession, Amazon invested heavily in technology to improve its supply chain and distribution capabilities, laying the foundation for its dominance in the e-commerce sector.

Collaborative innovation can also flourish during economic downturns. Businesses may partner with suppliers or even competitors to develop new solutions. For instance, during the COVID-19 pandemic, several pharmaceutical companies, including **Pfizer** and **BioNTech**, collaborated to develop and distribute vaccines rapidly. This partnership demonstrated the power of collaboration in addressing global challenges.

Examples of companies that thrived by innovating during downturns include **Apple**, which launched the first iPod during the 2001 recession, revolutionising the music industry. Similarly, **IBM** shifted its focus from hardware to services and software in response to the early 1990s economic challenges, allowing it to become a leader in technology services.

Fostering innovation during economic downturns requires a proactive approach and a willingness to embrace new ideas. Encouraging a **culture of experimentation**, investing in research and development, and focusing on customer needs can drive successful innovations. Companies can harness new technologies and expertise by collaborating with other businesses or research institutions, ultimately leading to more effective solutions.

14.8 Managing Costs and Efficiency

Managing **costs** and maintaining operational **efficiency** are critical for businesses to remain competitive, especially during economic uncertainty. Efficient operations not only help businesses reduce expenses but also enable them to deliver better value to customers. This section provides tips on how businesses can adjust their operations to maintain efficiency and control costs during different phases of the economic cycle, as well as strategies for flexible resource management.

Strategies for managing costs and efficiency include **process optimisation**, automation, and the use of technology. Optimising business processes involves identifying inefficiencies, eliminating waste, and streamlining workflows to enhance productivity. For instance, Toyota's adoption of lean manufacturing principles, such as just-in-time inventory management, has been instrumental in reducing costs and improving operational efficiency.

Automation can significantly enhance efficiency by reducing manual labour and minimising errors. Businesses should explore opportunities to automate routine tasks, freeing resources for more strategic activities. Amazon's use of automation in its fulfilment centres revolutionised its inventory management and order processing, resulting in faster delivery times and higher customer satisfaction.

Outsourcing non-core activities to specialised service providers can also help reduce costs. However, before outsourcing decisions, companies must evaluate potential risks, such as quality control and supply chain disruptions. Many technology companies, like Apple, have successfully outsourced manufacturing to lower-cost regions, allowing them to focus on design innovation while reducing production costs.

Maintaining flexible resource management is crucial for adapting to changing economic conditions. Businesses should consider flexible work arrangements, such as remote work or part-time contracts, to manage labour costs effectively. During the COVID-19 pandemic, many companies adopted flexible work arrangements, allowing employees to work from home, which helped reduce operational costs and maintain productivity.

Conducting **cost-benefit analyses** for major expenditures ensures that resources are allocated efficiently. For example, a manufacturing company considering purchasing new machinery should evaluate whether the investment will lead to efficiency gains and cost savings.

Strategies for maintaining efficiency during economic downturns include prioritising core activities and negotiating better terms with suppliers. Businesses should track key performance indicators (KPIs) related to cost management, efficiency, and productivity to identify areas for improvement. Implementing continuous improvement initiatives can further enhance operational efficiency.

14.9 Employee Morale and Retention

Maintaining employee **morale** and retention during economic uncertainty is crucial for sustaining productivity, fostering a positive workplace culture, and ensuring long-term success. Economic downturns can create employee anxiety, decreasing engagement and higher turnover. This section discusses strategies for keeping employees engaged and motivated during challenging times, focusing on communication, leadership, and maintaining a positive workplace culture.

Transparent communication is vital for maintaining trust and morale during periods of uncertainty. Leaders should keep employees informed about the company's financial situation, changes to operations, and potential workforce impacts. Regular updates and one-on-one discussions can address employee concerns and build confidence in leadership. For example, during the 2008 financial crisis, companies like General Electric maintained employee morale by regularly updating their financial position.

Recognising and appreciating employees' hard work is crucial for boosting morale. Small gestures like public recognition or thank-you notes can significantly impact engagement even during tough times. During the COVID-19 pandemic, companies like Salesforce used platforms to celebrate employees' contributions and maintain morale.

Supporting employee well-being is essential during uncertainty. Offering flexible work arrangements and access to mental health resources can help maintain morale and productivity. Unilever's commitment to employee well-being during the pandemic included providing access to counselling services and flexible work options, enhancing engagement.

Leadership visibility and accessibility are critical during uncertain times. Leaders should engage with employees at all levels, hosting regular Q&A sessions and visiting different departments. During the 2001 recession, Southwest Airlines CEO Herb Kelleher maintained high morale by being visible and approachable, which helped retain employees.

Providing opportunities for growth and development is also important. Offering training programs and mentorship opportunities helps employees build skills and advance their careers, enhancing morale. IBM's commitment to employee development during the 1990s included extensive training programs, allowing the company to retain top talent.

Fostering a positive workplace culture is crucial for employee morale and retention. Encouraging collaboration and teamwork, promoting work-life balance, and celebrating diversity and inclusion contribute to a resilient workplace. Empowering employees by giving them autonomy and responsibility can boost engagement and ownership.

Companies like Google, Salesforce, and Unilever exemplify the importance of maintaining employee morale and retention during challenging times. By implementing transparent communication, employee recognition, support for well-being, and growth opportunities, these companies keep their workforce engaged, motivated, and loyal.

14.10 Diversification Strategies

Diversification is a powerful strategy for managing risk, creating new revenue streams, and ensuring long-term business sustainability. By spreading risk across different products, markets, or industries, businesses can reduce their dependence on any single source of income and better navigate economic fluctuations. This section explores diversification strategies, including product, market, and geographic diversification, providing examples of companies successfully diversifying their operations.

Diversification strategies include **product diversification**, market diversification, and geographic diversification. Product diversification involves expanding a company's product or service offerings to reduce reliance on a single product line and tap into new customer segments. Apple's successful product diversification strategy includes expanding its portfolio from computers to a wide range of consumer electronics, allowing it to capture new markets.

Market diversification entails expanding into new customer segments, industries, or regions. Coca-Cola's market diversification strategy includes expanding product offerings to appeal to health-conscious consumers while increasing its presence in international markets to drive growth.

Geographic diversification involves expanding operations into new regions to spread risk. McDonald's geographic diversification strategy includes operating in over 100 countries worldwide, adapting menu offerings to local tastes, and capturing market share in diverse regions.

Vertical integration expands a company's operations along the supply chain, allowing greater control over costs and quality. Tesla's vertical integration strategy includes manufacturing its batteries and components, enhancing its competitive advantage. **Conglomerate diversification** involves entering entirely new industries unrelated to core operations, helping mitigate risk. General Electric exemplifies this strategy, expanding into aviation, healthcare, energy, and finance.

Diversification offers risk reduction, revenue growth, competitive advantage, and innovation opportunities. Spreading risk across different products, markets, and industries reduces the impact of failures. Expanding into new markets creates new revenue streams, leading to higher overall growth.

However, diversification presents challenges, including resource allocation, complexity, and cultural differences. Companies must allocate resources carefully to avoid diluting core operations. Diversifying can increase complexity, requiring strong leadership and effective communication.

Examples of successful diversification include Amazon's expansion from an online bookstore to a global e-commerce platform and cloud services. Disney's diversification includes theme parks and streaming services, enhancing its market position. Samsung has diversified into various industries, mitigating risk and becoming a global leader.

Businesses should conduct market research to identify opportunities and assess market demand when implementing a diversification strategy. Starting small and scaling gradually allows businesses to test strategies and gather feedback. Leveraging core competencies increases the chances of success in new ventures. Regularly monitoring performance metrics ensures adaptability and effectiveness.

14.11 Learning from Past Economic Cycles

Understanding how businesses have responded to past economic cycles can provide valuable insights into navigating future market changes. Historical examples offer lessons in **resilience**, innovation, and strategic decision-making that can help businesses prepare for and adapt to economic fluctuations. This section explores how businesses have responded to past economic cycles and the lessons applicable to future market changes.

Historical insights from past economic cycles include the **Great Depression** (1929-1939), which was characterised by severe economic downturns. Procter & Gamble navigated this period by investing in advertising and product innovation, introducing new products like Dreft. The lesson is that investing in innovation and understanding consumer needs can help businesses survive challenging economic conditions.

The **oil crisis** (1973-1974) forced industries reliant on energy to adapt. Toyota responded by accelerating the development of fuel-efficient vehicles, gaining market share as consumers shifted away from gas-guzzling options. This illustrates the importance of quickly adapting to changing market conditions and focusing on efficiency.

Many tech companies faced financial challenges during the dot-com bubble (1995-2001). Amazon survived by focusing on long-term growth and customer satisfaction, allowing it to emerge stronger. This highlights the value of prioritising sustainable growth over short-term gains.

The **global financial crisis** (2007-2008) prompted businesses to rethink strategies. Starbucks focused on operational efficiency and enhancing customer experience, successfully recovering from the downturn. The lesson is to concentrate on core strengths and stay true to company values during crises.

The **COVID-19 pandemic** (2020-present) presented unprecedented challenges. Zoom experienced rapid growth by scaling operations to meet demand for remote communication. This demonstrates the importance of agility and the ability to respond quickly to changing conditions.

Applying lessons from past economic cycles involves focusing on core strengths, investing in innovation, adapting to changing conditions, maintaining financial resilience, and staying true to core values. Companies prioritising customer satisfaction and ethical practices are more likely to build long-term success.

Conclusion

In this chapter, we explored the intricate dynamics of economic cycles and market changes, providing businesses with essential strategies to navigate periods of growth and downturns. By understanding the phases of economic cycles, **expansion**, **peak**, **contraction**, and **trough**, businesses can better anticipate challenges and seize opportunities, whether by recession-proofing their operations or capitalising on economic growth.

We discussed the importance of predicting market trends using economic indicators, technological advancements, and competitive analysis to guide strategic decisions. We also examined recession-proofing strategies like cost-cutting, diversification, and financial resilience, which are vital for sustaining businesses during economic downturns. Conversely, we explored how businesses can thrive during periods of economic growth by investing in expansion, innovation, and mergers and acquisitions.

The chapter highlighted the significance of financial planning in times of volatility, emphasising the need for healthy cash flow, debt management, and scenario planning. Moreover, we discussed how economic downturns foster innovation, encouraging businesses to develop cost-effective solutions, innovate business models, and leverage technology to stay competitive.

Cost management and operational efficiency were critical factors for maintaining competitiveness, particularly during uncertain times. We explored strategies such as process optimisation, automation, outsourcing, and flexible resource management.

Finally, we examined how maintaining employee morale and retention during economic uncertainty is vital for productivity and long-term success. Businesses prioritising employee well-being, transparent communication, and leadership visibility are better equipped to navigate challenging times.

By learning from historical examples, businesses can gain valuable insights into resilience, innovation, and strategic decision-making. Whether it is Procter & Gamble during the Great Depression, Toyota during the oil crisis, Amazon post-dot-com bubble, Starbucks during the financial crisis, or Zoom during the COVID-19 pandemic, these examples underscore the importance of adaptability and foresight in navigating economic cycles.

In conclusion, economic cycles and market changes are inevitable, but businesses can survive and thrive with the right strategies. Equipping themselves with the knowledge and tools discussed in this chapter, business leaders can confidently navigate the complexities of economic cycles, ensuring long-term success and sustainability for their organisations.

Chapter 15

Mergers and Acquisitions – Strategies for Growth and Consolidation

15.1 - Overview

Mergers and acquisitions (**M&A**) are indispensable strategic mechanisms for businesses striving to expand and consolidate their industry positions. Companies frequently utilise M&A to amplify their **market share**, enter untapped markets, and seize synergies that would be otherwise unattainable. Whether a business seeks to acquire a competitor to reduce market competition, merge with complementary enterprises to diversify its product offerings, or vertically integrate to secure better control over its supply chain, M&A transactions offer numerous **advantages**. These benefits include achieving **economies of scale**, bolstering competitive standing, and increasing market diversification. However, despite these benefits, M&A transactions come with significant challenges. The process is often highly **complex**, requiring meticulous due diligence, detailed planning, and a profound understanding of the financial, strategic, and cultural factors influencing the transaction's success.

Emphasising the importance of a well-conceived M&A strategy is crucial from the transaction's inception through execution. This ensures that companies and shareholders derive long-term value. The success of any merger or acquisition heavily depends on the company's ability to navigate the many challenges that arise. Even promising M&A deals can fail to deliver the anticipated outcomes without proper planning and strategic oversight, leaving companies vulnerable to financial strain, operational disruption, and cultural dissonance.

15.2 - Types of M&A Deals

M&A transactions manifest in various forms tailored to the specific strategic goals of the companies involved. Each type of deal has **advantages** and challenges, and the choice of structure largely depends on the companies' objectives. Let us delve into the concept of a horizontal merger, a strategic move where two companies within the same industry combine their resources. The primary aim of such a merger is to reduce competition, enhance **market share**, and achieve **economies of scale**. A well-documented example is the 1999 merger between Exxon and Mobil, which created one of the largest oil companies globally. This horizontal merger enabled both companies to streamline operations, reduce costs, and establish a stronger competitive stance within the global marketplace.

In contrast, a **vertical merger** involves companies coming together at different supply chain stages. This merger is often pursued to secure **supply lines**, lower operational costs, and increase efficiency. A prime example is Amazon's acquisition of Whole Foods in 2017. By acquiring Whole Foods, Amazon gained a physical retail presence and enhanced its grocery distribution network, solidifying its market position and expanding its service offerings.

Meanwhile, **conglomerate mergers** involve businesses from completely unrelated industries. These mergers are typically aimed at **diversifying risk** across different sectors, which can help protect companies from market volatility. For instance, General Electric's expansion into aviation, healthcare, and finance demonstrates how conglomerate mergers can reduce a company's exposure to risks in any single sector by spreading investments across various industries.

Acquisitions occur when one company takes control of another and can be **friendly** or hostile. A friendly acquisition takes place with the full support of the target company's management, while in a **hostile acquisition**, the acquiring company seeks control without the target company's consent. This can involve buying a significant share of the target company's stock or other strategies to gain a controlling interest.

Finally, a **joint venture** involves two or more companies pooling resources to collaborate on a specific project without fully merging their operations. This structure allows companies to share the **risks** and rewards of the project while maintaining their operational independence. Joint ventures are often seen as a viable alternative to full mergers or acquisitions, particularly when the companies wish to retain autonomy but still benefit from shared expertise and resources.

15.3 - Strategic Purposes of M&A

The **strategic motivations** behind mergers and acquisitions vary considerably, depending on the long-term objectives of the companies involved. While **market expansion** and the realisation of synergies are common reasons, businesses may also pursue M&A for purposes such as diversification, technology acquisition, or other strategic advantages.

One of the most frequently cited purposes of M&A is **market expansion**. Companies often engage in mergers or acquisitions to break into new geographic regions or tap into previously untapped market segments. A prime example of this is Facebook's 2014 acquisition of WhatsApp. This transaction allowed Facebook to significantly broaden its global user base and gain entry into emerging markets where WhatsApp had already established a strong foothold.

Another key driver of M&A is the realisation of **synergies**. Synergies may be cost savings, increased revenue, or improved operational efficiencies resulting from the two companies' combined strengths. The goal is to create an entity that is worth more together than the two businesses would have been separately. These synergies can range from streamlining supply chains to merging back-office operations, reducing overhead and improving profitability.

Additionally, M&A allows companies to **diversify** their revenue streams by entering new industries or adding new product lines. This diversification helps to reduce the company's reliance on a single market or product, thereby insulating it from market **volatility** and changes in consumer demand. A well-diversified business can better withstand economic fluctuations, as its revenue sources are spread across different sectors.

Another common reason companies pursue M&A is acquiring new technology, particularly in industries experiencing rapid technological change. A notable example is Google's 2005 acquisition of Android. Through this acquisition, Google positioned itself in the fast-growing mobile technology space, securing a platform for future growth as smartphones became an integral part of everyday life.

15.4 - Risks in M&A

While M&A transactions offer numerous benefits, they also come with significant **risks** that can endanger the deal's success. One of the most common risks is **financial**, specifically the danger of overpaying for the target company. Overpaying can occur when a company makes overly optimistic projections about future growth or becomes entangled in a competitive bidding war, driving the price beyond the target's actual value. Poor financial planning, including failing to account for integration costs adequately, can lead to unexpected financial strain, undermining the merger's potential benefits.

Operational risks also abound in M&A transactions, particularly during the **integration** process. Combining the systems, processes, and teams of two companies can lead to disruptions in daily operations. If operating models are misaligned or integration plans are poorly executed, the result can be losses in **productivity**, operational inefficiencies, and an increase in overall costs. This can negatively impact the short-term financial performance of both companies involved in the deal.

In addition to financial and operational risks, significant reputational risks are associated with M&A. A poorly executed merger or acquisition can lead to customer dissatisfaction, employee unrest, and even negative media coverage, damaging the company's brand and market perception. Moreover, suppose the merger fails to meet the expectations of shareholders or the wider market. In that case, the company may lose **investor confidence**, which can have long-term ramifications for its stock price and financial stability.

Regulatory hurdles represent yet another significant challenge in M&A transactions. Companies must navigate a complex **regulatory landscape**, as each jurisdiction may have different legal requirements to meet before the transaction can be finalised. Antitrust laws, for example, are designed to prevent deals that would reduce competition in a particular market, and securing regulatory approval can often delay or even derail an M&A deal entirely.

15.5 - Strategic Fit

The concept of **strategic fit** is a critical determinant of whether a merger or acquisition will ultimately succeed. Strategic fit refers to how well the acquiring company's financial, operational, and cultural goals align with the target company's goals. A strong strategic fit increases the likelihood that the companies will be able to realise the synergies and benefits envisioned during the planning stages. Conversely, a poor strategic fit can lead to significant long-term challenges that may hinder the integration process and prevent the merged entity from achieving its goals.

Assessing strategic fit involves evaluating several factors. Financial performance is one consideration, but cultural compatibility and the long-term vision of both companies are also important. A strong strategic fit should align with the merger's immediate operational goals and the business's future growth objectives.

For example, Disney's 2006 acquisition of Pixar was a strong example of **strategic alignment**. Disney wanted to revitalise its animation division, while Pixar had cutting-edge animation technology and creative talent that complemented Disney's goals. This alignment allowed both companies to leverage their strengths, resulting in a successful merger revitalising Disney's animation portfolio.

Cultural compatibility is another key factor in determining strategic fit. A lack of cultural alignment between two companies can lead to significant post-merger integration challenges, such as low employee morale, loss of **talent**, and operational inefficiencies. A thorough cultural assessment during the due diligence phase can help identify potential conflicts early and allow the acquiring company to develop strategies to mitigate these issues. The merger between Daimler-Benz and Chrysler in

1998 is a prime example of how cultural differences derail an otherwise promising deal. The two companies had vastly different approaches to management and leadership, which ultimately contributed to the merger's failure.

Beyond immediate financial and operational goals, it is essential to assess whether the **long-term vision** of the target company aligns with that of the acquirer. A merger or acquisition should not be driven solely by short-term financial gain. It should also reflect a shared vision for the **future direction** of both businesses. This long-term alignment is critical for ensuring the merged entity can thrive in the years ahead. A prime example of a merger with strong long-term strategic alignment is Microsoft's acquisition of LinkedIn in 2016. Both companies shared a vision of enhancing professional networking and connectivity, making this deal a strong strategic fit. This alignment has allowed LinkedIn to continue growing within Microsoft's ecosystem, contributing to the success of both companies.

15.6 - Conducting Due Diligence

Due diligence is one of the most critical phases in any M&A transaction. This process involves the acquiring company thoroughly investigating the target's financial, operational, legal, and cultural aspects. The primary goal of due diligence is to validate the **strategic fit**, identify potential risks, and uncover any hidden liabilities that could affect the transaction's success. A comprehensive due diligence process ensures that the acquirer makes an informed decision about whether to proceed with the deal.

Financial due diligence focuses on a detailed review of the target company's **financial statements**, including income statements, balance sheets, and cash flow reports. This process helps assess the company's profitability, liquidity, and financial stability. It also identifies potential financial risks, such as unsustainable debt levels or declining revenue trends, that could jeopardise the acquisition's success. Financial due diligence is essential to prevent overvaluation and ensure the acquirer pays a fair price for the target company.

Operational due diligence examines the target company's day-to-day operations, including its supply chain management, IT systems, and human resources. This examination aims to identify inefficiencies, potential synergies, and areas where the combined entity could reduce costs or improve performance. For example, evaluating how well the two companies' supply chains align can reveal opportunities to streamline logistics and reduce overhead. Operational due diligence is particularly important in industries where integration challenges, such as differing IT systems or supply chain processes, could create **disruptions**.

Legal due diligence is another vital component of the process. This involves reviewing the target company's contracts, intellectual property, litigation history, and compliance with regulatory standards. Identifying legal liabilities is critical to avoiding post-merger complications. For instance, unresolved lawsuits, intellectual property disputes, or non-compliance with regulatory requirements could expose the acquiring company to significant financial and reputational risks. Proper legal due diligence ensures the acquirer understands the target company's legal obligations before finalising the deal.

In addition to financial, operational, and legal due diligence, companies must assess the **cultural** fit between the acquirer and the target. Cultural due diligence involves examining the target company's values, leadership styles, communication practices, and innovation approach. This process often includes interviews with key executives, employee surveys, and on-site visits to observe how the target company operates. A thorough cultural assessment can help determine how well the two companies' cultures will integrate after the merger, reducing the risk of employee dissatisfaction and operational inefficiencies.

An excellent example of successful cultural due diligence is Facebook's acquisition of Instagram in 2012. Facebook recognised Instagram's unique culture and allowed the company to operate independently, contributing to the merger's success. By preserving Instagram's innovative and agile culture, Facebook was able to retain Instagram's core talent and maintain the platform's rapid growth.

15.7 - Integration Planning

Effective **integration planning** is essential to the success of any M&A transaction. Integration refers to combining the operations, systems, and cultures of the two companies involved in the merger. The success of a merger or acquisition often depends on how smoothly and efficiently this integration is executed. A well-defined integration strategy that addresses potential challenges, timelines, and responsibilities can significantly improve the chances of a successful outcome.

A comprehensive **integration strategy** should begin with clearly defined goals, timelines, and priorities for integrating the two companies. It should address operational, cultural, and human resource challenges while preserving both organisations' strengths. One of the most significant challenges in integration planning is merging two corporate cultures. Cultural integration can be particularly difficult when the companies have different values, leadership styles, and business practices. The failure to align cultures can lead to conflicts, low employee morale, and even **talent loss**.

The 1998 merger between Daimler-Benz and Chrysler exemplifies how cultural differences undermine an otherwise promising merger. The two companies had vastly different approaches to management, with Daimler-Benz being more hierarchical and formal, while Chrysler embraced a more relaxed and entrepreneurial culture. These cultural differences created friction and ultimately contributed to the merger's failure. To avoid such pitfalls, companies should assess cultural differences early in the integration process and develop strategies to bridge the gap between the two cultures.

Communication is another critical component of a successful integration plan. Employees from both companies need to be informed about the reasons for the merger, the expected benefits, and how the integration will affect them. Regular communication helps manage employee expectations and reduces uncertainty during the integration process. The Exxon-Mobil merger exemplifies how effective communication can help smooth the integration process. Exxon and Mobil's leadership teams prioritised transparent communication by holding town hall meetings and providing detailed employee updates throughout the integration process. This approach helped build trust and reduced employee anxiety during the transition.

Operational integration is equally important. Merging operational processes and systems, such as **supply chains**, IT infrastructures, and financial reporting mechanisms, is critical to realising the synergies envisioned during the M&A negotiations. Poorly planned operational integration can lead to significant disruptions and financial losses. A prime example of successful systems integration was Bank of America's acquisition of Merrill Lynch during the 2008 financial crisis. Bank of America meticulously planned the integration of Merrill Lynch's IT systems and financial operations, ensuring a smooth transition and business continuity.

Retaining key employees from both companies is essential for maintaining operational continuity and achieving the strategic goals of the merger. Offering **retention bonuses**, incentives, and career development opportunities can help ensure that top talent remains with the company post-merger. For instance, after Microsoft acquired LinkedIn, the retention of LinkedIn's leadership team played a pivotal role in the platform's smooth integration and continued success. The leadership team's expertise and institutional knowledge helped guide LinkedIn's operations within Microsoft, ensuring that the platform retained its unique culture while benefiting from Microsoft's resources.

15.8 - Cultural Integration

Cultural integration is one of mergers and acquisitions' most complex and often overlooked aspects. When two companies with distinct cultures come together, there is a high potential for **conflict** and misunderstandings. These conflicts manifest in different leadership styles, decision-making processes, and communication practices. If cultural differences are not adequately addressed, they can lead to employee dissatisfaction, decreased productivity, and increased turnover.

For example, the merger between Daimler-Benz and Chrysler highlighted how **cultural clashes** can undermine the success of an M&A transaction. Daimler-Benz's formal, hierarchical approach to management conflicted with Chrysler's more relaxed, entrepreneurial culture. This cultural mismatch led to friction between the two companies, contributing to the eventual dissolution of the merger.

In addition to cultural clashes, employees may resist changes brought about by a merger or acquisition, particularly if they feel that their company's culture is marginalised. Employee resistance can slow down the integration process and prevent the realisation of synergies. For example, the HP-Compaq merger in 2002 experienced significant employee resistance, particularly from Compaq employees, who felt that HP's bureaucratic culture stifled the innovation that had been a hallmark of Compaq.

Cultural integration can also lead to a perceived **loss of identity** for employees from the acquired company. This feeling of loss can result in disengagement, reduced loyalty, and lower job satisfaction, negatively impacting productivity. Following the merger between AOL and Time Warner in 2000, many AOL employees felt that their innovative, internet-focused culture was overshadowed by Time Warner's more traditional media culture. This cultural dissonance contributed to the merger's failure.

To address these challenges, companies must conduct thorough **cultural assessments** during the due diligence phase and develop strategies to integrate the two cultures post-merger. This often involves creating a unified vision and shared values that resonate with employees from both companies. Regular and transparent communication is essential to managing employee expectations and addressing concerns. By involving employees in the integration process and celebrating milestones that reflect the contributions of both companies, leadership can foster a sense of unity and shared purpose.

15.9 - Measuring Success

Measuring the success of a merger or acquisition is vital to ensure that the strategic objectives set at the outset have been achieved. The ability to assess the impact of the M&A deal lies in identifying and tracking specific **key performance indicators**

(KPIs). These KPIs may relate to financial performance, market share, employee retention, customer satisfaction, and cultural integration, providing valuable insights into the merger's progress.

Financial metrics are the most commonly used method to measure the success of a merger or acquisition. These include **revenue growth**, profitability, cost synergies, and return on investment (ROI). After the merger, companies should compare actual financial results with pre-merger projections to assess whether the deal has improved the overall financial performance. Revenue growth and enhanced profit margins indicate that the merger delivers the expected **financial benefits**.

Another critical indicator of success is whether the merger has strengthened the company's **market position**. This can be evaluated by tracking changes in market share and competitive positioning within the industry. An increase in market share, for example, suggests that the combined entity is performing well and capitalising on the synergies realised from the merger. The Exxon-Mobil merger provides a notable example of how the companies' consolidation strengthened their global competitive position in the oil industry.

Employee retention and engagement are important indicators of a successful merger or acquisition. **High turnover**, especially among key employees, can disrupt business operations and hinder integration. Tracking retention rates and employee engagement through surveys and feedback mechanisms is essential to understand how well employees adapt to the new organisational structure and culture.

Customer satisfaction is another crucial factor in evaluating the success of an M&A transaction, particularly when the target company has a strong customer-facing component. **Monitoring customer retention** rates and satisfaction levels can provide insight into whether the merger has positively or negatively impacted the customer experience. If customer churn increases or satisfaction declines, it may indicate that the integration process negatively affects service quality, requiring a reassessment of the integration strategy.

While more difficult to measure, **cultural integration** is essential for the long-term success of a merger or acquisition. Gauging cultural alignment through employee surveys, interviews, and engagement scores can help assess whether the two organisations are successfully merging their cultures. Strong cultural integration often leads to higher employee satisfaction, lower turnover, and a more cohesive organisational identity, all of which contribute to the overall success of the merger.

To ensure long-term success, companies must align their KPIs with the strategic objectives of the merger. Establishing a **performance baseline** before finalising the deal and regularly monitoring progress helps companies evaluate the overall success of the transaction. Involving key stakeholders, including leadership, employees, and customers, in setting targets and evaluating outcomes is also crucial. Flexibility and the willingness to adjust the integration strategy based on feedback and performance results can significantly enhance the chances of achieving long-term success.

15.10 - Common Pitfalls and How to Avoid Them

Mergers and acquisitions are inherently complex and often encounter pitfalls that undermine the transaction's success. The most common challenges include overvaluation, poor integration planning, cultural clashes, and operational disruptions. Understanding these pitfalls and taking proactive steps to avoid them can significantly increase the likelihood of a successful M&A deal.

One of the most frequent pitfalls is **overvaluation**. This occurs when the acquiring company pays more for the target company than it is worth. Overvaluation typically stems from overly optimistic growth projections or competitive bidding wars that drive the price higher than the target company's true market value. Overvaluation can place significant financial strain on the acquiring company, making achieving the expected return on investment difficult. A classic example of overvaluation is the AOL acquisition of Time Warner in 2000, where inflated expectations of synergies between the companies led to significant financial losses.

Another common pitfall is **inadequate planning** for post-merger integration. Poor integration planning can result in operational disruptions, inefficiencies, and the failure to realise expected synergies. The 2005 merger between Sprint and Nextel is a notable example of how poor planning can lead to disastrous results. The two companies struggled to integrate their operations, and their differing technologies created significant challenges. These operational difficulties ultimately contributed to the merger's failure.

Cultural differences between the merging companies can also pose significant challenges. **Misalignment** in values, leadership styles, and decision-making processes can create friction between employees and leadership teams, reducing productivity and high employee turnover. The Daimler-Benz and Chrysler merger is often cited as a cautionary tale of cultural clashes. The companies' differing approaches to management and organisational structure contributed to the eventual dissolution of the merger.

Operational disruptions are another significant pitfall that companies often underestimate. Merging **supply chains**, aligning IT systems, and streamlining processes are complex tasks that, if not handled properly, can lead to costly delays and disruptions. A notable example is the HP-Compaq merger, where the two companies faced major operational challenges, particularly in IT systems integration. These challenges delayed the realisation of cost synergies and caused frustration among employees and customers.

Clear communication with employees, customers, and stakeholders is critical to managing expectations and ensuring a smooth transition during a merger or acquisition. Failure to communicate effectively can lead to confusion, anxiety, and resistance to change. The 2006 merger between Alcatel and

Lucent was plagued by communication failures, which led to employee dissatisfaction and significant integration difficulties. Transparent and regular communication with all stakeholders is essential for fostering trust and managing expectations during the integration process.

Retaining **key employees** is crucial for maintaining operational continuity and achieving the strategic goals of the merger. Failure to identify and retain top talent during the integration process can result in losing institutional knowledge, negatively impacting the company's ability to execute its strategic plans. After AOL's merger with Time Warner, the departure of several key employees, including senior executives, weakened the company's leadership and contributed to the merger's failure.

To avoid these common pitfalls, companies should conduct **rigorous financial due diligence**, begin integration planning early, and address cultural differences head-on. Establishing a detailed integration plan that covers operational, cultural, and financial aspects is crucial for a smooth transition. **Clear and transparent communication** with employees and stakeholders helps manage expectations and build trust throughout the integration process. Additionally, offering incentives, career development opportunities, and open communication about future roles can help retain top talent and ensure continuity.

15.11 - Case Studies of Successful M&As

Examining **successful M&A transactions** can provide valuable insights into how companies navigate the complexities of mergers and acquisitions to achieve long-term growth and success. Several notable examples demonstrate how thoughtful strategies and execution can lead to successful outcomes.

One such example is **Disney's acquisition of Pixar** in 2006. The Walt Disney Company acquired Pixar Animation Studios for $7.4 billion in an all-stock deal. Disney sought to revitalise its struggling animation division, while Pixar was known for its creative talent and innovative approach to animation. This merger's success was partly due to Disney's decision to allow Pixar to maintain its creative independence, preserving its unique **culture** and operating structure. At the same time, Disney leveraged its global distribution network and marketing expertise to maximise the commercial success of Pixar's films. This merger is regarded as one of the most successful in the entertainment industry, producing critically acclaimed and commercially successful films such as *Toy Story 3* and *Up* while revitalising Disney's animation division.

Another notable example is **Facebook's acquisition of Instagram** in 2012. Facebook acquired Instagram for $1 billion in cash and stock at a time when Instagram was a rapidly growing photo-sharing platform with a loyal user base but no revenue model. Facebook's strategy was to allow Instagram to operate independently, preserving its brand and user experience while leveraging Facebook's resources for growth. This approach enabled Instagram to retain its core identity while expanding its user base and becoming a key driver of Facebook's advertising revenue. Since the acquisition, Instagram has grown exponentially and remains one of the most significant contributors to Facebook's overall success.

In 1999, **Exxon and Mobil** merged to form ExxonMobil, creating the world's largest publicly traded oil company. The $81 billion merger was driven by a desire to achieve **economies of scale**, improve operational efficiency, and enhance competitive positioning in the global energy market. The success of this merger was due to the companies' focus on cost savings and operational efficiency, streamlining operations and reducing redundancies. Leadership also prioritised cultural integration, emphasising shared values of operational excellence and environmental responsibility. The ExxonMobil merger resulted in significant cost savings and improved operational performance, and the company continues to be one of the world's largest and most profitable energy firms.

Google's acquisition of YouTube in 2006 is another successful M&A transaction. Google acquired YouTube for $1.65 billion in stock at a time when YouTube was the leading video-sharing platform but faced challenges related to copyright infringement and monetisation. Google addressed these challenges by developing the **Content ID system**, which allowed rights holders to manage and monetise their content. Google also integrated YouTube into its broader ecosystem, leveraging its search engine and advertising platform to generate revenue. Since the acquisition, YouTube has grown into the largest video-sharing platform in the world, with over 2 billion monthly active users. The acquisition has been a major driver of Google's advertising revenue, making it one of the most successful deals in the tech industry.

Amazon's acquisition of Whole Foods in 2017 marked its entry into the brick-and-mortar grocery industry. The $13.7 billion deal was part of Amazon's strategy to expand its **physical retail presence** and enhance its grocery delivery services. Amazon successfully integrated Whole Foods into its e-commerce platform, offering online grocery ordering and delivery through **Amazon Prime**. At the same time, Amazon maintained Whole Foods' focus on high-quality, organic products, preserving its brand identity. This acquisition significantly expanded Amazon's footprint in the grocery market and increased sales and customer engagement, making it a successful M&A deal.

Conclusion

Mergers and acquisitions offer businesses substantial opportunities for **growth**, market consolidation, and innovation. However, they also present significant risks and challenges. Companies prioritising **strategic fit**, cultural integration, and thorough due diligence are more likely to achieve long-term success. By learning from successful M&A case studies, such as Disney and Pixar, Facebook and Instagram, and Exxon and Mobil, companies can develop effective strategies to ensure their mergers and acquisitions create lasting value for shareholders. The ability to navigate the complexities of integration, manage cultural differences, and focus on long-term strategic objectives is key to the success of any M&A transaction.

Chapter 16

Technology and Digital Transformation: Leveraging the Digital Age

16.1 Overview

Technology and digital transformation have become essential for growth and survival in today's business environment. Companies that fail to adapt risk being left behind as innovation and digital tools reshape entire industries. The modern business landscape is characterised by rapid technological advancements that have forced organisations to embrace change at an unprecedented pace. Adopting digital tools is no longer a luxury but a necessity. Digital transformation is the cornerstone of business success in the 21st century, enabling businesses to remain competitive, efficient, and innovative.

The digital revolution is affecting nearly every aspect of business operations. Whether automating internal processes, enhancing customer experience, or unlocking new revenue streams, technology's role has expanded beyond the IT department to touch every function within a company. The traditional business model is being redefined, and companies are beginning to understand that **innovation** is crucial to maintaining relevance. Those who can effectively harness digital tools can expect increased operational efficiency, stronger customer engagement, and enhanced decision-making capabilities.

At its core, digital transformation involves more than adopting the latest technologies. It requires a strategic shift in mindset. Leaders must recognise that this is an ongoing, continuous improvement, adaptation, and evolution journey. As the competitive landscape becomes increasingly digitised, organisations that strategically implement technology across all operations are better equipped to meet evolving customer expectations and navigate market shifts. Throughout this chapter, we will explore the far-reaching impact of technology on businesses, the challenges of digital transformation, and how to effectively integrate technological advancements to drive long-term growth and success.

16.2 The Digital Revolution

The **digital revolution** has profoundly changed how businesses function, compete, and engage with customers. Traditional ways of operating, often reliant on physical locations, face-to-face transactions, and time-consuming processes, have been disrupted by the rise of digital platforms, the **explosion of data**, and the introduction of new technologies that fundamentally change how we interact with the world. No industry has been left untouched, and businesses must grapple with the consequences of a rapidly evolving technological landscape.

One of the most significant outcomes of the digital revolution has been the shift from brick-and-mortar operations to **online platforms**. In previous decades, a company's success was often constrained by geographic limitations and the capacity of physical stores. Today, businesses can reach global markets through **e-commerce** and **digital services**, transcending the traditional boundaries that once defined their operations. Companies like **Amazon, Alibaba**, and **Shopify** have taken full advantage of this shift by creating digital ecosystems that allow them to serve customers worldwide. The scalability of these platforms is unmatched, allowing businesses to grow at an unprecedented rate and with far fewer physical constraints.

This transition to digital platforms is a trend and fundamental transformation in business operations. Companies that embrace these platforms can provide customers with seamless, personalised experiences that meet their needs in real-time. This level of convenience and accessibility has dramatically shifted customer expectations. Consumers now expect businesses to offer fast, efficient, and custom-tailored interactions across multiple channels, including mobile, desktop, and in-store experiences. For businesses, this has meant investing in **responsive, user-friendly platforms** that can deliver a cohesive experience across all devices.

The role of **digital platforms** in shaping business strategies cannot be overstated. They have become central to how businesses communicate, collaborate, and execute transactions. Social media networks, Software as a Service (SaaS) applications, and **cloud computing** services have revolutionised businesses' operations, offering greater efficiency, broader reach, and deeper customer engagement opportunities. Social media platforms like Facebook, Instagram, and LinkedIn have become vital tools for building brand loyalty, engaging directly with customers, and driving sales. SaaS platforms like **Salesforce** and **HubSpot** streamline customer relationship management, improving how businesses manage their sales pipelines and customer interactions.

Moreover, cloud computing services, such as **Amazon Web Services (AWS)** and **Microsoft Azure**, have transformed how companies store, manage, and process data. These platforms have allowed businesses to operate more flexibly and efficiently by eliminating the need for expensive on-premises infrastructure and enabling scalable, cost-effective IT solutions. **Big data**, in particular, has become an invaluable asset in the digital age. The ability to collect, analyse, and interpret vast amounts of data allows businesses to make more informed, data-driven decisions. Companies like **Google** and **Netflix** have harnessed the power of data analytics to refine their services, personalise user experiences, and optimise their offerings.

However, with these new technologies come new challenges. The **rapid pace of change** means that businesses must constantly evolve and adapt to stay competitive. The failure to do so can lead to missed opportunities or, worse, the inability to survive in an increasingly digitised world. The key to successfully navigating this transformation lies in leveraging technology to improve efficiency and drive innovation. The digital revolution presents both challenges and opportunities, and businesses that embrace these changes stand to benefit greatly.

16.3 Challenges and Opportunities

The **rapid pace of technological innovation** has undoubtedly created immense opportunities for businesses to thrive in the digital age. However, with these opportunities come significant challenges. The rate at which new technologies are being introduced and the sheer scale of disruption they bring can be overwhelming. Businesses are under constant pressure to innovate, adopt new tools, and refine their strategies to stay ahead of the competition. This has often meant completely rethinking traditional business models, favouring more agile, technology-driven approaches.

One of the primary challenges businesses face is continually adapting to **rapid technological changes**. The innovation cycle is accelerating, with new tools, platforms, and systems being developed quickly. This requires companies to remain **agile** and responsive, ready to integrate new technologies into their operations as soon as they emerge. Staying ahead of technological trends can give businesses a competitive edge, allowing them to leverage emerging technologies before their competitors. However, this also places immense pressure on companies to continuously invest in **research and development** and the upskilling of their workforce.

Another major challenge the digital revolution poses is the **disruption of traditional industries**. The rise of **digital-first companies** has upended long-established business models, forcing traditional players to rethink their approach. This has been more evident than in the **retail**, **media**, and **finance** industries. The retail sector, in particular, has been transformed by e-commerce, with brick-and-mortar retailers struggling to compete against online giants like **Amazon** and **Walmart**. Companies that were slow to adapt to the digital revolution, such as **Sears** and **Toys "R" Us**, found themselves unable to keep pace with the rapid changes and were eventually forced into bankruptcy.

At the same time, digital transformation has created opportunities for businesses willing to embrace change. Companies can gain a significant advantage over competitors by adopting new technologies and shifting their business models. Early adopters of **emerging technologies**, such as **artificial intelligence (AI)**, **blockchain**, and the **Internet of Things (IoT)**, are well-positioned to drive innovation and differentiate themselves in crowded markets. These technologies offer the potential to streamline operations, improve customer experiences, and unlock new revenue streams. However, success in the digital age requires more than just investing in technology; it requires a **strategic approach** that aligns technology investments with long-term business objectives.

The expectations of **customers** have also evolved in the digital age, creating both challenges and opportunities for businesses. Customers today are more informed, empowered, and discerning than ever before. They can access a wealth of information and easily compare products, services, and prices across multiple platforms. As a result, businesses must meet **higher expectations** for convenience, speed, and personalisation. Companies that fail to deliver seamless,

digitally enhanced customer experiences risk losing market share to more agile competitors who can better meet these demands. Conversely, businesses that successfully harness digital tools to provide personalised, frictionless experiences can foster customer loyalty and create lasting competitive advantages.

A compelling case study that illustrates the digital revolution's impact on traditional industries is the transformation of the retail sector. Established retail giants such as **Sears** and **Toys "R" Us** struggled to adapt to the changing landscape, failing to embrace **e-commerce** and digital customer engagement. In contrast, companies like **Amazon** and **Walmart** invested heavily in digital platforms, logistics, and data analytics, allowing them to survive and thrive in the digital age. **Amazon**, in particular, has set new standards for customer-centric innovation, from one-click ordering to **same-day delivery**, forcing others in the industry to follow suit or face extinction.

By embracing digital transformation, businesses can position themselves for long-term success. Rapid technological change and evolving customer expectations present significant challenges, but they also present an opportunity for companies to innovate, improve their operations, and create meaningful value for their customers. Those who can navigate this complex landscape with **agility** and strategic foresight will be well-positioned to lead in the digital age.

16.4 Strategic Technology Planning

The importance of **strategic technology planning** cannot be overstated in today's digital economy. Technology is no longer just a support function for business operations; it has become a critical driver of innovation, competitive advantage, and long-term growth. Businesses that fail to align their technology investments with their overarching business objectives will likely fall behind in an increasingly digital world. Strategic technology planning involves adopting new technologies and a thoughtful, structured approach to ensure that these investments contribute to achieving business goals.

A successful technology plan must begin with a **deep understanding of the organisation's objectives**. Whether the aim is to increase market share, enhance customer engagement, or improve operational efficiency, the company's technology initiatives should directly support these goals. For example, a business looking to increase customer engagement might prioritise investments in **Customer Relationship Management (CRM)** systems or **artificial intelligence (AI)** solutions that allow for personalised customer interactions at scale. In contrast, a company focused on reducing operational costs may invest in automation technologies that streamline processes and reduce manual intervention.

Assessing the organisation's **current technology capabilities** is a crucial step in planning. Before making new technology investments, businesses must evaluate their existing IT infrastructure, systems, and processes to identify gaps and areas for improvement. This assessment helps companies understand where they are currently strong and vulnerable. For instance, a company might discover that its legacy systems are hindering growth by making it difficult to scale or integrate with newer, more flexible technologies. In such cases, upgrading or replacing outdated infrastructure becomes a critical priority.

Once a thorough assessment has been conducted, the next step is prioritising **technology initiatives**. Not all technology investments will have the same impact on the business, and some may carry higher levels of risk or require more resources than others. Companies must carefully consider the potential **return on investment (ROI)** of each initiative and how well it aligns with the company's broader strategic objectives. For example, investing in a new e-commerce platform may be a higher priority for a retail business looking to expand its online presence, whereas upgrading back-office systems may be postponed if the immediate focus is on customer-facing technologies.

A well-thought-out **technology roadmap** is essential for successful implementation. This roadmap should outline the company's IT strategy over a specific timeframe, typically three to five years, and provide a clear vision of where it is headed technologically. It should also detail the goals for each technology initiative, ensuring that they are **Specific, Measurable, Achievable, Relevant, and Time-bound (SMART)**. Setting clear, actionable goals helps ensure that the organisation remains focused and accountable throughout the implementation process.

A key element of strategic technology planning is ensuring that **key stakeholders** are actively involved in the planning process. Too often, technology initiatives are driven solely by the IT department, with limited input from other parts of the business. However, engaging stakeholders from all areas of the organisation, especially those directly affected by the changes, ensures that the technology strategy is aligned with business needs and has buy-in from employees at every level. Leaders from departments such as operations, marketing, finance, and human resources should all have a say in how technology is implemented, as their unique perspectives will help shape a more holistic and effective plan.

Of course, technology planning is not a one-time activity. The digital landscape is constantly evolving, and businesses must remain **flexible** and **adaptable** in their approach to technology. As new technologies emerge and business needs change, the technology roadmap should be revisited and adjusted accordingly. This agile approach allows companies to stay responsive to technological advancements and quickly capitalise on new opportunities.

One company that exemplifies the importance of strategic technology planning is **General Electric (GE)**. Under the leadership of **Jeff Immelt**, GE embarked on a transformative digital journey that fundamentally reshaped the company's business model. GE recognised early on that the **Industrial Internet of Things (IIoT)** could revolutionise its industry, and the company made significant investments in developing the **Predix platform**, a cloud-based software platform designed to collect and analyse data from industrial machines. GE enhanced its products, improved operational efficiency, and created new revenue streams through digital services by aligning its IT strategy with its business goals. This case demonstrates how a strategic approach to technology planning can lead to significant competitive advantages and drive innovation.

16.5 Developing a Technology Roadmap

A **technology roadmap** is a critical tool businesses use to guide their digital transformation efforts over a defined period. It serves as a strategic blueprint that outlines the organisation's technology initiatives, sets clear objectives, and ensures that IT investments are aligned with the company's long-term goals. A well-crafted technology roadmap provides structure and direction, helping businesses navigate the complexities of the digital age while remaining agile enough to adapt to new challenges and opportunities.

The first step in developing a successful technology roadmap is to **set clear goals** for each technology initiative. These goals should be aligned with the company's overall business strategy and reflect the organisation's priorities. For instance, a company looking to enhance its data analytics capabilities might set a goal to implement a **business intelligence platform** allowing real-time insights into customer behaviour and market trends. Alternatively, a company focused on improving its cybersecurity posture might set a goal to invest in advanced security tools that protect against cyber threats and ensure compliance with data protection regulations. Whatever the specific goals, they should be articulated in a measurable and achievable way to provide clarity and accountability throughout the implementation process.

Successful technology roadmaps are not developed in isolation; they require the active participation of **key stakeholders** from across the organisation. Business leaders, IT professionals, and end-users all have valuable perspectives to contribute, and their involvement ensures that the roadmap is comprehensive and aligned with the organisation's needs. By engaging stakeholders early in the planning process, businesses can foster a sense of ownership and buy-in, which is critical to the success of any technology initiative. Furthermore, involving stakeholders helps identify challenges and opportunities that may not be immediately apparent to the IT team, resulting in a more well-rounded and effective plan.

While a technology roadmap provides structure and direction, it must also be **adaptable** to accommodate changes in the business environment and technological landscape. Technology planning is an ongoing process, and companies must be prepared to revise their roadmap as new technologies emerge, market conditions change, and business priorities evolve. This flexibility is essential for ensuring the company remains responsive to technological advancements and quickly seizes new opportunities. For example, a business that initially planned to invest in a particular technology may find that a more advanced or cost-effective solution becomes available, requiring an adjustment to the roadmap.

A powerful example of a successful technology roadmap is General Electric's (GE) transformation, which developed a long-term strategy to integrate digital capabilities into its industrial products. Recognising the growing importance of digital technologies in the industrial sector, GE invested heavily in the **Industrial Internet of Things (IIoT)** and the development of the **Predix platform**. This cloud-based platform allowed GE to collect and analyse data from its machines, providing customers with valuable insights that improved operational efficiency and reduced downtime. By aligning its technology roadmap with its business goals, GE enhanced its product offerings and positioned itself as a leader in the digital industrial space. This case highlights the importance of a strategic, forward-looking technology roadmap in driving innovation and competitive advantage.

16.6 Digital Transformation Roadmap

Digital transformation is a complex, multi-faceted process that requires businesses to fundamentally rethink how they use technology, processes, and people to drive innovation and improve performance. A successful digital transformation requires a clear, well-defined roadmap that outlines the steps, strategies, and milestones necessary to achieve the company's digital goals. This roadmap acts as a guide, helping businesses navigate the challenges of digital transformation while staying focused on their objectives.

The first step in the digital transformation journey is to **assess the company's current digital capabilities**. This involves evaluating the organisation's existing technology infrastructure, digital tools, and overall digital maturity. By understanding where the company currently stands regarding its digital readiness, businesses can identify gaps and areas for improvement. For example, a traditional manufacturing company looking to adopt **Industry 4.0** practices might begin by assessing its current use of automation, data analytics, and connectivity to determine where digital technologies can be integrated to improve production efficiency and reduce costs.

Once the current capabilities have been assessed, the next step is to **set clear digital goals** that align with the company's overall business objectives. These goals should be focused on areas where digital transformation can have the most significant impact, such as improving **customer experience**, increasing operational efficiency, or developing new digital products and services. For example, a retail company might aim to implement an **omnichannel strategy** that integrates online and offline shopping experiences, creating a seamless and personalised customer journey across all touchpoints.

The next step is to **develop a comprehensive digital transformation strategy**. This strategy should outline the specific initiatives, technologies, and processes that will be implemented to achieve the company's digital goals. It should also include a timeline, budget, and resource allocation plan to ensure the transformation is properly managed and executed. A financial services company, for example, might develop a strategy to digitise its core banking operations by adopting

blockchain technology, automating back-office processes, and launching digital banking services.

Engaging stakeholders is critical for building a digital culture that embraces change and **innovation**. Digital transformation is not just about adopting new technologies; it also requires a cultural shift within the organisation. By involving employees, customers, and partners in the transformation process, businesses can foster a culture of **collaboration** and continuous improvement. For example, a global logistics company might engage employees through workshops and training programs to ensure they can adopt and integrate new digital practices into their daily workflows.

As businesses implement their digital transformation strategies, they must **monitor progress** and remain flexible, adjusting their approach to reflect changing market conditions or new technological advancements. Digital transformation is an ongoing process, and agile businesses are better positioned to stay ahead of their competitors and capitalise on emerging opportunities.

16.7 Adopting New Technologies

In today's rapidly evolving business environment, adopting **new technologies** is crucial for maintaining competitiveness and driving innovation. Emerging technologies such as **artificial intelligence (AI)**, **blockchain**, and the **Internet of Things (IoT)** offer businesses new opportunities to enhance efficiency, create new products and services, and gain a competitive edge.

However, successfully adopting these technologies requires a thoughtful, strategic approach that ensures alignment with the company's broader goals and objectives.

The first step in adopting new technologies is identifying a **clear use case** that directly aligns with the company's strategic goals. This involves understanding the specific problem the technology will address, its benefits, and how it will integrate with existing systems and processes. For example, a financial services company looking to adopt **blockchain** technology might focus on improving transparency and security in cross-border transactions. By clearly defining the business case for the technology, companies can ensure that their investments are focused on delivering measurable results.

Once a use case has been identified, businesses should consider **piloting** the technology in a controlled environment before rolling it out across the organisation. A **pilot project** allows companies to test the technology, assess its feasibility, and identify potential challenges before full-scale implementation. This phased approach minimises risk and provides valuable insights for future adoption efforts. For instance, a manufacturing company might pilot **IoT** technology on a single production line to monitor machine performance and predict maintenance needs. If the pilot is successful, the company can expand the use of IoT across all its facilities, gradually scaling up the implementation as confidence in the technology grows.

Engaging **cross-functional teams** is another critical element of successful technology adoption. Implementing new technologies often requires collaboration across multiple departments, including IT, operations, finance, and human resources. By involving cross-functional teams early in the process, businesses can ensure that the technology is integrated effectively and that all stakeholders are aligned with the project's goals. For example, a retail company adopting **AI** for personalised recommendations might involve marketing, IT, and customer service teams to ensure the AI system is properly integrated with its e-commerce platform and customer engagement strategies.

Investing in skills and training is also essential for maximising the benefits of new technologies. Many emerging technologies require new skill sets, and businesses must ensure their employees can effectively use these tools. This may involve upskilling existing staff, hiring new talent, or partnering with external experts to provide the necessary training. For example, a healthcare provider adopting **AI** for diagnostic purposes might invest in training programs for doctors and medical staff to help them understand how to interpret AI-generated insights and integrate them into patient care. By investing in skills development, businesses can maximise the value of their technology investments and foster a culture of **innovation** and continuous improvement.

One of the most exciting emerging technologies is **artificial intelligence (AI)**, which transforms industries by enabling machines to learn from data, make decisions, and perform tasks that previously required human intelligence. AI is already used in various applications, from chatbots and virtual assistants to **predictive analytics** and autonomous vehicles. In the retail sector, for example, AI is used to deliver personalised product recommendations, manage inventory, and improve customer service. In healthcare, AI is applied in diagnostics, drug discovery, and patient care, while manufacturing companies use AI for predictive maintenance, quality control, and production optimisation.

Another game-changing technology is **blockchain**, a decentralised and distributed ledger that enables secure and transparent transactions without intermediaries. Blockchain can potentially disrupt industries such as finance, supply chain management, and healthcare by providing a trusted way to record and verify transactions. For example, blockchain can be used in supply chain management to track the provenance of goods, ensuring transparency and reducing the risk of fraud. In finance, blockchain enables secure and efficient cross-border transactions, while in healthcare, it is applied to manage patient records and ensure data privacy.

The **Internet of Things (IoT)** refers to the network of connected devices that communicate and exchange data over the Internet. IoT is transforming industries by enabling businesses to collect real-time data, automate processes, and create new business models. In manufacturing, for example, IoT is used to create **smart factories**, where machines communicate with each other to optimise production processes. In retail, IoT enables **smart shelves** and personalised shopping experiences, while in agriculture, IoT devices monitor soil conditions, weather patterns, and crop health to improve yields.

One key strategy for adopting new technologies is to start with a **clear use case**. Before investing in a new technology, it is important to identify a specific problem or opportunity the technology will address. For example, a financial services company looking to adopt blockchain technology might focus on improving the transparency and security of cross-border transactions. By identifying a clear use case, businesses can ensure that their technology investments are focused on solving a real problem and delivering tangible benefits.

The next step is to **pilot** the technology in a controlled environment. Piloting allows businesses to test the technology, assess its feasibility, and identify potential challenges before full-scale implementation. For example, a manufacturing company might pilot IoT technology on a single production line to monitor machine performance and predict maintenance needs. If the pilot is successful, the company can scale the technology across its operations.

16.8 Cybersecurity

Cybersecurity has become a critical priority as businesses increasingly rely on digital technologies and online platforms. Protecting digital assets, safeguarding sensitive data, and managing cyber risks are essential for maintaining trust, ensuring compliance, and avoiding costly breaches. In the digital age, **cyber threats** have become more sophisticated, and businesses face a growing range of risks, from data breaches and ransomware attacks to phishing schemes and insider threats.

One primary reason for cybersecurity's growing importance is the **increasing frequency and complexity of cyberattacks**. Cybercriminals constantly develop new methods to exploit IT systems, networks, and device vulnerabilities. As businesses continue to digitise their operations and store more data online, they become attractive targets for cyberattacks. A successful breach can have devastating financial and reputational consequences, making it imperative for businesses to invest in robust cybersecurity measures.

In addition to the direct threats posed by cybercriminals, businesses must also comply with many **regulatory requirements** related to data protection and cybersecurity. Governments and regulatory bodies worldwide have introduced stricter data protection laws to safeguard consumer privacy and ensure businesses are held accountable for managing data. Compliance with regulations such as the **General Data Protection Regulation (GDPR)** in Europe, the **California Consumer Privacy Act (CCPA)** in the US, and China's **Cybersecurity Law** is essential for avoiding legal penalties and maintaining customer trust.

Beyond regulatory compliance, cybersecurity is essential for protecting **customer trust**. In the digital age, customers expect businesses to safeguard their personal and financial information. A data breach can erode customer confidence, damage a company's reputation, and lead to a loss of business. For this reason, building a strong cybersecurity framework is not just about preventing attacks; it is also about maintaining the trust and loyalty of customers who entrust businesses with their most sensitive information.

Businesses must conduct a cybersecurity risk assessment to build a robust cybersecurity framework. This assessment involves identifying and evaluating potential threats to the company's IT systems, data, and digital assets. It should also include an analysis of internal and external risks and vulnerabilities in the organisation's hardware, software, and network infrastructure. By identifying where the company is most vulnerable, businesses can take steps to mitigate these risks before they are exploited.

A **multi-layered approach** to cybersecurity provides the best protection against cyber threats. This involves implementing multiple lines of defence, including **technical, administrative, and physical security measures**. On the technical side, businesses should implement **firewalls**, **intrusion detection systems**, **encryption**, and **antivirus software** to protect their IT systems from unauthorised access and cyberattacks. Regularly updating and patching software is also essential for addressing known vulnerabilities.

In terms of administrative measures, businesses should establish clear **cybersecurity policies and procedures**, including access controls, password management, and data protection protocols. Employee training is also critical, as many cyberattacks exploit human error. By providing regular cybersecurity training and awareness programs, businesses can educate employees on the risks of phishing, social engineering, and other common attack vectors.

Physical security measures are equally important. Businesses must secure physical access to their IT infrastructure, including **data centres**, **servers**, and **network equipment**. This may involve implementing biometric access controls, security cameras, and secure storage for sensitive data. For example, a healthcare provider might implement multi-layered security measures to protect patient data, including encrypting **electronic health records (EHRs)**, requiring **multi-factor authentication** to access sensitive information, and conducting regular security audits to identify and address vulnerabilities.

Even with the best cybersecurity measures, no system is completely immune to cyberattacks. For this reason, businesses must develop a comprehensive **incident response plan** to respond quickly and effectively to security breaches. This plan should outline the organisation's steps during a cyber incident, including containment, eradication, recovery, and communication. A well-prepared incident response plan can help minimise the damage caused by a breach and ensure a swift return to normal operations.

Continuous **monitoring and testing** are essential for maintaining a strong cybersecurity posture. This includes monitoring network traffic for unusual activity, conducting vulnerability assessments, and performing penetration testing to identify and address weaknesses in the organisation's security framework. By regularly assessing and improving their cybersecurity measures, businesses can stay ahead of cyber threats and reduce risk exposure.

16.9 Data-Driven Decision-Making

In the digital age, **data** has become one of the most valuable assets for businesses, often called the "new oil." However, having vast amounts of data is not enough; the ability to analyse and interpret this data is what creates value. **Data-driven decision-making** allows businesses to move beyond intuition and make choices based on real insights, leading to more informed and strategic outcomes. This capability is becoming increasingly essential as businesses face complex and fast-changing environments where traditional decision-making methods can no longer keep pace.

To successfully embrace data-driven decision-making, a business must cultivate a **data-centric culture**. This begins at the top, with leadership championing data as a critical component in all decision-making processes. Leaders and managers need to exemplify a reliance on data rather than instinct or tradition, setting the standard for the rest of the organisation. By embedding data analysis into everyday operations, businesses can optimise their decision-making and unlock new opportunities for **innovation** and **growth**.

However, building a data-centric culture requires significant **investment in training** and tools. Employees at all levels must be empowered to use data in their roles. This means investing in **data literacy** programs that demystify data analysis and make it accessible to non-technical staff. Workshops, seminars, and continuous education can help employees learn how to interpret data, make predictions, and use analytics tools effectively. This ensures that data becomes a shared resource that everyone in the organisation can utilise to improve processes, solve problems, and create new business opportunities.

Choosing the right **tools and technologies** to support data-driven decision-making is also crucial. Businesses need systems capable of collecting, storing, and analysing data in ways relevant to their operations. This can range from basic spreadsheet software to advanced analytics platforms incorporating **machine learning** and **AI** to uncover hidden patterns and trends. When selecting a data analytics tool, companies should consider their specific needs, such as the volume of data they process, the complexity of the analysis required, and the level of technical expertise within their teams. For instance, a retail company might benefit from a **Customer Relationship Management (CRM)** system integrated with analytics tools to track consumer behaviour, preferences, and buying patterns, allowing them to personalise marketing efforts and improve customer retention.

Data-driven decision-making provides significant **competitive advantages**, particularly in understanding customer behaviour and market trends. By analysing data from multiple sources, businesses can identify patterns that would otherwise go unnoticed, enabling them to fine-tune their strategies. For example, a company might use data analytics to segment its customer base, tailoring products and services to specific demographics and increasing the likelihood of customer satisfaction and repeat business. Businesses that effectively utilise data can respond more swiftly to market changes, adjusting their operations or offerings based on real-time information.

A strong example of a company that has successfully embraced data-driven decision-making is **Netflix**. The streaming giant uses data analytics to inform nearly every aspect of its business, from content creation to user recommendations. By analysing user viewing habits, Netflix can predict what types of shows and movies will be popular and invest in original content accordingly. Additionally, its recommendation engine, which suggests content based on user preferences, has been a key factor in driving engagement and retaining customers. Netflix's data-driven approach has allowed it to stay ahead in a highly competitive market, continuously adapting its offerings to meet customer needs.

In the digital era, the companies that excel use data to drive their decision-making processes. By embracing a data-centric culture, investing in the right tools, and continuously analysing data, businesses can make smarter, more informed choices that lead to sustained growth and success.

16.10 Customer Experience in the Digital Age

The rise of **digital technologies** has transformed the way businesses engage with their customers. In today's highly competitive marketplace, **customer experience (CX)** has become one of the most important differentiators. Businesses delivering seamless, personalised, and engaging experiences gain a significant advantage over their competitors. As customers now interact with businesses through various digital channels, websites, mobile apps, social media, and more, the ability to deliver a consistent and satisfying experience across all touchpoints has become a crucial element of success.

At its core, customer experience encompasses every interaction with a business, from the moment they first engage with the brand to post-purchase support. In the digital age, many of these interactions occur online, and businesses must ensure that their **digital touchpoints** are functional, intuitive, and responsive to customer needs. **Usability** is key, if a customer encounters difficulty navigating a website or a mobile app, they are likely to abandon their journey in favour of a competitor who offers a more seamless experience.

Studies have shown that customers are willing to pay more for a superior experience, and businesses prioritising CX tend to see higher levels of **customer satisfaction**, loyalty, and advocacy. Conversely, a poor customer experience can harm a company's reputation. In the age of social media and online reviews, negative experiences can spread rapidly, resulting in lost customers and damage to the brand. Therefore, businesses must invest in creating exceptional experiences at every stage of the customer journey, from pre-purchase interactions to post-purchase engagement.

One of the most effective strategies for improving customer experience in the digital age is through **personalisation**. Businesses can tailor their interactions to meet specific needs and create a more engaging experience by using data to understand customer preferences and behaviours. For example, **e-commerce** platforms can use data analytics to recommend products based on a customer's browsing history and past purchases, creating a more personalised and relevant shopping experience. Similarly, email marketing campaigns can be customised to address individual customer interests, leading to higher engagement and conversion rates.

Another key aspect of CX in the digital age is **omnichannel integration**. Today's customers expect a consistent experience across all channels, whether shopping online, using a mobile app, or visiting a physical store. Businesses must ensure their systems are integrated, allowing customers to seamlessly move between channels without losing their place in the journey. For example, a customer might start browsing products on a company's website, visit a physical store to see the items in person, and finally purchase the mobile app. The experience should feel cohesive and connected across all these touchpoints.

Engagement is a driving force behind **customer loyalty**, and digital tools provide businesses with numerous opportunities to foster deeper connections with their customers. **Social media** platforms, for example, offer businesses a space to interact with customers directly, share content, and build communities around their brands. By regularly engaging with customers on social media, businesses can create a sense of loyalty and belonging that strengthens their relationship with the brand.

In addition, **loyalty programs** that reward customers for repeat purchases or referrals can be enhanced through digital tools. Mobile apps, for instance, can track customer rewards and offer personalised incentives to encourage repeat business. This increases engagement and helps businesses gather valuable data on customer preferences and behaviours, which can be used to personalise the experience further.

A standout example of a company that has mastered customer experience in the digital age is **Starbucks**. The coffee giant's mobile app is a cornerstone of its customer engagement strategy, offering features such as mobile ordering, payment, and a loyalty program that rewards customers with free drinks and other perks. The app's seamless integration with Starbucks' physical locations ensures customers can easily order ahead, skip lines, and pick up their drinks without hassle. Furthermore, the app provides personalised recommendations based on past purchases, enhancing the overall customer experience. This level of convenience and personalisation has helped Starbucks build a loyal customer base and drive repeat business.

In the digital age, **customer experience** has become critical to business success. By leveraging digital tools to provide personalised, seamless, and engaging experiences, businesses can create strong customer relationships, increase loyalty, and maintain a competitive edge. Companies prioritising CX and continuously innovating in this area will be well-positioned to thrive in the digital marketplace.

16.11 Digital Leadership

Effective leadership becomes increasingly crucial as businesses navigate the complexities of digital transformation. The role of a leader in the digital age is not just about managing technology; it's about fostering a culture of **innovation**, agility, and continuous learning. Digital leaders must understand the technologies driving transformation and guide their organisations through the changes these technologies bring. In essence, **digital leadership** requires a combination of strategic foresight, technological proficiency, and people management skills.

The traditional concept of leadership has evolved in the digital era. Leaders are now expected to be more than just effective managers; they must be **visionaries** who can anticipate and respond to the rapid pace of technological change. This requires a deep understanding of **emerging technologies** and their potential to reshape industries. Leaders must be able to translate complex technical concepts into actionable business strategies, ensuring that digital initiatives align with the organisation's overall objectives.

Digital leaders are also responsible for guiding their teams through the often disruptive digital transformation process. This requires strong **change management** skills, as digital transformation can involve significant shifts in processes, systems, and even company culture. Leaders must communicate the vision for the future and inspire confidence among their teams. Moreover, they need to address any fears or resistance that may arise during the transformation process. By fostering an environment of trust and transparency, leaders can help their teams navigate the uncertainties of digital change with greater ease.

One of the most important aspects of digital leadership is the ability to foster a **culture of innovation**. In a rapidly changing technological landscape, businesses that innovate quickly and effectively are more likely to succeed. Digital leaders must create an environment where **experimentation** and **risk-taking** are encouraged, and failure is seen as a valuable learning opportunity rather than a setback. This can be achieved by providing employees with the resources and support they need to pursue new ideas, whether it's access to the latest technologies or opportunities for professional development.

At the same time, digital leaders must stay **ahead of digital trends**. To lead effectively in the digital age, it is essential to keep up with the latest technological advancements and understand their implications for the business. This requires staying informed about current trends, anticipating developments, and engaging with industry experts and thought leaders. Leaders who can stay ahead of the curve will be better positioned to guide their organisations through the complexities of digital transformation.

In addition to keeping abreast of digital trends, **digital leaders** must be adept at managing **tech-savvy teams**. As technology evolves, businesses increasingly rely on specialists in **artificial intelligence (AI)**, **data analytics**, **cybersecurity**, and **cloud computing**. Managing these highly skilled professionals requires a unique blend of technical understanding and strong **communication skills**. Leaders must be able to translate complex technological information into strategic business language, ensuring that teams understand how their work contributes to the broader organisational goals. This balance between technical and strategic leadership fosters innovation and drives the business forward.

Moreover, digital leaders must recognise the importance of **collaboration** in a digitally transformed business environment. The ability to work effectively across departments and break down traditional silos is critical for driving digital initiatives. In a successful digital transformation, cross-functional teams, including IT, marketing, operations, and finance, must collaborate closely to ensure that new technologies are fully integrated into the business. **Leaders** play a key role in facilitating this collaboration by promoting **open communication**, ensuring alignment on objectives, and fostering a **shared vision** across the organisation.

One of the most celebrated examples of **effective digital leadership** is **Satya Nadella**, CEO of **Microsoft**. When Nadella took over the helm in 2014, Microsoft was perceived as a company that had missed key trends, such as **mobile** and **cloud computing**. Nadella quickly set about transforming both the company's strategy and its culture. His "**mobile-first, cloud-first**" approach has been instrumental in revitalising Microsoft, positioning it as a leader in cloud computing through its **Azure** platform and making it one of the most valuable companies in the world. Nadella's focus on breaking down silos, encouraging collaboration, and fostering a more inclusive and innovative culture has been key to Microsoft's resurgence.

Through the lens of **digital leadership**, Nadella's example underscores the importance of combining **technical expertise** with strong **people management** and **strategic vision**. Microsoft's transformation under his leadership is a testament to how embracing change, fostering a culture of innovation, and investing in the right technologies can drive a business's success in the digital age.

16.12 Innovation Through Digital Channels

In today's interconnected world, **digital channels** have become powerful tools for businesses seeking to expand their reach, enter new markets, and foster **innovation**. These channels, from **websites**, **social media**, and **mobile apps** to **e-commerce platforms**, provide businesses unprecedented opportunities to connect with customers, gather insights, and offer **personalised** experiences. Leveraging digital platforms effectively enables businesses to grow in ways that were impossible just a decade ago.

Digital channels allow businesses to innovate by offering new **products** and **services**, refining business models, and engaging customers in real-time. The use of **web platforms** and **social media** has allowed businesses to crowdsource ideas and feedback from their customers, facilitating the rapid development and testing of new concepts. By embracing this **open innovation** approach, companies can reduce the risks associated with innovation and ensure that their products align with customer expectations.

One of the key advantages of digital channels is their ability to support **new business models**. For example, the rise of **subscription-based models** has been driven largely by digital platforms. Companies like **Netflix**, **Spotify**, and **Adobe** have shifted away from traditional sales models and embraced subscription services that generate recurring revenue and foster deeper customer relationships. Similarly, **platform-based business models** have emerged, where companies like **Uber**, **Airbnb**, and **Amazon** act as intermediaries connecting service providers with customers. These platforms create immense value through **network effects**, becoming more valuable as they scale and attract more users.

The **omnichannel strategy**, which integrates multiple digital and physical touchpoints, has become critical for businesses aiming to deliver a seamless customer experience. Consumers today expect consistency, whether they interact with a brand in-store, online, or via mobile. This expectation has led to integrating **e-commerce platforms** with physical stores, where digital tools like mobile apps and **click-and-collect services** allow customers to order online and pick up in-store or vice versa.

Reaching new markets is another benefit of leveraging digital channels. **E-commerce platforms** and **digital marketing** have made it easier than ever for businesses to expand internationally without needing a physical presence in each market. For example, a small artisan business can sell handmade goods to customers around the globe through platforms like **Etsy**. Digital channels provide the ability to scale quickly, allowing businesses to test new markets and refine their strategies without the significant upfront costs traditionally associated with international expansion.

A notable example of innovation through digital channels is **Airbnb**. By creating a platform that connects people offering short-term accommodations with travellers, Airbnb has transformed the **hospitality industry**. Airbnb's use of **digital channels** has allowed it to scale from a small startup to a global leader in a few short years. The platform's user-friendly design and reliance on **peer reviews** create trust between hosts and guests, enabling millions of people to book unique accommodations worldwide. Airbnb's success highlights how digital channels can be used to create new business models, disrupt traditional industries, and scale rapidly.

In conclusion, digital channels provide businesses with various tools to drive innovation, enter new markets, and refine their business models. Companies that effectively leverage these platforms are well-positioned to stay ahead in a competitive and rapidly evolving digital landscape.

16.13 Case Studies in Digital Transformation

Examining real-world examples of businesses that have successfully navigated **digital transformation** offers valuable insights into the challenges, strategies, and outcomes associated with these efforts. These case studies illustrate how companies can harness **digital technologies** to drive innovation, improve efficiency, and gain a competitive advantage.

One of the most iconic examples of successful digital transformation is **General Electric (GE)**. GE, a long-established industrial giant, recognised that its traditional business model needed to evolve to remain competitive in a rapidly digitising world. Under the leadership of **Jeff Immelt**, GE embarked on a comprehensive digital transformation strategy that focused on integrating **digital capabilities** into its industrial products and services. A cornerstone of GE's transformation was the development of the **Predix platform**, a cloud-based software platform designed for the **Industrial Internet of Things (IIoT)**. Predix allows GE to collect and analyse data from industrial machines, providing customers with valuable insights to improve operational efficiency and reduce downtime.

GE's digital transformation also involved a significant cultural shift. The company embraced a more agile, software-focused approach, hiring thousands of software engineers and investing heavily in **data analytics** and **AI**. Although GE's transformation was not without challenges, its efforts to digitise its industrial operations have positioned it as a leader in the IIoT space. GE's experience highlights the importance of aligning **digital**

initiatives with core business objectives and the need for cultural change to support digital transformation.

Another compelling example of digital transformation is **Domino's Pizza**, which revitalised its business by embracing technology. In the early 2000s, Domino's faced declining sales and stiff competition in the fast-food industry. Recognising the need for change, the company boldly became a technology-driven business. Central to Domino's digital transformation was developing its digital ordering and delivery platforms. Domino's invested in **digital tools**, including a mobile app, an online ordering system, and even voice-activated ordering through **Amazon Alexa**. These innovations made it easier for customers to order pizza, track their deliveries, and engage with the brand.

Domino's also embraced **data analytics** to optimise its operations, from supply chain management to marketing. By analysing customer data, Domino's was able to **personalise promotions**, predict demand, and improve delivery times. The company's digital initiatives have been highly successful, driving significant sales and market share growth. Today, a substantial portion of Domino's revenue comes from its digital channels, and the company is regarded as one of the most innovative players in the fast-food industry. Domino's success demonstrates how **digital transformation** can revitalise a brand and drive long-term growth.

Burberry, the British luxury fashion brand, offers another example of successful digital transformation. With declining sales and growing competition in the luxury market, Burberry turned to digital technologies to strengthen its brand and enhance the **customer experience**. The company's digital transformation strategy focused on integrating digital and physical retail experiences. Burberry introduced **digital mirrors** in its stores, allowing customers to see how clothing would look without trying it on. Burberry also embraced **social media** and **live streaming**, becoming one of the first luxury brands to broadcast its runway shows online. These efforts helped Burberry modernise its brand, connect with a younger audience, and differentiate itself in a crowded market.

These case studies illustrate the transformative power of digital technologies and the importance of aligning digital initiatives with business goals. By embracing **innovation**, investing in digital tools, and fostering a culture of agility, businesses can successfully navigate the complexities of digital transformation and position themselves for long-term success.

Conclusion

The rapid rise of **technology** and **digital transformation** has fundamentally altered how businesses operate, interact with customers, and compete in the marketplace. As explored throughout this chapter, the digital revolution offers businesses both **challenges** and **opportunities**. Companies must now embrace **digital tools**, develop **data-driven strategies**, and foster a culture of **innovation** to remain relevant in an increasingly competitive and fast-paced environment.

Successful digital transformation requires more than just adopting new technologies; it demands a **strategic approach** that aligns technology investments with business goals. Businesses must invest in building the right infrastructure, upskilling their workforce, and fostering an **agile culture** that can adapt to technological changes. Leaders play a critical role in guiding their organisations through digital transformation, ensuring that teams remain aligned with the company's vision while encouraging **collaboration**, **innovation**, and **continuous learning**.

The GE, Domino's Pizza, and Burberry case studies demonstrate how embracing digital transformation can drive business growth, create new revenue streams, and improve operational efficiency. By investing in technologies like **AI**, **IoT**, **data analytics**, and **cloud computing**, businesses can unlock new opportunities and gain a competitive edge in their respective industries.

In conclusion, businesses that successfully leverage digital tools and embrace data-driven decision-making will be well-positioned to thrive; those who resist change or fail to invest in **digital transformation** risk being left behind. The **digital age** is here to stay, and companies embracing this new reality will lead their industries in the coming years.

Chapter 17

Leadership in Crisis: Managing Through Turbulence

17.1 Overview

Crises are inevitable in any business's journey, testing even the most seasoned leaders. These challenges, whether caused by **economic disruptions**, natural disasters, pandemics, or internal upheavals, demand more than survival; they require leaders to **steer** their organisations through turbulence, not merely to endure but to emerge stronger and more resilient. Effective crisis leadership means more than navigating through chaos; it involves finding **opportunities** within adversity and setting a course for long-term success. This chapter aims to equip aspiring leaders and entrepreneurs with the **mindset**, tools, and strategies to face crises confidently and resiliently. From early detection and crisis management planning to effective communication and post-crisis recovery, this comprehensive guide prepares leaders to handle difficult times and transform them into stepping stones for growth and improvement.

17.2 Recognising Signs of a Crisis

Recognising the early signs of a crisis is not just a skill; it's a proactive stance that every leader should adopt. Crises rarely appear without warning; they often start as minor issues that, if left unchecked, can escalate into major disruptions. By staying alert to **internal** and **external signals**, leaders can detect potential crises early and take pre-emptive action to mitigate their impact. External indicators like **market fluctuations**, regulatory changes, competitive pressures, and public perception shifts can be warning signs. For example, a sharp drop in consumer confidence may indicate an impending economic downturn, adversely affecting business operations. Similarly, new **legislation** in highly regulated sectors such as finance or healthcare can pose unforeseen challenges, making it crucial for leaders to stay informed and anticipate the potential impacts on their organisations.

Internal indicators also require close attention. Persistent **operational inefficiencies**, financial strain, and declining employee morale are all potential signs of trouble. For example, rising debt levels, shrinking profit margins or frequent equipment failures could signal deeper financial or operational issues that demand immediate attention. High employee turnover or visible drops in morale might indicate more profound **organisational problems**, such as leadership shortcomings or a toxic work environment, which, if left unaddressed, can exacerbate the crisis. Leaders must be vigilant, monitoring these signs and taking swift action to prevent them from escalating.

Proactive monitoring and response are essential for effective crisis management. Leveraging **data-driven insights** allows leaders to track key performance indicators (KPIs) and use predictive analytics to foresee potential issues, such as supply chain disruptions. Regular audits of financial, operational, and compliance processes can identify vulnerabilities before they become crises. Additionally, **scenario planning** helps leaders anticipate potential crisis scenarios and develop strategic responses, fostering a culture of adaptability and preparedness. By maintaining a vigilant and proactive approach, leaders can prevent minor issues from escalating into full-blown crises, safeguarding the organisation's stability and long-term success.

17.3 Crisis Management Planning

Effective crisis management begins long before a crisis occurs. Developing a comprehensive **crisis management plan** ensures that an organisation is prepared to respond promptly and effectively to unexpected events. A robust plan minimises the impact of a crisis and helps the organisation recover quickly and emerge stronger. A crucial component of crisis management planning is assembling a **crisis response team** composed of key personnel from across the organisation, including leadership, communications, legal, operations, HR, and IT. Each team member must have clearly defined roles and responsibilities to ensure all aspects of the crisis are managed with precision and clarity.

Creating detailed **contingency plans** is another fundamental aspect of crisis management. The crisis management plan should address various crises the organisation might face, such as natural disasters, cyberattacks, financial downturns, and public relations scandals. Based on a thorough risk assessment, specific contingency measures must be outlined for each type of crisis. Business continuity planning is a critical component of this process. It focuses on identifying essential business functions that must be maintained during a crisis and developing strategies to ensure continued operation. For instance, companies might establish **backup data centres** or alternative supply chain routes to ensure uninterrupted operations during a disruption.

Communication protocols are also a vital element of crisis management. The crisis management plan should outline how and when to communicate with various stakeholders, including employees, customers, investors, and regulators. Pre-prepared templates for press releases, internal communications, and social media updates can expedite communication, ensuring information is disseminated quickly and accurately. Regular **drills and simulations** are essential to test the effectiveness of the crisis management plan. These exercises allow the crisis response team to practice their roles, identify weaknesses in the plan, and refine strategies as needed. They also help familiarise the team with the plan, reducing response time during a crisis. A well-prepared organisation is better equipped to handle a crisis and more likely to emerge stronger and more resilient.

17.4 Effective Communication During a Crisis

One of the most critical components of crisis management is **communication**. During crises, stakeholders expect leaders to provide clear information, reassurance, and direction. How leaders communicate can significantly influence public perception, employee morale, and reputation. **Transparency** is key to maintaining credibility. For instance, leaders should provide honest and accurate information about the situation during a financial crisis, even when delivering bad news. Attempts to downplay or obscure the severity of a crisis can lead to a loss of trust and long-term damage to the organisation's reputation.

Sticking to the **facts** is crucial to prevent the spread of rumours and misinformation, which can intensify the crisis. Leaders should ensure that all communication is based on verified information and avoid making promises that may not be possible to keep. Consistency in messaging across all channels is also vital to avoid confusion. All spokespersons and stakeholders must be aligned with the organisation's crisis response strategy to ensure everyone delivers the same key messages to their respective audiences.

Managing **media relations** is a critical aspect of crisis communication. Designating a single spokesperson, or a small group of spokespersons, ensures that the organisation speaks with one voice. This individual should be well-prepared to handle challenging questions and effectively communicate the organisation's key messages during the crisis. Being proactive with the media helps the organisation maintain control over the narrative, and timely responses to media inquiries are crucial for shaping public perception. Delayed or incomplete responses can lead to negative coverage and speculation.

Internal communication is just as important as external communication during a crisis. Keeping employees informed helps maintain **morale** and cohesion. Leaders should provide regular updates on the crisis status, the organisation's response, and any changes that may affect the team. Encouraging feedback and providing a platform for questions and input can also alleviate anxiety among employees, helping them feel more engaged and informed. Effective communication with the public, media, or internal teams is foundational to successful crisis management. Leaders can maintain trust and guide their organisations through turbulent times by being transparent, responsive, and consistent.

17.5 Decision Making Under Pressure

Decision-making during a crisis often requires leaders to act swiftly and decisively under immense pressure. The stakes are high, and the margin for error is narrow. Making sound decisions in such circumstances demands a **calm mindset**, clarity, and the ability to collaborate effectively. One of the most important qualities of a crisis leader is the ability to **maintain composure** under pressure. Stress and panic can impair judgment, leading to hasty and potentially damaging decisions. Composed leaders can think clearly, objectively assess the situation, and make more informed decisions.

Prioritising **critical issues** is another essential aspect of crisis decision-making. Not all problems require immediate attention, so leaders must focus on those with the greatest impact on the organisation's survival and recovery. This process involves triaging the situation to address the most immediate threats first, ensuring that resources are allocated where they are most needed. Mindfulness and stress management techniques, such as deep breathing or meditation, can help leaders manage their stress levels and maintain a clear, focused mindset during high-pressure situations.

Gathering **accurate information** is crucial for making informed decisions. Leaders should seek reliable data from internal and external sources to understand the full scope of the crisis. This might involve consulting experts, reviewing data analytics, or gathering input from key stakeholders. However, avoiding information overload is essential, as too much data can overwhelm decision-making. Leaders should focus on the most relevant information and validate assumptions wherever possible to reduce uncertainty and ensure that decisions are based on accurate insights.

Involving the right people in the decision-making process is also key. Collaboration often benefits crisis decision-making, as diverse perspectives can lead to stronger decisions and help identify potential blind spots. Leaders should assemble a decision-making team with individuals who have varied expertise and encourage open dialogue, allowing team members to share their opinions freely. This approach fosters a more comprehensive understanding of the situation and helps ensure that all potential solutions are considered.

Making **decisive choices** is critical during a crisis. Indecision can be as damaging as making the wrong choice. Leaders must be willing to make tough decisions and act decisively, even in the face of uncertainty. Balancing speed with careful consideration is important, ensuring that decisions are made quickly but not recklessly. Leaders should also consider the long-term impact of their decisions, avoiding quick fixes that may create more significant problems. Being flexible and willing to adjust decisions as new information emerges is also crucial, as crises are often fluid and unpredictable.

17.6 Maintaining Team Morale and Cohesion

Maintaining team morale and cohesion during a crisis can be incredibly challenging. Uncertainty, stress, and fear can undermine trust, collaboration, and motivation. Leaders must focus on providing support, fostering resilience, and maintaining a sense of unity within the team. One of the most effective ways to support the team is by being visible and accessible. Regular check-ins and open lines of communication help reassure team members that leadership is engaged and responsive to their concerns.

Frequent and transparent communication is essential for sustaining morale. Leaders should provide regular updates on the crisis status, the organisation's response, and any changes that may affect the team. Even when there is little new information to share, simply checking in demonstrates that leadership is committed to keeping everyone informed. Acknowledging the emotional impact of the crisis is also crucial. Crises can evoke a wide range of emotions, from anxiety and frustration to anger and despair. Leaders should create a safe space for team members to express their feelings, demonstrating empathy and understanding, which can significantly strengthen team cohesion and trust.

Encouraging a growth mindset can help foster resilience within the team. This involves viewing challenges and setbacks as opportunities for learning and development rather than insurmountable obstacles. Leaders can promote this mindset by recognising and celebrating small wins, no matter how minor they may seem. These victories can boost morale and reinforce the belief that the team can overcome the crisis. Providing resources to support team members' physical and mental well-being is also essential. Access to mental health services, flexible work schedules, and opportunities for rest can help prevent burnout and maintain overall resilience.

Promoting cross-functional collaboration can enhance problem-solving and foster a sense of unity within the organisation. Crises often require teams from different departments to work together to address complex challenges. Leaders should encourage sharing information, resources, and expertise across departments to facilitate effective collaboration. Reminding the team of the organisation's mission and the importance of their work can also help sustain motivation and cohesion. When team members feel they are contributing to a larger purpose, they are more likely to remain engaged and committed, even during difficult times.

Leading by example is perhaps the most powerful way for leaders to inspire their teams during a crisis. Demonstrating calmness, resilience, and a collaborative spirit sets the tone for the entire organisation. Leaders should be willing to work alongside their teams, showing that they are not above the challenges and are fully committed to overcoming them together.

Maintaining trust and accountability is also essential. Leaders can build trust by being transparent about the organisation's challenges and decisions and holding team members accountable for their roles and responsibilities.

17.7 Business Continuity Planning

Ensuring the continuation of critical business functions during a crisis can determine whether an organisation **survives** or fails. Business continuity planning (BCP) is a crucial aspect of crisis management designed to help organisations maintain essential functions during and after a disruption. While crisis management focuses on the immediate response, BCP addresses the longer-term ability to sustain operations. A well-crafted BCP involves identifying potential **threats** to the organisation and developing strategies to ensure critical business functions can continue during and after a crisis. Potential disruptions can range from natural disasters and cyberattacks to pandemics and geopolitical events.

Maintaining critical operations during a crisis is the foundation of any BCP. This includes identifying **essential business functions** such as customer support, IT infrastructure, and supply chain management and ensuring they can be sustained despite significant disruptions. For example, a financial services firm may prioritise maintaining its trading platforms and customer service operations, even if other business functions need to be scaled back temporarily. Protecting physical and digital assets is also a key component of business continuity. Physical assets, such as facilities and equipment, must be safeguarded through secure storage and contingency plans for relocation if necessary. Digital assets, particularly **data**, require robust cybersecurity measures, including regular backups, encryption, and access controls. Establishing secure, remote work environments for employees can also help ensure business continuity if physical office access is disrupted.

Managing supply chain disruptions is a common challenge during crises. Companies should develop **contingency plans** to identify alternative suppliers, stockpile critical materials, and diversify supply chains geographically. The COVID-19 pandemic highlighted the vulnerabilities of global supply chains and underscored the need for flexible and resilient supply chain strategies. Regular testing and updating of the business continuity plan are essential to ensure its **effectiveness**. Drills and simulations can help identify weaknesses and refine strategies. At the same time, periodic reviews ensure that the plan remains relevant in the face of new risks, business changes, or shifts in market conditions.

A well-prepared business continuity plan enables an organisation to survive a crisis and positions it for a strong **recovery**. Organisations can build resilience and ensure continuity during challenging times by identifying critical operations, safeguarding assets, managing supply chain disruptions, and regularly testing and updating the plan.

17.8 Learning from Crisis

Crises are not only challenges to be overcome but also valuable opportunities for **learning** and growth. One of the most important outcomes of any crisis is the lessons learned, which can provide critical insights to help organisations improve their crisis management strategies and build greater resilience. Conducting a thorough **post-crisis review** is essential for understanding what happened, how the crisis was managed, and what could have been done differently. This review should involve input from all relevant stakeholders, including employees, customers, suppliers, and external partners, to ensure a comprehensive understanding of the crisis and identify areas for improvement.

During the post-crisis review, it is crucial to identify specific **lessons learned**. This might include recognising missed early warning signs, evaluating which crisis management strategies were effective, and understanding the weaknesses in the organisation's response. For example, if a crisis exposed vulnerabilities in the supply chain, this could lead to new strategies for supplier management in the future. Implementing these lessons is key to ensuring the organisation is better prepared for future crises and avoids repeating past mistakes.

Implementing changes based on the lessons learned from a crisis is essential for continuous improvement. This means translating insights from the post-crisis review into tangible actions, such as updating crisis management plans, improving employee training, investing in new technology, or changing organisational structures. These changes help the organisation be better prepared for future crises and demonstrate a commitment to learning and growth, which can enhance stakeholder trust and confidence.

Building a **culture of continuous improvement** is crucial for ensuring that the lessons learned from a crisis are applied and that the organisation becomes more resilient over time. Leaders play a vital role in fostering this environment by being open to feedback, encouraging innovation, and recognising those who contribute to the organisation's learning and growth. By creating a culture where continuous improvement is valued and rewarded, organisations can turn adversity into an opportunity for **strengthening** and growth, ensuring they are better equipped to face future challenges.

17.9 Rebuilding Trust and Confidence

Rebuilding **trust** and confidence after a crisis is one of leaders' most challenging tasks. Whether it involves customers, employees, investors, or the broader public, restoring trust is essential for long-term recovery and success. This process requires transparency, consistency, and a commitment to following through on promises. **Transparent communication** is the cornerstone of rebuilding trust. After a crisis, stakeholders need to understand what happened, why, and what the organisation is doing to prevent it from happening again. This requires honest communication from leadership, acknowledging any mistakes made during the crisis and avoiding the assignment of blame. Taking responsibility for failures and explaining the corrective measures can go a long way in restoring confidence.

Delivering on promises made during the crisis is also critical for rebuilding trust. Whether the promise involves improving safety standards, enhancing customer service, or compensating those affected, these commitments must be fulfilled. Stakeholders will be closely watching to see if the organisation follows through on its promises, and failure to do so can further damage trust and credibility. Demonstrating a commitment to recovery and long-term improvement is equally important. This may involve investments in new technologies, enhancements to risk management practices, or even leadership changes. Keeping stakeholders informed about the recovery process and soliciting their input can help demonstrate that the organisation is serious about making meaningful, lasting improvements.

Rebuilding **relationships** with key stakeholders often requires personal engagement beyond public communication. This might include direct outreach to major customers, investors, or partners to reassure them of the organisation's commitment to recovery. These relationships are crucial to the organisation's future success, and thoughtful, personalised engagement can help rebuild trust and confidence.

Ultimately, rebuilding trust and confidence after a crisis is challenging but essential. By being transparent, delivering on promises, demonstrating a commitment to recovery, and actively engaging with stakeholders, leaders can lay the foundation for long-term success. Trust is hard to regain, so leaders must handle this process carefully, ensuring **transparency** and follow-through at every stage.

17.10 Resilience and Adaptability

Resilience and adaptability are two essential traits for leaders navigating crises. These qualities help leaders guide their organisations through difficult times and position them to emerge stronger and more prepared for future challenges. Resilience involves the ability to withstand adversity and recover from setbacks, while adaptability refers to the capacity to **adjust** to new conditions and pivot when necessary. These traits enable leaders to respond effectively to crises and ensure their organisations remain agile and responsive.

Resilience is about maintaining a positive outlook, staying focused on long-term goals, and not letting temporary challenges derail progress. Resilient leaders can keep their teams motivated and focused despite difficult circumstances. This is especially important during crises when the pressure can be overwhelming, and challenges can come from many directions. Building resilience requires adopting **coping strategies** such as stress management techniques and fostering a growth mindset, which views challenges as opportunities for learning and development.

Adaptability is equally crucial during a crisis, as situations can evolve rapidly, and initial plans may no longer be viable. Adaptable leaders are open to change, can find new solutions, and are willing to take **decisive action** when necessary. This flexibility enables them to pivot quickly, keep their organisations moving forward, and capitalise on emerging opportunities. Cultivating adaptability involves encouraging **innovation**, being open to feedback, and empowering teams to experiment and take calculated risks.

Leading by example is essential for fostering resilience and adaptability within an organisation. Leaders who remain calm, demonstrate flexibility and are willing to adapt to changing circumstances inspire their teams to do the same. This helps the organisation navigate the current crisis and builds a **culture of resilience** and adaptability that will serve the organisation well. History is filled with examples of resilient and adaptable leaders who successfully navigated crises, such as CEOs who made difficult decisions during the 2008 financial crisis, ensuring their companies' survival and positioning them for recovery.

By developing resilience and adaptability, leaders can successfully guide their organisations through crises, inspire their teams, and ensure their organisations are well-positioned for long-term success. In a world where constant change and crises can strike at any time, the ability to remain **resilient and adaptable** is more important than ever.

17.11 Case Studies in Crisis Leadership

One of the most powerful ways to learn about crisis leadership is through **case studies**. These examples provide valuable insights into how leaders navigated crises, what strategies worked, and what could have been done differently. Johnson & Johnson's handling of the Tylenol tampering incident in 1982 is a classic example of successful crisis management. When seven people died after taking Tylenol capsules laced with cyanide, the company faced a potential disaster. Public fear was widespread, and the future of the Tylenol brand seemed in jeopardy. James Burke, the company's CEO, quickly prioritised **public safety** over profits, recalling all Tylenol products nationwide for $100 million. This decisive action and transparent communication helped the company rebuild consumer trust and emerge stronger from the crisis.

In contrast, BP's handling of the Deepwater Horizon oil spill in 2010 illustrates the **consequences** of poor crisis management. The explosion on the BP-operated rig led to one of the worst environmental disasters in history. BP's initial response was criticised for being slow and ineffective, and CEO Tony Hayward's infamous remark, "I would like my life back," further damaged the company's reputation. BP's communication failure and perceived prioritisation of legal liabilities over environmental responsibility severely damaged its reputation. The company was eventually forced to spend billions on clean-up efforts, compensation, and legal settlements.

Toyota's recall crisis in 2009-2010 is another example of crisis management, where the company faced significant challenges due to reports of unintended acceleration in several vehicle models. Initially, Toyota was slow to acknowledge the severity of the problem and communicate with regulators and the public. However, once the crisis escalated, the company took significant steps to address the issue. The company's president, Akio Toyoda, publicly apologised and took personal responsibility for the failures, implementing rigorous **quality control** measures and making substantial changes to production processes to prevent similar issues in the future.

The 2008 financial crisis and the collapse of Lehman Brothers highlight the dangers of poor risk management and failure to act decisively in a crisis. Lehman's leadership, under CEO Richard Fuld, failed to manage the firm's exposure to the subprime mortgage market, and when the crisis hit, they could not secure a bailout or find a buyer. This led to the company's collapse, contributing significantly to the global economic downturn. Lehman's failure underscores the importance of **risk management** and the need for decisive action during a crisis.

These case studies provide essential lessons for aspiring leaders. Whether through swift, transparent action or learning from missteps, each example offers valuable insights into what works and does not in crisis management. By learning from these successes and failures, leaders can better prepare to handle future crises and guide their organisations through turbulent times.

Conclusion

Leadership during times of crisis is a true test of an organisation's **resilience**, adaptability, and core values. Navigating through turbulence requires more than technical skills or strategic foresight; it demands a deep commitment to transparency, decisive action, effective communication, and a focus on stakeholder well-being. This chapter has explored the many facets of crisis leadership, from early detection and proactive planning to making tough decisions under pressure and maintaining team morale. Real-world case studies have provided valuable lessons on what works in crisis management and what can go wrong.

Crises are inevitable, and an organisation's long-term success depends on its ability to handle them effectively. Leaders who remain calm, make swift decisions, prioritise the safety and trust of stakeholders, and learn from their experiences will not only survive the storm but also emerge stronger. In the end, crisis leadership is about more than overcoming immediate challenges; it is about learning from those experiences, building resilience, and fostering a culture of continuous improvement. By embracing these principles, leaders can turn adversity into opportunity and ensure their organisations are better prepared for challenges.

Chapter 18

Personal Development for CEOs: Continuous Learning and Adaptation

18.1 Overview

The role of a **CEO** is one of constant evolution and adaptation, demanding a dynamic leadership style that can guide an organisation through both triumphs and challenges. To be effective, CEOs must commit to **continuous personal development** to lead their companies successfully and manage their growth and well-being. This chapter delves into the essential aspects of personal development for CEOs, emphasising the importance of **ongoing learning**, self-awareness, and adaptability. It offers actionable strategies for enhancing leadership abilities, maintaining a healthy work-life balance, and staying abreast of industry trends. By focusing on their personal growth, CEOs can better navigate the complexities of their roles and drive their organisations towards long-term success in an ever-evolving competitive landscape.

18.2 The Importance of Self-Awareness

Self-awareness is the **foundation** of effective leadership. It involves a deep understanding of one's strengths, weaknesses, values, and leadership style, significantly influencing decision-making, team management, and the organisation's overall direction. For CEOs, self-awareness is crucial as it enables them to regulate their emotions, build stronger relationships, and foster a positive organisational culture. By understanding their capabilities and those of their team members, CEOs can create an environment where employees feel valued and connected, thereby enhancing overall **performance** and organisational cohesion. This heightened self-awareness empowers CEOs to lead with greater confidence, control, and authenticity.

Gaining insights through various **feedback** mechanisms is vital for developing self-awareness. Tools like 360-degree feedback provide a comprehensive view of how others perceive a CEO's leadership style and performance, revealing blind spots that may not be apparent through self-reflection alone. Regular check-ins and one-on-one meetings with direct reports foster open communication, allowing leaders to gauge the effectiveness of their approach and build stronger connections. Alongside external feedback, self-reflection plays a crucial role. Practices such as journaling or meditation can help CEOs clarify their motivations and understand the impact of their actions, contributing to a deeper sense of self-awareness and more thoughtful leadership.

Understanding one's **leadership style** is also essential. Tools like the Myers-Briggs Type Indicator (MBTI) or the DISC profile can offer valuable insights into a CEO's natural leadership tendencies, helping them adapt their approach to fit different situations and team dynamics. Emotional intelligence (EQ) is another critical component of self-awareness, involving the ability to recognise and manage one's emotions while being attuned to the feelings of others. High EQ enables CEOs to navigate interpersonal relationships effectively, resolve conflicts, and lead with empathy. It is an indispensable asset for any leader seeking a supportive and productive organisational culture.

Balancing strengths and weaknesses is a key aspect of effective leadership. Self-aware CEOs leverage their strengths while actively addressing their weaknesses. For example, a CEO who excels in strategic thinking but struggles with operational details can delegate these responsibilities to capable team members, focusing instead on steering the organisation's long-term direction. Acknowledging and working on weaknesses is not about dwelling on shortcomings but continuous **improvement**. Professional development opportunities like workshops or mentorship can help bridge knowledge gaps and enhance leadership effectiveness. Self-awareness is a continuous journey that underpins effective leadership, fostering a transparent, empathetic, and adaptive leadership style that benefits both the CEO and the organisation.

18.3 Lifelong Learning

In a rapidly evolving world, **lifelong learning** is not merely a personal choice for CEOs but a professional imperative. The most successful leaders continually expand their knowledge, refine their skills, and stay ahead of industry changes to remain effective in their roles. Engaging in lifelong learning enables CEOs to adapt to the complex landscape of modern business, ensuring they are well-prepared to lead their organisations through change and uncertainty.

Staying current with **industry trends** is a fundamental aspect of lifelong learning. Attending industry conferences and seminars provides CEOs with valuable insights into emerging technologies, best practices, and market shifts. These events also offer opportunities to learn from thought leaders and network with peers, which can inspire new ideas and strategic approaches. For instance, a CEO in the technology sector might attend events like CES or the Gartner Symposium to gain a deeper understanding of the latest innovations and how they might impact their business. Joining professional associations also provides access to exclusive research, webinars, and publications, keeping CEOs informed and connected with the broader professional community.

Acquiring new **skills** is equally important for lifelong learning. Formal education, such as executive programs at prestigious institutions like Harvard or INSEAD, can provide advanced knowledge in areas like strategy, finance, and leadership. Online learning platforms like Coursera and LinkedIn Learning make it easier for CEOs to learn at their own pace, covering topics such as data science, digital marketing, and negotiation. Additionally, workshops and boot camps offer hands-on learning experiences that allow CEOs to quickly acquire new skills and apply them directly to their organisations. These continuous learning efforts help CEOs stay agile and capable of navigating complex business environments.

Expanding knowledge through self-study is another valuable aspect of lifelong learning. Reading beyond the immediate industry, whether books on **leadership**, economics, or psychology, provides fresh perspectives that can be applied to business challenges. Resources like "The Innovator's Dilemma" by Clayton Christensen offer insights into managing disruption, while books on behavioural economics or cognitive science can enhance strategic thinking and decision-making. Podcasts and webinars are also excellent tools for learning on the go, offering insights from industry experts and thought leaders. Reflecting on what has been learned and finding ways to integrate new knowledge into leadership and strategy ensures that lifelong learning translates into tangible organisational benefits.

Lifelong learning is integral to effective leadership. By staying informed about industry trends, acquiring new skills, and dedicating themselves to continuous self-study, CEOs can remain agile, relevant, and prepared to lead their organisations in an ever-changing world.

18.4 Mentorship and Coaching

Mentorship and coaching provide invaluable support for CEOs seeking personal and professional growth. These relationships offer guidance, perspective, and accountability, helping leaders navigate challenges, refine their leadership approach, and achieve their full potential. Engaging with mentors and coaches allows CEOs to benefit from the experiences of others, accelerating their learning and enhancing their leadership capabilities.

The benefits of mentorship are significant. A mentor can provide an external perspective that helps CEOs see challenges and opportunities differently. For example, a mentor who has navigated similar business challenges can offer lessons learned and prevent the CEO from repeating common mistakes. Mentorship can also accelerate learning by drawing on the mentor's experiences and networks, saving the CEO time that might otherwise be spent on trial and error. Having a mentor to turn to during difficult times can boost a CEO's confidence, providing encouragement and validation that strengthens their belief in their judgment and decision-making abilities.

Finding the right **mentor** involves seeking someone with relevant experience and a leadership approach that aligns with the CEO's values. While the mentors must not be from the same industry, they must understand similar leadership challenges. Professional networks, industry events, and leadership forums provide opportunities to connect with potential mentors. When approaching a potential mentor, it is important to communicate what the CEO hopes to gain from the relationship and be open to formal and informal mentoring opportunities.

Building a productive mentor-mentee relationship requires clear expectations, openness, and honesty. CEOs should establish mutual expectations regarding the frequency of meetings, communication methods, and goals to ensure the relationship is productive and beneficial for both parties. Effective mentorship also requires transparency; CEOs should be open about their challenges and receptive to the mentor's feedback and advice. Taking ownership of the relationship means proactively scheduling meetings, preparing for discussions, and acting on the mentor's guidance.

Executive coaching is another valuable resource for CEOs. Unlike mentorship, coaching is a more structured process focused on specific leadership goals. Coaches work closely with CEOs to develop decision-making, communication, and strategic thinking skills. They provide accountability and support, helping CEOs stay on track with their development goals. Coaches are also skilled at identifying blind spots and areas where a CEO may lack awareness, enabling leaders to make more informed decisions and avoid potential pitfalls.

Mentorship and coaching are crucial to a CEO's personal and professional development. By building relationships with mentors and engaging in coaching, CEOs can accelerate their learning, build confidence, and develop their leadership abilities in a supportive and structured way.

18.5 Balancing Personal and Professional Life

Finding a healthy **balance** between personal and professional life is one of the greatest challenges for CEOs. The intense demands of leading an organisation often leave little room for personal time, yet maintaining this balance is crucial for a CEO's long-term effectiveness and well-being. Striking a balance improves personal satisfaction and enhances leadership performance by preventing burnout and ensuring CEOs have the energy and focus to lead effectively.

The challenges of work-life balance for CEOs are significant. High expectations and constant pressure to deliver results can lead to long work hours, where personal time is often sacrificed. While sometimes necessary in the short term, this approach can lead to burnout, decreased effectiveness, and strained relationships over time. The rise of digital tools and communication platforms has also blurred the boundaries between work and personal life, making it difficult for CEOs to disconnect from work-related responsibilities fully. This constant connectivity can create ongoing stress and disrupt the ability to recharge during personal time.

To manage these challenges, CEOs can adopt stress management and self-care strategies. Setting clear boundaries between work and personal life is essential. CEOs should establish specific times when work is off-limits, such as family meals, weekends, or vacations. Communicating these boundaries to colleagues and employees helps manage expectations and ensures that personal time is respected. Effective delegation is another key strategy. By trusting their teams to take ownership of certain tasks, CEOs can step back from day-to-day operations and focus on strategic priorities, reducing their workload and improving their work-life balance.

Scheduling personal time with the same priority as business activities is crucial. Regular exercise, family activities, hobbies, or relaxation should be considered non-negotiable commitments. Practices such as mindfulness, meditation, or deep breathing can also help manage stress, encouraging CEOs to stay present in the moment and reduce anxiety. Techniques like yoga or running alleviate stress and promote physical and mental well-being.

Setting boundaries is essential for ensuring well-being. CEOs should actively disconnect from work-related communication during personal time, using strategies such as turning off notifications, setting out-of-office messages, and putting away devices during family activities. This allows them to engage in non-work activities and recharge their energy fully. A strong support system, including a supportive partner, family, friends, or a mentor who understands the challenges of leadership, can also provide emotional support and serve as a sounding board for difficult decisions.

Practising self-compassion is equally important. CEOs should be kind to themselves, acknowledging that it is okay to make mistakes or take time to recharge. Self-compassion helps reduce guilt and supports a healthier relationship with work, enabling CEOs to maintain their effectiveness and resilience over the long term. Celebrating small wins, personal and professional, contributes to motivation and morale, reinforcing the importance of balancing personal and professional life.

Achieving a healthy work-life balance is an ongoing challenge for CEOs, but it is essential for their well-being and leadership effectiveness. By setting boundaries, practising self-care, and showing self-compassion, CEOs can find a balance that supports their satisfaction and enhances their ability to lead successfully.

18.6 Adapting to Change

In the fast-paced business world, **adaptability** is an essential trait for CEOs. The ability to respond to market shifts, technological innovations, and organisational challenges is crucial for maintaining competitiveness and driving success. Adaptability enables leaders to navigate uncertainty, embrace new opportunities, and steer their organisations through periods of transformation and disruption.

One of the most important aspects of adaptability is the ability to respond to **market changes**. Rapid technological shifts, consumer behaviour, and regulatory landscapes can significantly impact a business, requiring CEOs to adjust strategies and business models quickly. For example, e-commerce has forced traditional retailers to invest in online platforms to meet changing consumer preferences. CEOs anticipating these changes and pivoting their strategies are better positioned to lead their organisations through disruption.

Fostering a culture of **innovation** is another critical element of adaptable leadership. CEOs who encourage new ideas, experimentation, and creativity within their organisations create an environment where employees feel empowered to explore new approaches and challenge the status quo. This innovative mindset helps organisations stay ahead of competitors and thrive in changing environments. Leaders who view disruption as an opportunity rather than a threat are more likely to guide their organisations successfully through turbulent periods.

To stay flexible, CEOs must embrace a **growth mindset**, believing their abilities can be developed through effort and learning. This mindset encourages leaders to see challenges and failures as opportunities for growth and improvement rather

456

than insurmountable obstacles. Staying curious and open-minded, questioning assumptions, and seeking new perspectives are all traits of adaptable leaders who remain responsive to change.

Being willing to pivot is also essential for staying adaptable. Whether it involves altering a business strategy, adjusting product offerings, or exploring new markets, the ability to change course when necessary ensures that the organisation remains agile and responsive to evolving conditions. Encouraging diverse perspectives within the leadership team can also enhance adaptability, as different viewpoints can lead to more innovative solutions and a better understanding of complex issues.

Leading through change requires clear communication and the ability to manage **resistance**. CEOs must articulate a clear vision for the change, explaining why it is necessary and how it aligns with the organisation's goals. Addressing employee concerns and involving them in the change process can help build buy-in and reduce resistance. Demonstrating flexibility and a positive attitude towards change sets a powerful example, inspiring employees to embrace new directions confidently.

Adaptability is a critical leadership trait in today's dynamic business environment. CEOs who embrace change, foster innovation, and create a learning and continuous improvement culture are better equipped to navigate uncertainty and lead their organisations to long-term success.

18.7 Networking and Building Relationships

Building and maintaining strong **professional networks** is a critical component of CEO success. Networking provides access to valuable resources, knowledge, and opportunities, which can foster personal and organisational growth. Effective networking goes beyond exchanging business cards; it involves building meaningful relationships that support a CEO's strategic goals and personal development.

Networking offers numerous benefits, including access to **resources and opportunities** that may not be available internally. A robust professional network can connect CEOs with business partners, investors, mentors, and specialists in various fields. These connections can lead to collaborations, strategic alliances, and new business opportunities that drive growth and innovation. Networking also facilitates knowledge sharing and learning, allowing CEOs to gain new insights into market trends, business innovations, and leadership strategies through interactions with peers and industry leaders.

Effective networking requires a strategic approach. Attending **industry events** such as conferences and seminars provides opportunities to expand professional connections, share ideas, and build relationships that could lead to future collaborations. Joining professional associations also offers structured networking opportunities, connecting CEOs with peers who share similar leadership challenges. Leveraging social media platforms like LinkedIn allows CEOs to engage with a broader audience, share insights, and establish themselves as thought leaders.

Building mutually beneficial relationships is key to successful networking. Networking should not be solely about seeking what can be gained; it should be reciprocal. CEOs who approach networking with a mindset of offering value through insights, introductions, or support build stronger, more lasting relationships. Nurturing these relationships over time through regular check-ins and sharing relevant information ensures they remain productive and mutually beneficial.

Leveraging connections effectively can provide valuable **advice and feedback**. CEOs should not hesitate to seek input from their professional networks when facing difficult decisions or considering new strategies. This external perspective can offer fresh insights and innovative solutions. Identifying opportunities for collaboration, whether through joint ventures, partnerships, or shared initiatives, can also create new avenues for growth and innovation. CEOs can enhance their competitive advantage and achieve mutual success by building strategic alliances with organisations that share complementary goals and values.

Networking and building relationships are essential aspects of effective leadership. By developing and leveraging a strong professional network, CEOs can access valuable resources and opportunities that accelerate personal and organisational growth. Focusing on reciprocity, authenticity, and nurturing relationships over time creates a support system that enhances leadership effectiveness and contributes to long-term success.

18.8 Physical and Mental Health

Maintaining **physical and mental health** is crucial for CEOs. Leadership demands require high energy, resilience, and focus, all closely linked to overall well-being. CEOs must prioritise their physical and mental health to sustain long-term performance and lead effectively.

Effective leadership is directly tied to a CEO's health. A healthy body and mind enable CEOs to think, manage stress, and make sound decisions. Neglecting health can lead to burnout, impaired judgment, and decreased leadership effectiveness. Therefore, prioritising well-being is not just a personal concern but a professional necessity for CEOs striving to maintain their effectiveness and longevity in their roles.

Physical health should be a priority, not an option. Regular **exercise** is one of the most effective ways for CEOs to reduce stress and improve mental clarity. Incorporating physical activity into the daily routine, whether through morning runs, yoga, or even short walks during the workday, helps maintain the energy and stamina required for demanding leadership roles. Nutrition also plays a crucial role in sustaining energy levels and cognitive function. CEOs should avoid relying on quick, unhealthy meals due to time constraints and instead prioritise a balanced diet rich in whole foods, lean proteins, and healthy fats. Adequate sleep is essential for optimal cognitive performance; CEOs should aim for 7-8 hours of sleep per night and establish a routine that promotes restful sleep, such as reducing screen time before bed and practising relaxation techniques.

Mental health is often overlooked but equally important. Mindfulness practices, such as **meditation**, can significantly impact a CEO's mental well-being by promoting clarity and helping leaders stay grounded in high-pressure situations. When necessary, seeking professional mental health support, such as therapy or coaching, can provide valuable perspectives and coping strategies. Work-life integration, rather than strict separation, can also help maintain mental health, allowing CEOs to find synergies between personal and professional activities that support overall well-being.

Integrating health into a busy schedule requires strategic planning. Time-blocking can help CEOs prioritise health by scheduling specific times for exercise, relaxation, and meal planning. Delegating tasks to capable team members free up time, allowing CEOs to focus on their well-being without sacrificing leadership responsibilities. Health-related technologies, such as fitness trackers and meditation apps, can also support CEOs in maintaining their physical and mental health, ensuring these practices are incorporated into their daily routines.

Prioritising physical and mental health is foundational to a CEO's ability to lead effectively. By focusing on their well-being, CEOs can enhance their cognitive functions, emotional resilience, and leadership capabilities, setting a positive example for their organisations and fostering a culture of health and well-being.

18.9 Time Management and Productivity

Time management is a critical skill for any CEO. With numerous competing demands for their attention, CEOs must manage their time effectively to focus on the activities that impact their organisation's success. Effective time management enables CEOs to achieve goals, drive growth, and balance work and personal life.

The power of **prioritisation** is one of the most important aspects of time management. CEOs must distinguish between tasks of varying importance and focus on those that drive organisational success. Tools like the Eisenhower Matrix, which categorises tasks based on urgency and importance, can help CEOs allocate their time to activities with the most significant impact. Strategic delegation is also crucial; understanding which tasks require direct attention and which can be delegated to trusted team members allows CEOs to free up time for high-impact decisions and strategic priorities. The 80/20 rule, or Pareto Principle, suggests that 80% of outcomes come from 20% of efforts, guiding CEOs to identify and focus on the critical few activities that yield the most results.

Productivity techniques such as time-blocking and the Pomodoro Technique can further enhance time management. Time-blocking involves scheduling specific blocks of time for different tasks, preventing distractions and enabling focused work. The Pomodoro Technique, which breaks work into intervals followed by short breaks, helps manage fatigue and maintain concentration. Leveraging technology, such as task management apps and scheduling tools, can streamline workflows and reduce administrative burdens, allowing CEOs to use their time more efficiently.

Establishing **routines** can also boost productivity. Morning routines that include exercise, meditation, or reviewing priorities set a positive tone for the day, while evening routines help CEOs unwind, reflect, and plan for the next day. Regular reflection on time management strategies and productivity outcomes allows CEOs to identify the most effective activities and make necessary adjustments to optimise their time use.

Balancing productivity with well-being is essential. Overworking can lead to burnout, negatively affecting productivity and overall effectiveness. Scheduling regular breaks and downtime, such as weekends or vacations, allows CEOs to recharge and maintain high performance. Rather than striving for a strict separation between work and personal life, integrating personal activities into the workday, such as combining family time with exercise, can help maintain productivity while fulfilling personal obligations.

Mastering time management is essential for leadership effectiveness. By prioritising tasks, adopting productivity techniques, and balancing work with personal well-being, CEOs can maximise efficiency, achieve their goals, and lead their organisations more successfully.

18.10 Personal Branding

In today's interconnected world, **personal branding** is a vital element of leadership for CEOs. A strong personal brand enhances a CEO's credibility, influence, and ability to lead effectively. This chapter explores the concept of personal branding and offers strategies for building and maintaining a leadership identity that resonates with stakeholders and contributes to organisational success.

A CEO's brand reflects how they are perceived by employees, customers, investors, and the broader public. It encompasses values, communication style, expertise, and public image. In an increasingly competitive business environment, a well-defined personal brand can differentiate a CEO and their organisation, build trust, and attract opportunities. Identifying core values is the first step in building a personal brand. These values might include integrity, innovation, or a commitment to customer service and should align with the organisation's vision and be reflected in every action and decision.

Authenticity is crucial for personal branding. CEOs should aim to be genuine in their leadership style, communication, and public interactions. Authenticity builds trust with stakeholders and ensures that the CEO's brand is credible and relatable. Storytelling is a powerful tool for building a personal brand. Sharing personal experiences that reflect their values and leadership philosophy helps humanise the CEO's brand and forge deeper connections with stakeholders.

Maintaining a consistent public image reinforces a CEO's brand. Public speaking engagements, media interviews, and other appearances provide opportunities to communicate a CEO's values and vision. Social media platforms like LinkedIn and Twitter are powerful tools for building a personal brand. CEOs should actively manage their profiles, share insights, and engage with their audience to establish themselves as thought leaders. A cohesive visual identity, including professional photographs and personal style, further strengthens credibility and enhances brand recognition.

Leveraging personal branding for organisational success involves aligning the CEO's brand with the organisation's mission and values. Thought leadership, through articles, books, and public speaking, positions the CEO as an expert, influencing industry trends and public discourse. During crises, a strong personal brand can help stabilise the organisation. Transparent, empathetic communication is key to maintaining trust and protecting the CEO's and organisation's reputations.

Personal branding is not static; it evolves as the CEO grows and the business environment changes. Continuous learning and adapting to new trends ensure the CEO's brand remains relevant. Reflecting on feedback and personal growth helps CEOs adjust their brand to reflect their evolving leadership style and values. Building a legacy through consistent, value-driven leadership leaves a lasting impact on the organisation and industry.

For CEOs, personal branding is a powerful tool for driving organisational success and creating a lasting legacy. By defining their core values, crafting a consistent public image, and leveraging their brand, CEOs can enhance their leadership effectiveness and align with their organisation's mission.

18.11 Inspirational Reads and Resources

Access to the right resources is essential for a CEO's ongoing personal and professional development. Books, articles, podcasts, and courses provide inspiration, knowledge, and strategies for leadership growth. Recommended resources include classics like "Good to Great" by Jim Collins and "The Innovator's Dilemma" by Clayton Christensen, which offer valuable insights into leadership and innovation. "Leaders Eat Last" by Simon Sinek and "The Hard Thing About Hard Things" by Ben Horowitz provide practical advice on creating strong organisational cultures and navigating leadership challenges.

Staying informed on industry trends is crucial. Subscribing to publications like Harvard Business Review and The Economist keeps CEOs updated on market dynamics and leadership strategies. Podcasts such as "How I Built This" and "The Tim Ferriss Show" offer insights from successful entrepreneurs and thought leaders, while online courses from platforms like Coursera and Harvard Business School Online provide opportunities for skill development and continuous learning.

These resources empower CEOs to expand their horizons, deepen their insights, and stay ahead of industry changes. By engaging with diverse materials, CEOs can enhance their leadership capabilities and drive organisational success.

Conclusion

In the modern business world, the role of a CEO requires a commitment to continuous personal development, adaptability, and a holistic approach to leadership. The strategies and insights outlined in this chapter highlight the importance of self-awareness, lifelong learning, and maintaining a healthy balance between work and personal life. By focusing on these areas, CEOs can navigate the complexities of their role with confidence and resilience. Adaptability remains a cornerstone of effective leadership, enabling CEOs to guide their organisations through disruption and change while fostering a culture of innovation. Building strong professional networks further enhances a CEO's ability to access resources and opportunities that drive growth and success. In addition, the power of personal branding cannot be overstated; an authentic, well-crafted brand elevates a CEO's influence and aligns with their organisation's mission.

As the business landscape continues to evolve, CEOs must prioritise their personal and professional development to remain effective and ensure the long-term success of their organisations. The approaches discussed in this chapter offer a comprehensive roadmap for CEOs to refine their leadership, stay ahead of industry trends, and lead with purpose and integrity. By integrating these practices into their leadership approach, CEOs can create a lasting legacy of excellence and guide their organisations toward a prosperous future.

Chapter 19

Building and Leveraging Networks: The Power of Relationships

19.1 Overview

A well-cultivated **network** is beneficial and indispensable in modern business's complex and interconnected world. Networking extends beyond collecting contacts or adding connections on platforms like LinkedIn. It involves cultivating **authentic, meaningful relationships** that unlock opportunities, provide invaluable insights, and build a supportive community. This chapter delves into how building and leveraging networks is fundamental to business success. It will explore practical strategies for creating and maintaining valuable connections, which are crucial for personal growth and achieving organisational objectives. Furthermore, this chapter will highlight different forms of networking, from strategic partnerships to community engagement, each playing a pivotal role in today's professional landscape.

19.2 The Value of Networking

Networking is often seen as a supplementary activity in business, yet its role is central to success. A strong network is a collection of contacts and a powerful gateway to resources, opportunities, and knowledge that can significantly impact business growth and sustainability. Accessing and nurturing a robust network can make the difference between thriving and struggling in an increasingly competitive environment. For leaders, networking is a strategic tool that can open doors to new opportunities, foster innovation, and provide the support necessary to navigate challenges.

A supportive network extends beyond professional contacts, offering **emotional and practical support**. Business leaders, particularly those in high-stakes roles, often face isolation when making critical decisions. A well-nurtured network provides access to mentors, peers, and advisors who understand the unique pressures of leadership. For instance, a CEO might turn to a trusted mentor within their network for guidance on a difficult strategic decision, benefiting from the mentor's experience and insight. This support system fosters community and provides a safe space to discuss challenges, brainstorm ideas, and receive constructive feedback.

Networking also plays a pivotal role in creating and accessing new **growth opportunities**. Entrepreneurs and executives with expansive networks can uncover partnerships, market expansions, or client referrals that may not be available through conventional channels. A serendipitous conversation at an industry event could lead to a lucrative deal or a strategic partnership that accelerates growth. Networking interactions often lead to innovative solutions and collaborations, exposing leaders to new ideas and diverse perspectives that can be applied to their businesses.

Moreover, networking is crucial for staying informed about **industry trends, challenges, and opportunities**. Regular interactions with peers, competitors, and experts facilitate the exchange of vital information, helping leaders stay ahead of the curve. Attending conferences or participating in industry associations can provide insights into emerging technologies, regulatory changes, and market dynamics. Learning from the experiences of others can prevent costly mistakes and accelerate personal and organisational growth, leading to more informed decision-making.

A strong network also significantly enhances a leader's **credibility and reputation**. Cultivating relationships with influential figures in one's industry can help leaders become recognised as thought leaders, opening doors to opportunities such as speaking at conferences, publishing articles, or receiving endorsements from respected colleagues. In times of crisis, a robust network can be critical for managing and maintaining one's professional reputation. Trusted contacts may offer public support, provide strategic advice, or assist in managing communications with key stakeholders, helping to preserve and protect one's professional standing.

In summary, networking is not just about making connections. It encompasses emotional support, access to new opportunities, fostering innovation, and enhancing credibility. Leaders can leverage these relationships to gain resources and insights contributing to business success. Networking should be regarded as a strategic asset, requiring time, effort, and the cultivation of genuine relationships.

19.3 Building Strategic Partnerships

Strategic partnerships are a powerful means businesses can achieve growth, innovation, and a competitive edge. These partnerships extend beyond surface-level collaborations, evolving into deliberate alliances that align with the long-term goals of all parties involved. For example, the collaboration between Apple and Mastercard in developing Apple Pay showcases a successful strategic alliance that leveraged the strengths of both companies. Establishing such partnerships requires thorough planning, skilful negotiation, and careful management to ensure that both parties benefit equally.

The first step in forming a strategic partnership is **identifying potential partners** whose goals and values align with yours. This alignment ensures the partnership is mutually beneficial, with both parties working towards common objectives. Potential partners can be identified through research, networking, or attending industry events. For instance, a technology company seeking to diversify its offerings might partner with a software development firm that provides complementary expertise. Identifying complementary strengths is also essential. The most successful partnerships often arise when each party offers something the other lacks, such as technology, market access, or specialised knowledge.

Cultural fit between organisations is another critical factor in the success of a partnership. Shared values, work ethics, and approaches to business can facilitate smoother communication, decision-making, and conflict resolution. This cultural alignment helps build trust and ensures that both parties agree regarding the partnership's objectives and expectations.

Negotiating strategic partnerships requires creating **win-win scenarios** where both parties feel they are receiving value. Understanding your partner's needs and priorities and aligning them with your own is key to building trust and ensuring both parties are satisfied with the partnership's terms. Setting clear objectives and expectations from the outset is essential. This includes defining roles and responsibilities, setting performance metrics, and agreeing on timelines to avoid misunderstandings and keep both parties focused on the partnership's long-term success. Additionally, the legal and financial aspects of the partnership must be meticulously outlined in contracts, covering intellectual property rights, revenue sharing, and dispute resolution mechanisms. Seeking legal advice ensures that both parties' interests are protected and the partnership is built on a solid foundation.

Once a partnership is established, **ongoing communication** is essential to its success. Regular meetings, updates, and discussions about challenges and progress are vital. Consistent communication fosters trust and ensures that both parties remain aligned as the partnership evolves. Flexibility and adaptability are also key to maintaining a successful partnership. The business landscape constantly changes, and strategic partnerships must be flexible enough to adapt to new opportunities, market shifts, or internal changes. Being willing to revisit and adjust the terms of the partnership ensures its continued relevance and effectiveness over time.

Measuring success is another crucial aspect of maintaining partnerships. Regular evaluations of the partnership's outcomes against the objectives and metrics established during negotiations allow both parties to assess its impact. These evaluations ensure that the partnership delivers value and provides opportunities to make necessary adjustments. Strategic partnerships offer significant advantages for growth and innovation. Leaders who choose their partners wisely, negotiate agreements that provide mutual value, and maintain open communication can build long-lasting partnerships that drive sustained success. These partnerships allow organisations to leverage complementary strengths and work together toward shared goals, creating a powerful competitive advantage when executed effectively.

19.4 Effective Networking Strategies

Networking is a skill that can be honed over time. The most effective networking is not about collecting as many contacts as possible but about building **meaningful, lasting relationships** that lead to mutually beneficial opportunities. This section provides practical advice for networking online and offline to help build a diverse, valuable network that can support personal and professional growth.

Regarding networking at industry events, being **strategic** about which events to attend is important. Not all networking events are equally valuable, and attending every event is not necessarily the best approach. Instead, professionals should carefully select events that align with their industry, goals, and the connections they wish to make. For instance, attending a niche conference within your sector may provide more relevant and valuable connections than a broader, more general networking event. Preparing in advance is essential for maximising the value of networking at events. Researching the attendees, speakers, and sponsors can help identify key individuals to connect with. Going in with a plan allows for more effective use of time and increases the likelihood of leaving with meaningful new contacts.

During the event, it is important to focus on engaging in substantial conversations rather than simply exchanging business cards. Asking open-ended questions, listening carefully, and showing genuine interest in the people you meet builds rapport and can lead to deeper, more lasting connections. Following up with new contacts after the event is critical. A personalised message referencing your conversation demonstrates interest in maintaining the relationship. Depending on the context, this follow-up can be carried out via email, LinkedIn, or even a handwritten note.

Leveraging **online networks** such as LinkedIn is also essential. Optimising your LinkedIn profile to ensure it is professional, complete, and up-to-date is the first step. This includes using a high-quality photo, writing a compelling summary, and showcasing your accomplishments and areas of expertise. A well-crafted profile enhances your visibility and attracts more professional opportunities. Joining relevant LinkedIn groups allows professionals to connect with others who share similar interests or work within the same industry. Active participation in these groups, engaging in discussions, sharing insights, or posting relevant content can increase visibility and help forge new relationships.

Consistency is key when networking online. **Regularly sharing relevant content**, commenting on others' posts, and participating in discussions will keep you visible within your network. Consistent engagement helps build your reputation as a thought leader and ensures you remain at the top of your mind for potential opportunities. When reaching out to new connections on LinkedIn, it is important to personalise your connection requests, including a message that explains why you want to connect, whether based on shared interests, mutual connections, or admiration for their work, significantly increases the chances of your request being accepted and lays the foundation for a meaningful professional relationship.

Building a **diverse network** involves connecting with professionals from various industries, backgrounds, and experience levels. Limiting networking efforts to one's immediate industry or peer group can lead to missed opportunities. By connecting with individuals from different sectors, professionals gain access to new perspectives and ideas that can be applied to their businesses. Cross-industry networking can generate fresh insights and approaches. For example, a CEO in the healthcare sector may benefit from connecting with a technology entrepreneur, leading to the implementation of innovative business models or technologies.

Effective networking is about accumulating contacts and cultivating meaningful, long-term relationships that offer

mutual value. A strategic approach to online and offline networking, combined with efforts to diversify one's network, can create a web of professional relationships supporting career and business objectives. While networking requires time and genuine interest in others, the rewards, such as new opportunities, valuable knowledge, and emotional support, are substantial.

19.5 Cultivating Investor Relations

Strong relationships with investors are essential for many businesses, providing the **funding and support** necessary for growth. Cultivating and maintaining these relationships requires regular communication, transparency, and demonstrating progress. This section outlines strategies for building robust investor relations and ensuring continued support.

Investors provide more than just financial capital; they also offer strategic guidance, industry connections, and credibility. Maintaining strong relationships with investors ensures ongoing support, particularly during challenging times. A solid relationship can make a critical difference when seeking additional funding or navigating periods of uncertainty. Building trust and confidence is foundational to successful investor relations. Investors need to trust that their capital is being utilised effectively and that the business is on a solid path toward success. This trust is built through consistent communication, transparency, and a clear demonstration of progress.

Regular updates are crucial to keeping investors informed and engaged. These updates should include key financial reports, milestones, and significant business developments or challenges. Providing consistent and transparent communication reduces the risk of misunderstandings and keeps investors confident in the business's direction. Transparency and honesty are essential to maintaining trust with investors. Being open about both successes and challenges demonstrates integrity and fosters stronger relationships. When difficulties arise, communicating them honestly and explaining the steps to address them reassures investors that the business is proactive and solutions-oriented.

Tailoring communication to the **interests and concerns** of individual investors can also strengthen these relationships. For example, some investors may be particularly interested in sustainability efforts, while others may focus more on financial performance. Personalised communication demonstrates an understanding of each investor's priorities and builds rapport.

Demonstrating **progress and value** is crucial for maintaining investor confidence. Regularly reporting on key milestones, such as product launches, market expansions, or revenue growth, reassures investors that the business is progressing toward its long-term goals. Demonstrating tangible progress helps strengthen investor confidence in the company's ability to deliver on its promises. Highlighting success stories is another effective way to demonstrate value. Whether it involves new client wins, successful marketing campaigns, or industry awards, sharing these achievements creates a positive narrative around the business. Success stories can be shared through newsletters, investor reports, or presentations, showcasing the company's accomplishments and future potential.

Building **long-term relationships** with investors involves more than just providing regular updates. Engaging with investors beyond financial performance is key to building long-term relationships. Understanding investors' broader goals and values allows for more meaningful engagement. For instance, some investors may be passionate about social impact or innovation. Engaging with them on these topics fosters a deeper connection and encourages continued support.

Inviting feedback and input from investors can also be valuable. Investors often possess extensive experience and insights that can benefit the business. Seeking their input leverages their expertise and makes them feel more personally invested in the company's success. Celebrating success with investors by hosting events or sending personalised thank-you notes strengthens the relationship. Acknowledging their role in the business's achievements fosters loyalty and solidifies the partnership.

Building strong investor relations requires more than simply managing expectations; it is about cultivating **long-term partnerships** built on trust, mutual respect, and shared success. By maintaining transparent communication, demonstrating progress, and engaging with investors personally, leaders can ensure continued support and a stable foundation for growth.

19.6 Community Engagement

Engaging with local communities is an effective way for businesses to build **brand loyalty, foster goodwill, and create a positive social impact**. Community engagement involves more than traditional marketing; it entails building genuine relationships with the people and organisations in the areas where the business operates. This section explores the benefits of community engagement and offers strategies for participating in local initiatives effectively.

Companies that engage with local communities often enjoy higher levels of **brand loyalty**. When a business is seen as a positive force within the community, customers are more likely to support it, not only for its products or services but also for its contributions to the community's well-being. Community engagement can significantly enhance a company's reputation. By participating in local initiatives, supporting charitable causes, or sponsoring community events, businesses demonstrate their commitment to social responsibility. This, in turn, strengthens customer trust and builds a stronger brand image.

Beyond business benefits, community engagement allows companies to make a **meaningful social impact**. Through volunteer work, donations, or educational programmes, businesses can contribute to improving their communities. This aligns with growing consumer expectations that companies act as responsible corporate citizens. Effective community engagement involves participating in local events, supporting CSR initiatives, and organising employee volunteer programmes.

These efforts benefit the community and strengthen the company's ties to its local environment.

Building **long-term relationships** with local leaders, such as city officials, community organisers, and non-profit directors, is key to successful community engagement. These leaders provide valuable insights into the community's needs and can help identify opportunities for collaboration. Regular communication ensures that the company's efforts are aligned with the community's priorities. Supporting local businesses is another way to contribute to the community's economic health. This can involve sourcing materials locally, partnering with vendors, or promoting other small businesses. By contributing to the local economy, companies build goodwill and deepen their ties to the community.

Listening to the community is an important aspect of effective engagement. Businesses should seek feedback from community members through surveys, town hall meetings, or direct conversations. This feedback ensures that the company's engagement efforts are relevant and responsive to the community's needs. Tracking participation levels, initiatives' reach and outcomes is crucial for measuring the impact of community engagement. For example, suppose a business sponsors a charity event and tracks the money raised, the number of participants, and the effect on the community. In that case, these provide valuable insights into the initiative's success.

Sharing **success stories** from community engagement efforts further demonstrates the positive impact of the company's initiatives. These stories can be shared via the company's website, social media channels, or annual reports, showcasing the difference the company is making in the community. Regularly reviewing and adjusting community engagement strategies ensures their continued effectiveness. As community needs evolve, businesses should be open to refining their approaches to remain impactful and relevant.

Community engagement is a powerful tool for businesses to build strong local connections, enhance their reputation, and contribute to positive social change. By actively participating in local initiatives, supporting CSR programmes, and building long-term relationships with community leaders, businesses can become integral parts of the communities they serve. Effective community engagement benefits the business and the community, creating a win-win scenario.

19.7 Alumni Networks

Alumni networks are a unique and often underutilised resource for building and leveraging **connections** that can significantly impact business success. These networks typically consist of individuals with a common educational or professional background, such as attending the same university, business school, or professional training programme. The shared experiences within these networks create a strong foundation for building mutually beneficial relationships, leading to new opportunities, collaborations, and support systems that can be vital in various business contexts.

Reconnecting with former classmates and colleagues through alumni networks can be one of the most rewarding aspects of networking. These individuals often hold diverse roles across various industries and regions, offering a wealth of knowledge, experience, and potential partnerships. Attending alumni events, reunions, or gatherings designed to bring together past members of an institution provides an excellent opportunity to rekindle old friendships and form new professional relationships. In addition to formal events, reconnecting through platforms like LinkedIn or dedicated alumni networks can be highly effective. A simple message acknowledging shared history can open doors to deeper and more meaningful connections.

Alumni networks are more than personal relationships; they can be leveraged strategically for **business growth**. Many institutions provide platforms where alumni can connect, share job opportunities, and discuss industry trends. These platforms are invaluable for sourcing talent, finding mentors, or identifying potential investors. For example, if you want to expand your business into a new region, an alumnus with experience could offer valuable insights and introductions that might otherwise take years to cultivate. Similarly, alumni who have navigated similar business challenges can offer advice and guidance, helping you avoid common pitfalls and accelerate growth.

Alumni networks also offer an excellent opportunity to build and enhance your **brand**. Contributing to alumni discussions, offering mentorship to recent graduates, or speaking at alumni events positions you as a thought leader within the community, increasing your visibility among influential peers and raising your professional profile. Many alumni associations have publications or digital platforms where you can share articles, case studies, or professional insights. Contributing to these platforms allows you to establish your expertise further and attract opportunities that align with your business goals.

Staying active and giving back to your **alumni network** is crucial for maintaining and growing these valuable connections. Volunteering for alumni committees, supporting fundraising efforts, or mentoring current students are all ways to remain engaged and contribute to the community. This involvement strengthens the network and connects you to valuable resources and opportunities. By actively participating in these networks, you can unlock a wealth of connections, insights, and opportunities to propel your business forward and support your professional development.

19.8 Mastermind Groups and Think Tanks

Mastermind groups and think tanks are at the forefront of **collaborative networking**, providing structured environments for deep thinking, innovation, and problem-solving among like-minded professionals. Whether your goal is to overcome a specific challenge, innovate within your industry, or accelerate personal and professional development, joining or forming a mastermind group or think tank can be transformative. These groups bring together individuals with diverse backgrounds and expertise, creating a space for sharing knowledge and developing innovative solutions.

A mastermind group is a **peer-to-peer mentoring concept** where members help each other solve problems by providing advice and insights from their collective experiences. Napoleon Hill popularised the concept in his book *Think and Grow Rich*, describing mastermind groups as gatherings where individuals meet regularly to encourage and support one another in reaching their goals. The true power of a mastermind group lies in its members' collective intelligence. By bringing together individuals with diverse backgrounds and experiences, these groups offer solutions and perspectives that may not be apparent to someone working in isolation. Members hold each other accountable, provide feedback, and often collaborate on projects, making the group a powerful catalyst for personal and professional growth.

When forming or joining a mastermind group, it is crucial to select its members carefully. Ideally, the group should consist of individuals at similar career stages but with diverse industry backgrounds. This **diversity ensures a broad range of perspectives**, leading to more innovative ideas and solutions. If you are forming a mastermind group, begin by identifying peers whose judgment and experience you respect. Reach out with a clear proposal outlining the group's purpose, commitment, and expected benefits. Alternatively, many existing mastermind groups, both in-person and online, may align with your goals. Joining a well-established group allows one to contribute to and benefit from collective knowledge.

To gain the most value from a mastermind group, it is essential to approach it with the intent to both give and receive. Keys include active participation in discussions, offering insights, and remaining open to constructive feedback. The more you invest in the group, the greater the rewards you reap from its members' shared wisdom. Regular participation builds trust and strengthens relationships with other members, potentially leading to significant collaborations or shared opportunities.

On the other hand, think tanks are more formal entities that generate ideas, research, and policy recommendations in specific industries or areas of interest. Think tanks gather experts from various fields to address complex issues, innovate, and influence decision-making processes. **Participating in a think tank** is an excellent way for business leaders to stay ahead of industry trends. Think tanks provide access to cutting-edge knowledge and thought leadership, helping to inform business strategies and drive innovation.

Creating a think tank involves defining its purpose and focus, whether addressing industry-wide challenges or specific technological issues. Once the purpose is clear, recruit members with relevant expertise willing to contribute their time and knowledge. Meetings should be structured to facilitate in-depth discussions and brainstorming. The output from these meetings might include white papers, research reports, or policy recommendations that can then be shared with stakeholders to influence decision-making.

The long-term benefits of mastermind groups and think tanks are substantial. These groups provide continuous motivation, accountability, and inspiration, helping members stay committed to their goals. The **exposure to diverse perspectives** enhances problem-solving abilities and fosters innovation. Additionally, relationships formed within mastermind groups and think tanks often extend beyond the professional, resulting in lasting friendships and professional alliances. The collective wisdom and support gained from these groups can significantly impact an organisation's success and the leader's development.

19.9 Navigating Industry Associations

Industry associations are some of the most valuable resources for business leaders and entrepreneurs. These organisations bring together professionals from the same industry to **collaborate, share knowledge, and advocate for common interests**. Actively participating in industry associations provides access to exclusive resources, enables you to influence industry standards, and helps build a strong professional network that can support your business and career growth.

Joining an industry association offers numerous benefits, including access to specialised knowledge, networking opportunities, and the ability to influence industry trends and policies. Industry associations often host **conferences, seminars, and workshops** where members can learn from experts and engage with their peers. These events are invaluable for staying current on industry developments and connecting with professionals with similar challenges and goals.

In addition to education and networking, industry associations often serve as powerful lobbying forces. They represent their members in discussions with government bodies, regulatory agencies, and other key stakeholders. By becoming actively involved in an industry association, business leaders can ensure their interests are represented and have the opportunity to influence the future direction of their industry. Participating in **advocacy efforts** allows members to shape industry regulations, standards, and best practices, providing a competitive advantage.

Merely joining an industry association is not enough to reap the full range of benefits it offers. Active participation is essential. This includes attending events, participating in discussions, and volunteering for **committees or leadership positions** within the association. Active involvement increases visibility and positions you as a thought leader within your industry. Leadership roles within industry associations provide valuable opportunities to expand your network and influence the association's direction. Whether chairing a committee, organising an event, or contributing to a publication, these roles allow you to demonstrate your expertise and collaborate with other influential members.

Industry associations often provide members exclusive resources, such as **research reports, market data, legal advice, and training programmes**. These resources give businesses a competitive edge by informing them about their industry's latest developments and best practices. For example, some associations offer detailed market analyses or benchmarking studies to help guide strategic decision-making. Others provide legal and regulatory updates to assist businesses in complying with current laws. Leveraging these resources enables businesses to stay ahead of industry trends and position themselves for long-term success.

Networking and building relationships are also significant benefits of industry association membership. Events hosted by these associations bring together industry professionals, creating opportunities to build **relationships with potential partners, collaborators, and competitors**. The relationships built through industry associations often have long-lasting benefits throughout one's career. Many professionals find that their contacts within these associations become trusted advisors, mentors, or business partners, extending beyond the professional realm and fostering strong, supportive bonds.

Finally, industry associations provide members a platform to influence **industry standards and policies**. By contributing to developing best practices and advocating for change, business leaders demonstrate their commitment to the industry's future success, further enhancing their credibility and reputation. Participating in industry associations is a powerful way for business leaders to stay informed, expand their networks, and influence industry developments. Active participation in these associations and leveraging their resources can position businesses for long-term success and contribute to the growth and resilience of the industry as a whole.

19.10 Social Capital

Social capital refers to the networks, relationships, and trust individuals and organisations build over time, which can be leveraged to achieve various goals. In business, **social capital** is an intangible asset that significantly influences success. It encompasses the goodwill, influence, and access to resources that arise from the relationships you cultivate. High social capital provides increased access to information, resources, and opportunities that may not be available to others. It can also offer a competitive edge by opening doors that might otherwise remain closed.

For example, a CEO with strong social capital may have easier access to **venture capital, better negotiation terms, or opportunities to collaborate with top-tier talent**. People are more likely to offer help, share valuable information, or collaborate with someone they trust and respect. Building social capital requires time, effort, and a genuine interest in others. Relationships based on trust, reciprocity, and mutual respect form the foundation of social capital.

Being generous with your knowledge and resources is important to building social capital effectively. Sharing expertise, making introductions, and offering support when needed establishes you as a valuable and generous network member, encouraging others to reciprocate. Engaging in meaningful conversations and investing in long-term relationships are also key strategies. Building strong relationships requires more than casual exchanges. Engaging in deep, meaningful conversations with your contacts builds the trust and rapport essential to social capital.

Social capital can be leveraged to access **resources and opportunities** that may be difficult to obtain through traditional means. For example, a well-connected entrepreneur may secure venture capital more easily through their network than through formal channels. It can also enhance one's ability to influence and persuade others. When people trust and respect each other, they are more likely to support their ideas, invest in their business, or collaborate on projects. Social capital is critical in forming business alliances through partnerships, joint ventures, or strategic collaborations.

During times of crisis, **social capital becomes particularly valuable**. A strong network can provide the support and resources needed to navigate financial, reputational, or operational challenges. For example, during the 2008 financial crisis, many businesses survived due to the support of their networks. Companies with high social capital could secure bridge financing, negotiate favourable terms with suppliers, and receive advice from their peers, which were critical to survival. Social capital is an intangible yet powerful asset that can significantly influence business success. Building and maintaining strong relationships based on trust and reciprocity allows you to create a network that offers invaluable support, resources, and opportunities for growth and achievement.

19.11 Case Studies in Networking Success

To fully appreciate the power of networking, it is helpful to examine real-world examples of individuals and organisations that have achieved remarkable success through **effective networking**. These case studies illustrate various strategies, challenges, and lessons that can be applied to your networking efforts. They demonstrate how strategic partnerships, innovation through collaboration, and the ability to overcome challenges through community support have shaped the success of some of the most recognised global brands.

One of the most well-known examples of a successful strategic partnership is the collaboration between **Starbucks and Barnes & Noble**. In the 1990s, both companies sought to enhance their customer experience and expand their reach. Starbucks wanted to increase its presence in retail locations, while Barnes & Noble aimed to create a more inviting atmosphere in its stores. The partnership was mutually beneficial. Barnes & Noble began offering Starbucks coffee in its stores, creating a comfortable space where customers could relax, read, and enjoy a beverage. This strategic partnership significantly enhanced Barnes & Noble's in-store experience while providing Starbucks access to a new and loyal customer base.

The key takeaway from this partnership is the concept of **mutual benefit**. The collaboration succeeded because both companies gained significant value. Each organisation brought something valuable, and both benefited from the relationship. Another important factor was leveraging each company's

complementary strengths, Barnes & Noble's retail space and Starbucks' premium coffee experience. The long-term commitment to mutual success allowed the collaboration to flourish over the years, showing how strategic partnerships can elevate brand experiences and customer satisfaction.

Another example of successful networking is the collaboration between **Apple and Nike**. These iconic brands joined forces to create the Nike+ product line, integrating Apple's technology with Nike's athletic wear. The partnership led to innovative products, such as the Nike+ Running App and the Apple Watch Nike edition, blending fitness with technology in new ways. This collaboration was driven by a shared vision to enhance the athletic experience through technology. By combining their strengths, Apple's expertise in technology and Nike's in sportswear, the companies created groundbreaking products that neither could have developed.

The success of the Apple-Nike collaboration highlights the importance of a **shared vision**. Partners can innovate and create products that push boundaries when they share a common goal. This case also underscores the value of **cross-industry collaboration**. Networking beyond your immediate field can lead to fresh perspectives and innovative solutions that might not emerge in a more insular environment. Networking can drive innovation, and connecting with partners from different industries can open up new opportunities.

The rise of **LinkedIn** provides a prime example of how a company can leverage networking to build a global brand.

Founded in 2002, LinkedIn began as a platform for professionals to connect and network online. Over the years, it has evolved into the world's largest professional networking site, with over 700 million members. LinkedIn's success can be attributed to its relentless focus on networking as its core value proposition. By continuously evolving the platform to meet the needs of professionals, such as adding job postings, company pages, and content-sharing features, LinkedIn has become indispensable for professional networking. Strategic partnerships, such as its acquisition by Microsoft in 2016, have further expanded LinkedIn's capabilities and reach.

The key lesson from LinkedIn's story is the importance of focusing on **core strengths**. By remaining dedicated to its mission of professional networking, LinkedIn built a platform that meets the needs of professionals worldwide. Its strategic partnership with Microsoft shows how alliances can help a company grow and reach new heights. LinkedIn's success also highlights the necessity of **continuous evolution**. LinkedIn has maintained its position as the leading professional network by regularly introducing new features and adapting to changing market demands.

Airbnb's rise to success is a testament to the power of networking in overcoming challenges. Founded in 2008, the company faced significant obstacles, including legal challenges, investor scepticism, and resistance from the traditional hospitality industry. Despite these hurdles, Airbnb's founders leveraged their network to navigate these challenges. They sought advice from successful entrepreneurs, connected with investors who believed in their vision and built a strong community of hosts who became advocates for the brand. This network of supporters was crucial in helping Airbnb overcome early difficulties and grow into the global powerhouse it is today.

The story of Airbnb illustrates the importance of **resilience through networking**. The founders' ability to leverage their network was key to overcoming numerous challenges. By seeking advice, securing investment, and building a community, they persevered and succeeded. Airbnb's success also demonstrates the value of **community building**. The company's network of hosts and guests became its most valuable asset, driving growth and loyalty. The company's network also provided crucial advocacy, helping it navigate regulatory challenges and build credibility.

These case studies demonstrate how networking can open doors to new opportunities, foster innovation, and provide essential support during times of challenge. They highlight the importance of **strategic partnerships**, cross-industry collaboration, and community building. By learning from these examples, business leaders can better understand how to leverage their networks to drive success and navigate the complexities of the business world.

Conclusion

Chapter 19 has explored the significant role that **networking** plays in business success. The power of relationships is undeniable, from strategic partnerships and alumni networks to mastermind groups and industry associations. Effective networking is not just about making connections; it is about cultivating meaningful, mutually beneficial relationships that open doors to new opportunities, foster innovation, and provide essential support during challenging times.

Building a strong network requires more than just collecting contacts. It involves actively engaging with your network, contributing value, and being open to learning from others. The case studies presented demonstrate how strategic partnerships, innovation through collaboration, and the ability to overcome challenges through community support have shaped the success of some of the most recognised global brands. These examples remind business leaders that networking should be a critical part of their strategy for growth, resilience, and long-term success.

By applying the principles and strategies discussed in this chapter, you can build a strong network that supports your business goals and enhances your ability to navigate obstacles, access resources, and drive sustained success. Networking is an ongoing process that requires time, effort, and a genuine interest in the success of others, but the rewards, both personal and professional, are well worth the investment.

Chapter 20

The Future of Leadership: Trends, Challenges, and Opportunities

20.1 Overview

The leadership landscape is undergoing a significant shift due to profound global changes. This transformation, driven by technological advancements, evolving societal expectations, and the increasing interconnectedness of businesses, presents leaders with unprecedented challenges. However, it also brings significant opportunities. The leaders of tomorrow must be equipped with new skills, mindsets, and approaches. This chapter explores the trends, challenges, and opportunities that will shape the future of leadership, emphasising the crucial role of adaptability and innovation. These two qualities are not just key but are the fuel that will drive leaders to successfully navigate the changing landscape and ensure their organisations survive and thrive in an ever-evolving environment.

Modern leaders are no longer confined to traditional roles or rigid hierarchical structures. Instead, effective leadership now involves embracing flexibility, empathy, and inclusivity. These qualities are becoming essential as businesses operate in a more interconnected and culturally diverse world. Leaders who can successfully adapt to these changes will be better positioned to guide their organisations through periods of uncertainty and transformation. By understanding the key trends reshaping leadership, current and aspiring leaders can proactively develop strategies that address immediate challenges and prepare their organisations for long-term success in a rapidly changing world. This understanding empowers leaders to take control of their organisation's future and shape it according to their vision.

20.2 Emerging Leadership Trends

In today's fast-paced and complex world, the nature of leadership is undergoing a significant transformation. Traditional notions of authority and hierarchy give way to new models prioritising **agility, emotional intelligence, and inclusivity**. Modern leaders must navigate a landscape shaped by rapid technological advancements, shifting societal values, and a more interconnected global business environment. Several key trends are emerging that will redefine what it means to be an effective leader in the years to come. Leaders must anticipate and adapt to these trends. Doing so will better equip them to lead their organisations towards sustainable success in the face of uncertainty and transformation.

One of the most significant leadership changes is the shift from a command-and-control style to one emphasising empathy and emotional intelligence. Emotional intelligence (EI) is the ability to understand and manage your own emotions and to understand and influence the emotions of others. Historically, leadership was often associated with authority, decisiveness, and the ability to control others. However, the future of leadership increasingly centres around EI, recognising that skills such as empathy, self-awareness, and emotional regulation are crucial for building trust, fostering collaboration, and enhancing employee engagement. Leaders who can effectively harness their emotional intelligence are better equipped to navigate complex interpersonal dynamics, resolve conflicts, and inspire their teams to reach their full potential, making each member feel valued and integral to the team's success.

Another critical trend is the growing importance of **diversity and inclusivity** in leadership. What was once considered a matter of compliance is now recognised as a strategic imperative. Diverse teams bring diverse perspectives that can lead to more innovative solutions and better decision-making. This shift drives leaders to champion diversity and inclusivity by setting clear objectives, implementing inclusive hiring practices, and fostering a workplace culture where all employees feel valued and heard. For instance, leaders can create diversity and inclusion committees, implement blind hiring practices, and provide cultural sensitivity training. Leaders who embrace these values are better positioned to leverage their teams' diverse talents, leading to improved organisational performance and a more dynamic, innovative work environment.

The increasing need for **agility** is another trend that is reshaping leadership. In a world where disruption has become the norm, agility has emerged as a critical trait for leaders. Agile leaders are not tied to rigid plans but are open to experimentation and iterative learning. They can quickly adapt to changing circumstances, pivot strategies when necessary, and remain resilient in uncertainty. This requires promoting a culture of continuous improvement, encouraging innovation, and supporting calculated risk-taking within their teams. Leaders play a crucial role in fostering a growth mindset by providing opportunities for learning and development, encouraging feedback and reflection, and rewarding initiative and creativity. By doing so, they can inspire and motivate employees to think creatively, even in the most challenging conditions.

20.3 Navigating Globalisation

Globalisation has fundamentally changed businesses' operations, presenting leaders with new opportunities and challenges. As economies, cultures, and markets become more interconnected, effective leadership increasingly relies on the ability to navigate these diverse and complex environments. **Globalisation** opens new avenues for growth and expansion and requires leaders to develop the skills to lead across borders and manage culturally diverse teams. To succeed in this globalised landscape, leaders must cultivate cultural sensitivity and awareness, enabling them to build trust and promote collaboration among team members from different backgrounds.

Leading culturally diverse teams is one of the most significant challenges that globalisation poses for leaders. Differences in cultural backgrounds can lead to variations in communication styles, work ethics, and expectations. Leaders must develop a deep understanding of these **cultural nuances** and be sensitive to the diverse needs of their team members. This cultural intelligence is essential for building trust, promoting collaboration, and avoiding misunderstandings that could hinder team performance. Leaders can create a more inclusive and cohesive team environment by learning about their members' cultural backgrounds and engaging with them to understand their perspectives.

Another global challenge is managing teams across different **geographical locations** and time zones. Effective global collaboration requires flexible communication and collaborative tools to ensure that all team members remain aligned, regardless of their physical location. Leaders must establish clear communication protocols, set expectations for response times, and provide opportunities for team members to connect personally. Regular virtual meetings, cross-functional projects, and team-building activities can help bridge the gap between geographically dispersed teams, fostering a sense of unity and shared purpose.

Adapting business strategies to local markets is another crucial aspect of navigating globalisation. Leaders must balance maintaining a consistent global brand with adapting to local market conditions. This requires a deep understanding of local **consumer behaviour**, regulatory environments, and the competitive landscape. Leaders who can tailor their products, services, and marketing strategies to meet the specific needs of local customers while ensuring alignment with the broader corporate strategy are more likely to succeed in the global marketplace.

20.4 Sustainability and Ethical Leadership

As the world grapples with increasingly complex environmental and social challenges, sustainability and ethical leadership have become critical components of modern business strategy. Leaders must drive financial performance while committing to social and environmental responsibility. This shift reflects a growing recognition that businesses are crucial in addressing global challenges and that leaders must integrate sustainability into their decision-making processes. By prioritising sustainability, leaders can build more resilient brands and contribute to a more sustainable and equitable world.

Sustainability is no longer seen as merely a regulatory requirement; it has become a strategic priority for businesses aiming for long-term competitiveness. Consumers, investors, and employees increasingly demand that companies take meaningful action to reduce their environmental impact and contribute to societal well-being. Leaders who embed sustainability into every aspect of their business, from product development to supply chain management and corporate governance, can differentiate their organisations and build stronger, more resilient brands. For example, companies like Ørsted have demonstrated the potential of sustainability-focused leadership by transitioning from fossil fuels to renewable energy, setting a benchmark for sustainability in business.

In addition to sustainability, ethical leadership is becoming increasingly important in modern business. Ethical leadership goes beyond legal requirements; it involves making decisions aligned with the company's values and doing the right thing, even when faced with difficult choices. Leaders prioritising ethics create a culture of integrity, accountability, and transparency, which is essential in building stakeholder trust. By clearly defining and communicating the company's values, providing regular training on ethical decision-making, and establishing mechanisms for reporting and addressing unethical behaviour, leaders can foster an ethical culture that permeates every level of the organisation.

20.5 The Role of AI and Technology in Leadership

Artificial intelligence (AI) and emerging technologies rapidly transform how businesses operate and leaders make decisions. While these technologies offer significant opportunities for **innovation** and operational efficiency, they also present challenges that leaders must navigate to ensure responsible and ethical use. Integrating AI into business processes can enhance decision-making by providing insights from vast data, enabling leaders to make more informed and timely decisions. However, using AI also raises important ethical considerations, such as privacy, bias, and accountability, that leaders must address to maintain trust and credibility.

AI and data analytics provide leaders with powerful tools to enhance decision-making by uncovering patterns, trends, and insights that would be difficult for humans to detect independently. This enables leaders to make more informed decisions, optimise operations, and predict future trends more accurately. Beyond decision-making, AI can also drive **innovation** by enabling the development of new products, services, and business models. For instance, AI-powered customer service tools such as chatbots improve customer experiences, while IoT devices enhance supply chain management. Leaders who embrace these technologies can create new opportunities for growth and stay ahead of the competition.

However, using AI and technology in leadership also presents significant challenges, particularly in managing ethical risks. Leaders must ensure that AI systems are designed and implemented fairly, transparently, and with respect for individual rights. Establishing clear **ethical guidelines**, conducting regular audits of AI systems, and communicating openly with stakeholders about the use of AI are essential measures to address these concerns. Furthermore, as AI increasingly takes over tasks traditionally performed by humans, leaders must find the right balance between human and machine collaboration. This involves determining which tasks best suit AI and require human judgment and creativity.

To remain competitive in the digital age, leaders must invest in **digital transformation** initiatives that align with their business objectives. This involves adopting new technologies, rethinking organisational processes, and fostering a culture of innovation. Collaboration between leadership and IT teams is essential to ensure that technology investments are strategic, scalable, and aligned with the company's long-term vision. Creating a data-driven culture is also crucial in leveraging technology for competitive advantage. Leaders should encourage employees to use data in decision-making by providing the necessary tools and training, ultimately driving continuous improvement and innovation.

20.6 The Changing Nature of Work

The nature of work is rapidly evolving, driven by the rise of remote teams, the gig economy, and the increasing demand for **flexible work arrangements**. These changes reshape how leaders manage their teams, maintain organisational culture, and drive performance in a more dynamic and fluid work environment. The shift towards more flexible and distributed work models presents opportunities and challenges for leaders, requiring them to rethink traditional leadership and team management approaches.

Leading remote teams presents unique challenges, including maintaining clear communication, building trust, and ensuring accountability. Without interacting face-to-face, leaders must find new ways to engage their teams and ensure alignment with the organisation's goals. To effectively manage **distributed teams**, leaders should prioritise transparent communication, set clear expectations for deliverables, and use collaborative tools to facilitate teamwork. Regular virtual meetings, check-ins, and team-building activities are essential for maintaining connection and cohesion within remote teams. Leaders must also be mindful of their team members' different time zones and cultural backgrounds, ensuring everyone feels included and valued.

The gig economy, characterised by a growing number of professionals choosing freelance or contract work over traditional full-time employment, is also transforming the workplace. Leaders can capitalise on the **gig economy** by accessing specialised skills and expertise on a project-by-project basis. However, managing a workforce that includes both full-time and gig workers requires clear contracts, well-defined deliverables, and effective communication strategies. Supporting flexible work arrangements, such as remote work, flexible hours, and job-sharing, can help leaders attract and retain top talent, improve employee satisfaction, and boost productivity.

Maintaining a strong organisational culture in a virtual environment can be challenging, as employees may feel disconnected from the company's mission and values. Leaders must intentionally build and reinforce the organisational culture, even when team members are not physically present. This can be achieved by regularly communicating the company's **values**, recognising and celebrating achievements, and creating opportunities for social interaction. Virtual team-building activities and online events can help foster a sense of belonging and unity within distributed teams. Ensuring that all employees, regardless of location, have access to the same resources, support, and opportunities for development is also essential.

20.7 Inclusive Leadership: Embracing Diversity for Innovation

Inclusive leadership has emerged as both a **moral imperative** and a strategic advantage in today's evolving business landscape.

It goes beyond traditional diversity metrics like race, gender, and age. It involves creating an environment where all voices are heard, and diverse perspectives are actively sought and valued. This approach fosters innovation, drives team performance, and ensures global competitiveness. Leaders who embrace inclusivity are better positioned to harness the full potential of their teams, leading to more creative solutions and a more dynamic, innovative work environment.

In the past, inclusivity was often viewed as a compliance requirement or a positive cultural initiative. However, the future of leadership demands a more profound integration of **inclusivity** into organisations' core strategies. Leaders who champion inclusivity are better positioned to harness their teams' diverse talents and perspectives, leading to more innovative solutions and a more dynamic workplace. Research consistently demonstrates that diverse teams outperform homogeneous ones, particularly in areas of problem-solving and innovation, due to the wider range of perspectives that challenge conventional thinking and spark creativity.

To practise inclusive leadership effectively, leaders must actively create opportunities for diverse voices to be heard. This involves implementing diverse hiring panels, employee resource groups, and unconscious bias training. Leaders should also foster an open and respectful dialogue within their teams, creating a safe space for employees to share their perspectives and ideas. Regular "listening sessions" can be an excellent tool for leaders to engage with employees from different backgrounds, gaining insight into their experiences and suggestions for improving company practices. Organisations like Accenture have successfully embedded inclusivity into their corporate strategy through various initiatives, leading to enhanced innovation and client satisfaction.

20.8 Personalisation and Customisation: Tailoring Leadership Approaches

As leadership evolves, **one-size-fits-all approaches** are becoming increasingly ineffective. The future of leadership is moving towards personalisation and customisation, where leaders adapt their styles to meet their teams and individual employees' unique needs. This shift reflects the growing recognition that different individuals respond to varying leadership styles and that the most effective leaders can tailor their approach to fit specific circumstances. Leaders who understand and respond to their teams' diverse needs and preferences can create a more supportive and productive work environment, ultimately driving higher levels of engagement and performance.

Effective personalised leadership begins with deeply understanding each team member's strengths, needs, and motivations. Leaders who take the time to get to know their employees personally are better positioned to maximise each individual's potential. This may involve adapting communication styles, setting personalised goals, or offering tailored development opportunities. For example, some employees may excel in a more autonomous environment, while others may thrive under more guidance and feedback. Recognising these differences enables leaders to provide the necessary support to drive higher **productivity** and engagement.

Customised leadership approaches can significantly improve team performance and engagement. Employees who feel their leaders understand and support their unique needs are more likely to be motivated, engaged, and committed to their work. Personalised leadership fosters stronger relationships between leaders and their teams, building trust, loyalty, and mutual respect. For instance, Intuit has successfully aligned its leadership practices with individual strengths and allowed for rapid experimentation, leading to high employee engagement and innovation. By catering to the diverse needs of its workforce, the company has cultivated an environment that drives success.

Leaders must be adaptable and open to learning from their team members to implement personalised leadership effectively. This requires **active listening**, regular communication, and a willingness to adjust leadership styles based on feedback and evolving circumstances. Tools such as personality assessments, one-on-one meetings, and feedback loops can help leaders better understand their teams and refine their leadership approach. By doing so, leaders create a more responsive and supportive work environment, empowering employees to reach their full potential. This not only enhances individual performance but also contributes to the overall success and cohesion of the team.

20.9 Learning and Development: The Future of Executive Education

Continuous learning and development have become essential components of effective leadership in an era of **accelerating change**. The future of leadership will be defined by those who are committed to lifelong learning and who understand the importance of staying ahead of emerging trends, technologies, and best practices. Traditional executive education models, which rely on periodic training sessions or workshops, are no longer sufficient in today's fast-paced business environment. Instead, the future of leadership demands a commitment to lifelong learning, where leaders continually seek new knowledge, skills, and experiences to adapt to a rapidly changing business landscape.

Digital learning platforms have revolutionised how leaders acquire new skills and knowledge. These platforms offer **flexible, on-demand learning** opportunities that can be tailored to executives' busy schedules. Whether through online courses, webinars, or virtual workshops, leaders can now access educational content whenever and wherever they need it. This flexibility allows leaders to continuously update their knowledge and skills, keeping pace with the rapid changes in their industries. Additionally, digital learning platforms offer personalised learning paths, allowing leaders to focus on the areas most relevant to their roles and career goals.

As the business world becomes more complex, there is growing recognition of the importance of **soft skills** in leadership. While technical skills remain critical, soft skills such as emotional intelligence, communication, adaptability, and collaboration are increasingly seen as essential to effective leadership. The future of executive education will emphasise the development of these soft skills, equipping leaders with the interpersonal tools needed to build cohesive teams and navigate the complexities of modern leadership.

20.10 Entrepreneurship and Intrapreneurship: Cultivating Innovation

Innovation is the lifeblood of any successful organisation, and the future of leadership will be defined by those who can foster a **culture of innovation**. This involves encouraging entrepreneurship and intrapreneurship, empowering employees to take ownership of projects and drive new business initiatives from within the organisation. Leaders who create an environment that supports creativity and risk-taking can unlock innovation potential, enabling their organisations to stay ahead of emerging market trends and maintain a competitive edge.

To foster innovation, leaders must create an environment where creativity and risk-taking are encouraged. This may involve establishing **innovation labs**, providing resources for experimentation, or implementing incentive programmes that reward innovative ideas. Leaders should also be willing to take calculated risks and support their teams when they pursue unconventional ideas. By creating a safe space for innovation and supporting employees in their efforts to develop new solutions, leaders can drive significant growth and transformation within their organisations.

Intrapreneurship involves empowering employees to act as entrepreneurs within the organisation, giving them the freedom and resources to explore new ideas and develop new products or services. Leaders who encourage **intrapreneurship** foster a culture of innovation by enabling employees to take ownership of their projects and drive change. For instance, DBS Bank in Singapore has successfully fostered a culture of intrapreneurship through its platform-based approach. It empowers employees to think like entrepreneurs and develop new solutions that expand the bank's offerings and drive growth.

While fostering innovation is essential, leaders must ensure that innovation efforts align with the organisation's broader business goals. This requires balancing the pursuit of creative ideas with a clear focus on **strategic objectives**. Leaders can achieve this by setting innovation goals, establishing metrics for success, and regularly reviewing the progress of innovation projects. By aligning innovation with the company's long-term strategy, leaders can drive sustainable growth while encouraging a culture of creativity and experimentation.

20.11 Case Studies in Future-Focused Leadership

Real-world examples provide valuable insights into how organisations navigate the challenges and opportunities of future-focused leadership. The following case studies highlight companies and leaders at the forefront of embracing **inclusive**

leadership, personalised approaches, and fostering innovation. These examples demonstrate how forward-thinking organisations are already leveraging emerging trends and adapting their leadership strategies to drive success and build resilience in a rapidly changing business environment.

Accenture, a global professional services company, has made significant strides in fostering an **inclusive culture**. The organisation has implemented initiatives such as unconscious bias training and created platforms where diverse voices can be heard. Accenture's leadership team has prioritised inclusivity, resulting in a diverse and engaged workforce. The "Inclusion Starts with I" campaign has been instrumental in raising awareness and driving behavioural change across all levels of the organisation. Accenture has leveraged a broader range of perspectives by embedding inclusivity into its strategic framework, enhancing innovation and client satisfaction.

Intuit, a financial software company, has embraced **personalised leadership** to drive innovation and employee engagement. By shifting from a traditional hierarchical model to one that emphasises design thinking and rapid experimentation, Intuit allows employees to work on projects aligned with their strengths and interests. This personalised approach has enabled the company to remain agile in the face of market changes, leading to significant growth. Intuit's leadership model demonstrates how tailoring leadership styles to meet employees' unique needs can foster a culture of innovation and high performance.

DBS Bank, headquartered in Singapore, exemplifies how **intrapreneurship** can drive innovation within a large organisation. By adopting a platform-based approach, DBS has encouraged its employees to think like entrepreneurs, leading to the development of new solutions that expand the bank's offerings and drive growth. Through partnerships with over 400 companies across various sectors, DBS has significantly expanded its market reach while fostering a culture of innovation. The bank's focus on intrapreneurship has allowed it to continuously innovate and grow, positioning it as a leader in digital banking.

PwC's "Leaders Solving for Tomorrow" programme prepares senior leaders for the complexities of modern business by focusing on **rapid experimentation, execution, and learning**. This programme encourages continuous learning and equips leaders with the skills to navigate the evolving global business landscape. PwC's commitment to leadership development, particularly in the digital age, ensures its leaders are well-prepared to meet future challenges while fostering innovation and adaptability.

Ørsted, a Danish multinational power company, provides an exemplary sustainable leadership model. By transitioning from fossil fuels to renewable energy, Ørsted has significantly reduced its carbon footprint and positioned itself as a global leader in renewable energy. Ørsted's leadership in sustainability demonstrates how integrating ethical and environmental considerations into business strategy can lead to long-term success and differentiation in the marketplace.

Conclusion

The future of leadership is becoming increasingly complex, driven by **technological advancements, shifting societal expectations, and globalisation**. Leaders must be prepared to adapt, innovate, and guide their organisations through these profound changes. Emotional intelligence, inclusivity, agility, and a commitment to sustainability are now essential traits for effective leadership. The case studies presented in this chapter, Accenture's inclusive leadership, Intuit's personalised approach, DBS Bank's intrapreneurial culture, PwC's focus on continuous learning, and Ørsted's leadership in sustainability, highlight how forward-thinking organisations are already embracing these principles to drive success. These examples provide valuable lessons for aspiring leaders who wish to navigate the challenges and opportunities of the future. Ultimately, the most successful leaders will be those who can balance today's demands with tomorrow's possibilities, inspiring their teams to achieve greatness while positively impacting their organisations and society.

Printed in Great Britain
by Amazon